La Causa Chicana
The movement for justice

La Causa Chicana
The movement for justice

Margaret M. Mangold, Editor

Family Service Association of America   New York

234752

International Standard Book Number: 0-87304-100-3
Library of Congress Catalog Card Number: 72–92083

Printed in the United States of America

3

The publication of this book was made
possible in part by the contributions of the
Shell Companies Foundation, Inc., Houston, Texas,
and the Lois and Samuel Silberman Fund,
New York, New York.

Contents

Authors

LYDIA R. AGUIRRE, Social Worker, El Paso, Texas

TOMÁS C. ATENCIO, National Coordinator, La Academia de la Nueva Raza, Dixon, New Mexico

GRACE BURRUEL, Psychiatric Social Worker, Tucson Southern Counties Mental Health Services, La Frontera Center, Tucson, Arizona

MATEO R. CAMARILLO, Field Coordinator, Graduate School of Social Work, San Jose State College, San Jose, California

NELBA CHAVEZ, Psychiatric Social Worker, Tucson Southern Counties Mental Health Services, La Frontera Center, Tucson, Arizona

ANTONIO DEL BUONO, Barrio Professor, Graduate School of Social Work, San Jose State College, San Jose, California

JOHN FLOREZ, Assistant Director, Field Operations Division, National Urban Coalition, Washington, D.C.

ALEJANDRO GARCIA, Staff Associate, National Association of Social Workers, New York, New York

ALEX GONZALEZ, Student, Law School, Harvard University, Cambridge, Massachusetts

FAUSTINA RAMIREZ KNOLL, Social Worker, Detroit, Michigan

JORGE LARA-BRAUD, D.D., Director, Hispanic-American Institute, Austin, Texas

GLORIA LÓPEZ MCKNIGHT, Founder and President, Latin American Coordinating Council, Inc., Detroit, Michigan, and Social Worker, Wayne County Department of Social Services, Detroit, Michigan

ARMANDO MORALES, D.S.W., Assistant Professor, Department of Psychiatry, School of Medicine, University of California at Los Angeles, and Member, Trabajadores de la Raza, East Los Angeles, California

MARIO G. OBLEDO, General Counsel, Mexican-American Legal Defense and Educational Fund, San Francisco, California

PHILIP D. ORTEGO, Ph.D., Assistant to the President and Professor of Urban Affairs, Metropolitan State College, Denver, Colorado

AMADO M. PADILLA, Ph.D., Assistant Professor of Psychology and Chicano Studies, University of California, Santa Barbara, California

MANUEL RAMIREZ III, Ph.D., Associate Professor of Psychology and Mexican-American Studies, and Director, Bicultural/Bilingual Follow Through Model, University of California, Riverside, California

GUMECINDO SALAS, Director of Chicano Studies, Monteith College, Wayne State University, Detroit, Michigan

ISABEL SALAS, on leave from the Detroit Board of Education; formerly Assistant Professor, Monteith College, Wayne State University, Detroit, Michigan

FAUSTINA SOLIS, Associate Professor, Department of Community Medicine, University of California at San Diego, La Jolla, California; formerly Project Director, Farm Workers Health Service, California Department of Public Health, Berkeley, California

MARTA SOTOMAYOR, Doctoral Student, Graduate School of Social Work, University of Denver, Denver, Colorado, and *Asocida,* La Academia de la Nueva Raza, Dixon, New Mexico

Foreword

The intent of this book is to present information about Chicanos to social workers and members of other helping professions so they may become involved in the movement by Mexican Americans to be first-class citizens of the United States. In order to serve this group effectively, one needs to understand the historical background, the cultural derivatives, and the value system of this long-suppressed, neglected minority.

It is essential to understand the wide diversity of cultural patterns represented by the Mexican Americans. Knowledge of the Chicano culture that is derived from their Indian-Mexican-Spanish heritage can serve to enrich American culture and illuminate American history if other Americans give this heritage the opportunity for expression within our institutions. The time has come—in fact, it is long overdue —to recognize the myth of the melting pot for the false values it represents. Only when the people of the United States can relinquish this myth and can work to eradicate the fear of differentness that is the basis of racism will the myth and the fear be supplanted by a recognition and acceptance of the valuable contribution of each ethnic group. Moreover, only when no *one* person in this country is suppressed or discriminated against because of his color, religion, or cultural background can people truly be free. The spirit of the Chicano movement comes from a dedication and determination to achieve a life of full equality for *all* people.

The commitment to equality for all and the deep conviction that social change must continue have led the authors of this book to put forth a series of articles from their lives and professional experiences. These articles should increase awareness and understanding of a population group in need of direct services and in need of institutional recognition and commitment that reflect their unique cultural, religious, and language characteristics. The articles are an attempt to communicate the concern and anguish of the Chicano population group— specifically the Chicano family—to the people who must recognize that the group exists, who must comprehend those characteristics common to all groups and especially those characteristics unique to the Chicanos, who must modify their stance and move toward removing cultural and language barriers in social service agencies and educational institutions, and who must significantly involve all the strata within the Chicano population group in meaningful ways at all organizational levels. The tone of the appeal may seem mild to some and harsh to others; it may leave others untouched. The hope is that the message will generate thoughtful discussion and a compassionate organizational response.

The volume is dedicated to the Chicano family. *La familia Chicana* has withstood the negative impact of outside social and economic forces and continues to be the primary, and at times the only, social institution useful to the Spanish-speaking population group. Various social programs have disregarded and divided the family units and addressed themselves to children and youth and not to the parents—the youth could speak English, the parents could not. They have attempted to transform Chicano families into Anglo families, thus disrupting useful processes—social workers knew what was good for the families; to diagnose parent-child relationships and extended family relationships by utilizing alien concepts and terminology—social workers, even those who speak Spanish, cannot translate certain psychological terms into Spanish; and to disrupt family and community processes conducive to the mental health of the community—*el oro del barrio* has no value when one's perspective is alien to the barrio.

Some concerned people have indicated that more than half of the social workers in the Southwest should be accused of disrupting Chicano family life and negatively affecting the development of family life; other people feel strongly that they should be jailed. One may reflect on the inability of some members of helping professions to work effectively with Chicano families and on the grave negative consequences that are not articulated by those who suffer. It is not unusual for youngsters to serve as interpreters in the interaction between parents and professionals. The admission by professionals that they are incompetent in working effectively with Chicano families is a prerequisite in moving toward a constructive organizational response.

It is hoped that these articles will reduce ignorance, raise such vital issues as competency, and motivate the helping professions toward critical self-examination, significant search efforts, and the development of effective solutions. A vital campaign must be launched by a coalition of interest groups to formulate and implement a bilingual-bicultural human services delivery system.

The articles reflect the perspectives of persons working in various settings, geographical regions, and disciplines. Some of the authors articulate their concerns about social change and social service, whereas others provide profiles about the Chicano family and the community. The concerns of these authors must become your concerns, and, from a common commitment, effective efforts will evolve.

I appeal to you, the reader, to act on the basis of knowledge and understanding of need rather than to wait until demands are made on you. I feel strongly that all the authors of this book have faith that positive and constructive steps will follow as a result of your efforts. We need your help!

JUAN RAMOS, PH.D.
Chief
Interagency Liaison Branch
National Institute of Mental Health
Rockville, Maryland

Preface

In midsummer 1970, the Family Service Association of America held a two-day regional conference in Albuquerque, New Mexico, that focused on the Mexican-American family. Several Chicano social workers attended and, aware of the lack of accurate knowledge of Mexican-American family life, history, and culture, asked FSAA to publish a special issue of its journal, *Social Casework,* to be devoted to the needs, problems, and achievements of Mexican Americans.

Under the leadership of Dr. Juan Ramos, a planning committee met two months later in San Antonio with the Editor and W. Keith Daugherty, Assistant General Director of FSAA. The meeting afforded a stimulating exchange of ideas and suggestions spontaneously presented with a combination of scholarly seriousness and humor. Content and authors were agreed upon for nine articles. The enthusiasm for the special issue generated at this meeting sustained all of us through the months that had to elapse before *La Causa Chicana: Una Familia Unida* was published in May 1971.

When the manuscripts arrived in the FSAA office, the staff of Publications Service—editors and secretaries—began to enjoy a learning experience beyond our expectations. As we edited, retyped, and proofread the articles, we were struck by our ignorance concerning the second largest minority in the United States. When we realized the tremendous job to be done to destroy stereotyped thinking about Mexican Americans, our commitment to *la Causa* became even stronger. We are indebted to the authors, who so thoroughly opened our eyes.

The special issue was well received by practitioners and educators, and interest grew in producing a book which would include those nine articles as well as others prepared for this book—all representing interdisciplinary concerns. This volume is the result. To document the reality of Mexican Americans in the fight to achieve justice, the book presents the viewpoints of Chicano authors engaged in education, law, psychology, and the ministry, as well as social work.

The publication of *La Causa Chicana,* in addition to other projects and programs, attests to the commitment of FSAA to strengthen the family life of all people by eradicating the racism that so adversely affects families. It is our hope that the readers—members of the helping professions, students, and concerned laymen—will derive the understanding and conviction that will lead to action to support the Chicano movement toward dignity and justice.

MARGARET M. MANGOLD
Director
Publications Service
FSAA

Acknowledgements

I wish to express my gratitude to the many persons in addition to the authors who are responsible for this book. First is Dr. Juan Ramos who gave generously of his time and counsel and was the able chairman of the meetings of the planning committee. Other committee members who helped plan the content of this book were:

Lydia R. Aguirre and Ralph Aguirre, El Paso, Texas;

W. Keith Daugherty, New York, New York;

Janie Salinas Farris, Baytown, Texas;

Imelda Flores, Austin, Texas;

James R. Gamble, Jr., San Antonio, Texas;

Guadalupe Gibson, San Antonio, Texas;

Faustina Ramirez Knoll, Detroit, Michigan;

Helen Ramirez, Los Angeles, California;

Santos Reyes, Austin, Texas;

Marta Sotomayor, Denver, Colorado; and

Eduardo Villarreal, San Antonio, Texas.

Lydia R. Aguirre voluntarily served as liaison with the authors and gave valuable assistance to them and to the Editor. Mrs. Aguirre and Dr. Ramos also served as an advisory committee for the selection of manuscripts.

Publications staff, as I have indicated previously, offered continuous support and assistance. I am particularly grateful to Jennifer S. Villiger who, with unfailing good nature, dealt with the numerous problems that always beset the Production Editor.

M.M.M.

The Meaning of the Chicano Movement

Lydia R. Aguirre

The Chicano is an extremely diversified "individual." [1] We are as heterogeneous as our history. Without that background of history, it is difficult to understand us. *No somos Mexicanos.* We are citizens of the United States with cultural ties to Mexico and in some instances to Spain, but, within our ties of language and culture, we have developed a culture that is neither Spanish nor Mexican. *Entre nosotros habemos quien habla un espanol puro, pero tambien entre nosotros habemos los "batos" que no pueden conseguir "jale" por la razon que sea.*

We are bilingual. We are doctors, university professors, lawyers, and congressmen as well as farm laborers, maids, housewives, plumbers, mailmen, and engineers. There are some Mexican Americans who are *tio-tacos,* those who ride the fence and *cuando se les aprieta el cinto, nos dan en la torre.* Then, there are some Mexican Americans who would readily turn Chicano when they are scratched a little. By that I mean when they understand the true value of this, our diversified Chicano movement.

About the term *Chicano,* I can not as yet give you a scholarly explanation. From my adolescence in Edinburg, Texas, I remember Chicano as a derogatory term applied *only by us,* who we then insisted should be called Mexican Americans. We demanded that we be classified as Caucasian. Chicano was a term used self-consciously and degradingly only by ourselves. In his columns in the *Los Angeles Times,* Ruben Salazar attempted to define the term. In one column he wrote, "A Chicano is a Mexican American with a non-Anglo image of himself . . . actually the word Chicano is as difficult to define as 'soul'." In another instance, he wrote, "For those who like simplistic answers Chicano can be defined as short for Mexicano. For those who prefer complicated answers it has been suggested that Chicano may have come from the word Chihuahua—the name of a Mexican state bordering on the United States. Getting trickier this version contends that Mexicans who migrated to Texas call themselves Chicanos." In a third reference he said, "Chicanos then are merely fighting to become 'Americans'. Yes, but with a Chicano outlook."

As I understand the word *Chicano* in the Chicano movement, it is this: if there is no lowest of the low and no highest of the high and *each* will wear the label of *Chicano* with pride, he will have personal respect and with it *dignidad y unidad con sus hermanos Chicanos.* He will be proud to assume his heritage guaranteed in the Treaty of Guadalupe Hidalgo and proud to use the language and customs that are his by heritage, treaty, and *corazon.* Chicano power simply means that in the finding of identity—that is, a right to be *as he is,* not Mexican, not Spanish, not speaking either a "pure" English or a "pure" Spanish, but *as he is,* a product of a Spanish-Mexican-Indian heritage and an Anglo-Saxon (American, or, as they say, in Mexico, *Estado Unidense*) influence—he will unite with his brothers in heritage. As he has pride and unity, so will he lose his self-consciousness and self-degradation and thereby will gain status and power.

Collectively, the Chicano in unity can influence the social systems that have perpetuated social injustices. Some say we are in the midst of a social revolution. I prefer to state that we are in the midst of a renaissance. We challenge the educational system to recognize our "differentness." We challenge ourselves to be proud of this differentness. We challenge the educational system to teach Hispanic history, to teach bilingually, and to give us adequate schools where students are largely Chicano. We demand not to be segregated. We demand that others recognize our differentness and work within that differentness rather than make the Chicano suppress his Chicanismo and adopt Anglo-Saxon ideals.

We demand that our side of the story be told. From this demand grew the Ruben Salazar Memorial Scholarship Foundation. Ruben Salazar dared to speak the truth. His voice was silenced when he was killed in Los Angeles in the line of duty, covering the 1970 Chicano Moratorium for his paper. Through the mass communications scholarships we are offering, we hope to educate young people in television, radio, and journalism to continue Ruben Salazar's message. Needless to say, the present mass media sometimes distort the truth. What may really be a justified confrontation on a social injustice can be reported as a riotous disruption.

Some of us feel that we need parallel institutions to have real justice. The Ruben Salazar memorial foundation has a long-range goal of establishing or sponsoring a daily newspaper. Later on, who knows—perhaps even Chicano radio and television!

We continue being so terribly diversified, yet we have so many cultural values that unite us. Each area has problems unique to that area. Northern New Mexico is rural and communal. The people there are fighting for their lands and grazing and water rights. Urban areas fight both discrimination and racism. Racism is so difficult to fight because it is so intangible and difficult to pinpoint. Yet it is all around us.

Take, for example, El Paso. People with Spanish surnames number almost half of the population of El Paso. Yet we have very few businessmen proportionately. If we look at executive positions of the major companies, we are lucky to find a sprinkling of Spanish surnames. Many of our educated young people have to leave this community to find jobs. I personally know several young people who looked diligently for jobs for months and either left town or took a menial job. Recently, however, I received a call from an Anglo-Saxon young lady friend of mine who found a good job after only three days of looking in a city strange to her. Were the former just unfortunate incidents and was the latter a fortunate incident?

In approaching the problems facing us, the Chicano uses different methods. Each in his own way is striving to achieve human dignity, self-respect, and just equality. Some Chicanos (and I include myself) attempt to effect change within established systems, and if that does not work, attempt to establish parallel systems. Hence, we have separate newspapers, Chicano conferences, businesses. We attempt to change the educational system better to meet our needs. We demand justice in courts and from police within the established order.

Other Chicanos prefer isolationism or brown separatism. These are in the minority. Very few would want a separate nation.

Others, particularly in New Mexico, who brought from Spain and continued the system of an agrarian, communal society into this century, want a return to that system which in that climate and region is almost imperative to survival. It is interesting to note that the Pueblo Indian who lived in that region when the Spaniards arrived had a similar system already in operation.

In our search for identity, we are researching and, I feel, perhaps creating, the concept of *Aztlan.* Supposedly, we are descendants, through our Indian heritage, of the native peoples of the Southwest. The Aztlan people had a civilization that is still with us in a modified form through Mexican-Spanish influences. *Aztlan* lives in any land where a Chicano lives: in his mind and heart and in the land he walks. The emblem used extensively in Chicano circles is a black Aztec eagle on a red background.

Carnalismo, a feeling or an allegiance that permeates the movement, means a type of brotherhood within members of La Raza characterized by depth of feeling and allegiance to other *carnales.* It is the type of feeling and allegiance that many blood relatives have for one another. Once a Chicano is your *carnal,* he will stand with you through thick or thin.

In social work circles (I am a social worker by training), we are looking at the aspects of the Chicano (Mexican-American) family that are conducive to mental health. We are attempting to break the stereotypes associated with the Chicano family and show the Chicano family with its healthful components as well as with its harmful components. We are looking at the extended family and at the social welfare institutions that penalize the Chicano for preserving these family ties. In a sense, our culture has retained the "people orientation" lost to many in our materialistic society.

One of our leaders in the movement has been César Chávez with his organization of farm workers. His is a nonviolent movement. From the frustration of the strikes originated the Teatro Campesino (in Delano, California, in 1965). Out of the need for laughter, the strikers began a fast-paced, almost slapstick style of comedy mimicking those pertinent to the strikers: the patron, the contractor, the scab, and so forth. It is now a tremendously effective mode of showing the problems faced by Chicanos. It is raw; it is realistic; it is life itself!

Reies López Tijerina is another leader. His leadership is primarily in Tierra Amarilla in New Mexico. He is a land grant spokesman, who was imprisoned, charged with destroying federal property in one of the National Forests. Tijerina is a native of southern Texas. He saw his father run off his land in a most humiliating fashion. He was from humble origins, and he drifted around in farm camps. He was an extremely eloquent, fiery speaker for his *Alianza,* fighting for return of lands to land grantees and communal rights, but, most important, for full recognition of the Treaty of Guadalupe Hidalgo. Ranchers have distorted laws in this area to suit their needs.

Rodolfo "Corky" González from Colorado has been a leader in the migratory labor area. He is an ex-boxer, lecturer, poet, political activist, and community organizer, as well as a businessman and philanthropist. He is presently president and director of the Crusade for Justice, a Chicano civil rights organization in Denver. His poem, "Yo Soy Joaquín," should be required reading for everyone. Joaquín's first words poignantly describe the anguish of the Chicano who is confused and lost in the Anglo society.

José Angel Gutierrez of Crystal City, Texas, is a young man who is devoting his most capable energies toward establishing a base of political power in Texas. Chicanos who have become disillusioned with both political parties have created a third party, La Raza Unida.

The Mexican press was a strong ally to the Mexican Americans who fought injustices during and after World War II. We are still fighting these injustices, but now with a better self-concept, with a sustaining and lasting dedication and determination, and with more sophisticated and greater manpower. The dedication is courageous and contagious. We are fighting the vast racism that is rampant in our country and that seems unable to tolerate differentness. We are fighting for the right to be *as we are*—Chicanos. And within our culture we demand the right to be first class citizens within this our United States.

Por mi Raza hablará el Espíritu.

Note

1 This article is a composite of excerpts from a letter to a journalist in Mexico. The letter attempted to interpret the dedicated, courageous struggle of a people to retain ethnic individuality and achieve equality.

Mexican Americans and the Media

Mario G. Obledo

Mexican Americans are the second largest minority in the United States. Ninety percent of them live in the five southwestern states of Arizona, California, Colorado, New Mexico, and Texas. In 1960, Chicanos constituted 15 percent of the total population of the Southwest. Throughout the Southwest more than one-third of all Mexican-American families live at poverty levels on incomes of less than $3,000 per year. A Mexican American is seven times more likely than an Anglo American to live in substandard housing. The chance that his baby will be born dead or will die before his first birthday is about twice as great. The educational level is four years below that of the Anglos. The Mexican-American school dropout rate is twice the national average. The unemployment rate is about twice that of Anglos. When employed, almost 80 percent of Chicanos work at unskilled or semiskilled, low-paying jobs.[1]

The pattern of Mexican-American poverty, as well as many of the causes, is similar to that of all other poverty in the United States.

Verification of legal citations in this chapter and additional research were done by Robert Joselow, former staff attorney, Mexican American Legal Defense and Educational Fund.

However, certain characteristics of the community and its experience in this country are unique. Lack of understanding by the dominant culture community in the Southwest is typical. Nationally, ignorance is almost universal. The media, with their preoccupation in portraying Mexican Americans in stereotypes, have reinforced this ignorance. Resulting from this widespread ignorance is the fact that although most minority groups are stereotyped and subject to misunderstanding, Mexican Americans are particularly subject to such characterization. One example is the popular misconception that Mexican Americans are primarily engaged in farm labor. In actuality, 80 percent live in crowded urban barrios.

Statistics are sterile things, but just as real people are watching their lives decay in the ghettos of Bedford-Stuyvesant, Watts, and Newark, so are human beings being destroyed in the barrios of San Antonio, East Los Angeles, and migrant labor camps throughout the United States. Considering the realities of their lives, it is no wonder that Chicanos are distrustful of federal and state governments whose concern, in their eyes, has been solely directed at more advantaged citizens. One Mexican American in El Paso said:

> We who have for thirty years seen the Department of Labor stand by, and at times connive, while farm labor unions were destroyed by agri-business; we who have seen the Immigration and Naturalization Service see-saw with the seasonal tides of wetbacks; we who are now seeing the Department of Housing and Urban Development assist in the demolishment of the urban barrios where ex-farm laborers have sought a final refuge; we who have waited for a Secretary of Education who would bristle with indignation, back it with action, at a system that continues to produce that shameful anachronism—the migrant child; we who have seen the Office of Economic Opportunity retreat with its shield, not on it, after calling the Mexican poor to do battle for maximum feasible participation in their own destinies . . . we, may I say, are profoundly skeptical.[2]

A significant part of the problem arises from the media's failure to portray the Mexican American with any degree of depth. To state a truism—a basic prerequisite for a response is a stimulus. Meaningful change in the status of the Chicano simply cannot occur unless the communications media convey some information beyond caricatures. Ignoring the real problems can only exacerbate the situation. To say that the realities of Mexican-American life and the identity of such a large number of people in the larger society does not raise an issue of public importance is to ignore a basic fact of life for millions of struggling citizens.

The racial, stereotypic commercial

Often young Chicanos are deeply offended by the recurring caricatures of Mexicans as lazy, slovenly morons. They, more than their fathers and grandfathers, feel great pride in their Mexican heritage and are repulsed when they see it demeaned. They want these stereotypic myths destroyed, so that they may become contributing members of the dominant community. Mexican-American youths, like young blacks, are striving for a sense of identity through race consciousness. To this end, *La Raza* (literally translated as "the race") has become the focal point of organized efforts against school segregation, housing discrimination, job discrimination, and other injustices.

Mexican Americans are demanding their rights, and the overwhelming majority wants to achieve the objectives through peaceful means. This accomplishment is possible if the Anglo community will help rather than smother such activity with overt or subtle repression. Stereotypic commercials represent the antithesis of a positive identity around which the Chicano might peacefully rally. In effect, such commercials indicate the dominant culture's denial of a rich heritage.

The effect of stereotypic representations on the perceiver is a subtle but significant one. Therefore, any survey conducted by an advertising agency is of limited value. First, its validity is questionable on the grounds that it is obviously self-serving. Secondly, the effect of such characterizations is far more subtle than the "man on the street" can understand. A recent article stated:

> It is well known that American culture is saturated with images and caricatures of various ethnic groups. These "pictures in our heads" which Lippmann (1922) called stereotypes have come to be regarded as highly significant factors in intergroup and interpersonal relations.[3]

In a complaint against stereotyping, affidavits from experts would be necessary to demonstrate the cause and effect relationship between media portrayal of stereotypes and socioeconomic status and social attitudes. These affidavits would be presented to reinforce the following specific allegations.

1. *That stereotypes presented by the electronic media have contributed substantially to keeping Mexican Americans socially and economically repressed.* Generalities replace interpersonal dealings. As one study reported, when one analyzes stereotypes, response is not in terms of an individual human being "but as a personification of the symbol we have learned to look down upon. Walter Lippmann has called this type of belief a stereotype—by which is meant a fixed impression which conforms very little to the facts it pretends to represent and results from our defining first and observing second." [4]

2. *That although stereotypic advertising might be intended to sell a product, the actual effect and methodology is subtle and persuasive in influencing social thinking and attitudes.* [5]

3. *That such stereotypic ads actually reinforce feelings of racial superiority in one group by implying racial inferiority in others.* Axiomatic to this concept is the belief that stereotypic advertising encourages and reinforces feelings of inferiority in those groups that are derided; it is perhaps unfortunate that "What people think of us is bound to some degree to fashion what we are." [6] Elaborating on his term—*the self-fulfilling prophecy*—Robert K. Merton commented:

> It serves to call attention to the reciprocal conduct of human beings when in interaction. Too often we think of out-groups as simply possessing certain qualities . . . and in-groups as having certain false images of these qualities. . . . The truth of the matter is that these two conditions interact. The way we perceive qualities in others cannot help but have an effect on what qualities others will display. It is not true, of course, that every grim image we have of hated groups results in the development of hateful traits to confirm our worst expectations. Yet there is likely to be some kind of unpleasant reflex of our unpleasant opinions. And thus a vicious circle is established that tends, unless specifically halted, to augment social distance and enhance the grounds of prejudice. [7]

4. *That the effect of stereotypic advertisements is far greater when the content of the media bombardment is most consistent and unbalanced and when no positive image is ever portrayed.* An im-

portant reason for the survival of stereotypes is the fact that "they are socially supported, continually revived and hammered in, by our media of mass communication." [8] The significant point—that Chicanos, as opposed to most other racial minorities, have had virtually no positive access to the media—is unquestioned. The electronic media's complete neglect of Mexican Americans except to sell corn chips and tacos has taken its toll.

Federal Communications Commission's Fairness Doctrine

Throughout the history of the federal government's regulation of the air waves, paramount importance has been placed upon the public interest as opposed to any private interests. Limitations in the number of available frequencies, in addition to the very pervasiveness of the electronic media, dictate that licensees have a great responsibility to those on the receiving end of their transmissions. This view was expressed as early as the 1926 Congressional debates considering the enactment of the Radio Act of 1927.[9]

> We have reached the definite conclusion that the right of all our people to enjoy this means of communication can be preserved only by repudiation of the idea underlying the 1912 law that anyone who will, may transmit and by the assertion in its stead of the doctrine that the right of the public to service is superior to the right of any individual to use the ether. This is the first and most fundamental difference between the pending bill and the present law. . . . If enacted into law, the broadcasting privilege will not be the right of selfishness. It will rest upon an assurance of public interest to be served.[10]

The cases following the 1927 Act implicitly suggested a doctrine of "fairness" based on the requirement that the broadcasting must be "public," that is, "something other than private merchandising." [11] At this stage in the development of the public interest to be served, the concept of fairness was a negative idea. There was no affirmative obligation to do anything. There were "shall nots" but no "shalls"; thou shall not use the public air waves strictly for private gain.

These early principles were affirmed by the FCC, operating in accordance with the Communications Act of 1934.[12] The classic case in this regard was *Mayflower Broadcasting Corp.*[13] In *Mayflower,* the Commission stated that:

Under the American system of broadcasting it is clear that responsibility for the conduct of a broadcast station must rest
initially with the broadcaster. It is equally clear that with the
limitations in frequencies inherent in the nature of radio, the
public interest can never be served by a dedication of any
broadcast facility to the support of his own partisan ends.
Radio can serve as an instrument of democracy only when devoted to the communication of information and the exchange
of ideas fairly and objectively presented.[14]

After *Mayflower* the FCC started speaking of an affirmative duty
on the part of a licensee to broadcast contrasting viewpoints.[15] In
Johnston Broadcasting Co., for example, the Commission considered
two mutually exclusive applications for a frequency in Birmingham,
Alabama. It based its decision on the program proposals of one ap-
plicant rather than on the qualifications of either of the parties to
run a radio station. The FCC reasoned as follows:

Although the Johnston Broadcasting Company has a policy of
permitting the presentation of conflicting views on controversial matters, there is nothing in this record to indicate that an
affirmative effort will be made to encourage broadcasts of
forums or discussion groups dealing with controversial issues.
. . . On the other hand, Thomas N. Beach's station . . . has
a policy which provides not only for equal opportunities to be
heard for both sides on controversial issues but also for positive action on the part of the station in planning public forums
and round-table discussions to deal with those questions.[16]

The foundation of the Commission's Fairness Doctrine, issued in
1949, is to be found in its Report on Editorializing by Broadcast
Licensees.[17] In the Report, the FCC "recognized that there can be
no one all-embracing formula which licensees can hope to apply
to insure the fair and balanced presentation of all public issues." [18]
As a result of the FCC's consideration of the *Lar Daly* case,[19]
which concerned news broadcasts covering certain political events
by Chicago television stations, Congress amended Section 315 of the
Communications Act to its present form.[20] This 1959 amendment
provides that broadcasters in their coverage of the news are not
relieved of the "obligation imposed upon them under this Act to
operate in the public interest and to afford reasonable opportunity
for the discussion of conflicting views on issues of public impor-

tance." [21] The Supreme Court in *Red Lion Broadcasting Co.* v. *F.C.C.*, followed the FCC's interpretation of this statute:

> This language makes it very plain that Congress, in 1959, announced that the phrase "public interest," which had been in the Act since 1927, imposed a duty on broadcasters to discuss both sides of controversial public issues. In other words, the amendment vindicated the F.C.C.'s general view that the Fairness Doctrine inhered in the public interest.[22]

The FCC, as a result of the landmark decision in *Red Lion,* clearly has the Congressionally authorized power to compel broadcasters to use their facilities to show all sides of a controversial issue:

> Thirty years of consistent administrative construction left undisturbed by Congress until 1959, when that construction was expressly accepted, reinforce the natural conclusion that the public interest language of the Act authorized the Commission to require licensees to use their stations for discussion of public issues, and that the F.C.C. is free to implement this requirement by reasonable rules and regulations which fall short of abridgements of the freedom of speech and press, and of the censorship proscribed by 326 of the Act.[23]

The power is there; the problem now is in the implementation.

In a series of proceedings before the Commission in 1962, the personal attack aspect of the Fairness Doctrine was first crystallized.[24] The Commission issued a Public Notice in 1963.[25] After affirming its adherence to the views expressed in the 1949 Report on Editorializing by Broadcasting Licensees "that the licensee has an affirmative obligation to afford reasonable opportunity for the presentation of contrasting viewpoints on any controversial issue which he chooses to cover," the Commission enumerated three factual situations, including the personal attack context, in which the Fairness Doctrine has been applied.[26] Regarding personal attacks the Notice said:

> When a controversial program involves a personal attack upon an individual or organization, the licensee must transmit the text of the broadcast to the person or group attacked, wherever located, either prior to or at the time of the broadcast, with a specific offer of his station's facilities for an adequate response.[27]

In the 1963 Public Notice the Commission also announced it was going to conduct a study; the resultant Fairness Primer was released in 1964.[28] It is stated there that the FCC hopes that the Public Notice "will reduce significantly the number of fairness complaints made to the Commission" by apprising both the broadcasters and the general public of the Commission's attitude toward the Fairness Doctrine.[29] The Primer emphasized that the context of each case is of fundamental importance. It provided that if the complaint set forth sufficient facts to warrant further Commission consideration, "it will promptly advise the licensee of the complaint and request the licensee's comments on the matter. Full opportunity is given to the licensee to set out all programs which he has presented, or plans to present, with respect to the issue in question during an appropriate time period." [30]

The Primer contained a section specifically devoted to the personal attack issue. In summary, that section emphasized the affirmative duty of the broadcaster to take appropriate steps to insure that the persons attacked were made aware of the nature of the attacks and were also aware of their opportunities to respond.[31] This mandate applies "where there are statements, in connection with a controversial issue of public importance, attacking an individual's or group's integrity, character, or honesty or like personal qualities." [32]

Because of the ineffectiveness of the Public Notices of 1963 and 1964, the FCC issued a Notice of Proposed Rule Making in April 1966.[33] The dual purposes behind such a codification were:

> First, it will emphasize and make more precise licensee obligation in this important area. Second, it will assist the Commission in taking effective action in appropriate circumstances when the procedures are not followed.[34]

The rules themselves were adopted in July 1967.[35] Included in the memorandum opinion and order following the rules was the comment:

> Statements that the rules will discourage, rather than encourage controversial programming ignore the fact the rules do no more than restate existing substantive policy—a policy designed to encourage controversial programming by insuring that more than one viewpoint on issues of public importance are carried over licensee's facilities.[36]

The purpose of the above analysis is to outline the growth and demonstrate the spirit of the Doctrine. As has been discussed, the Fairness Doctrine is divided into the personal attack and the more general, controversial issue aspects. The personal attack regulations are as follows:

> Personal attacks; political editorials. (a) When, during the presentation of views on a controversial issue of public importance, an attack is made upon the honesty, character, integrity or like personal qualities of an identified person or group, the licensee shall, within a reasonable time and in no event later than one week after the attack, transmit to the person or group attacked (1) notification of the date, time and identification of the broadcast; (2) a script or tape (or an accurate summary if a script or tape is not available) of the attack; and (3) an offer of a reasonable opportunity to respond over licensee's facilities.[37]

Many recent cases have determined that the Mexican American is a significant, identifiable group. Therefore, this minority might fall within the ambit of the personal attack portion of these regulations. Essentially, the broadcasters must give adequate coverage to public issues, and the coverage must be fair and accurately reflect the opposing views. The Mexican-American community could insist on compliance with both aspects of the regulations by broadcasters who may be airing comments derogatory to this ethnic group.

In brief, the Fairness Doctrine provides that when a controversial issue of public importance is raised, the broadcast licensee is obligated to show all sides of that issue. "Fairness" thus applies to any controversial issue raised during a broadcast production.

Mexican Americans have had virtually no positive exposure in the electronic media. The advertising industry's selective presentation of exaggerated racial and cultural characteristics is strongly objected to by many concerned with the Chicano's role in American life. The consequences are necessarily ridicule of the Mexican American. To find no fault with a media bombardment of stereotypes is not only a tacit agreement with that image, but also encourages Anglo feelings of superiority over the Mexicans depicted.

Truth obviously cannot be a goal of "fairness." The entire concept of truth is much too vague and elusive. However, the Fairness Doctrine is designed to foster debate, to encourage the presentation of contrasting views, and to make the media responsive to persons other than sponsors. To this end, a denial of Mexican-American access to the media is the antithesis of responsive programming. Recently many examples of positive black images have been broadcast. Chicanos want the same treatment in order to inform the electronic media's mass audience that they are not all banditos or drunkards being loaded into ambulances after cantina brawls as implied by some local broadcasters in communities with large Chicano populations.

Chicanos should monitor all radio and television stations in their communities to ascertain if these stations are meeting their public responsibilities. If stations broadcast remarks, commercials, news programs, or talk shows that are slanted against Chicanos, these stations should be immediately approached with a request that they cease such activities or that Chicano spokesmen or spokeswomen be given fair time for purposes of response.

The media in America influence public opinion to an immeasurable degree and mold the feelings and outlooks of a vast number of persons who listen to radio broadcasts and view television programs. A person's outlook and his feelings about racial and ethnic minorities can be swayed and directed by the media. It is crucial that Chicanos take a closer look at the media operations in their communities and report to the Federal Communications Commission any suspected violations of the law. It is imperative that the Mexican American in this country begin to receive a more positive image in radio broadcasts and on television screens. Only when the Mexican American receives a positive image will this ethnic group have equal footing in the social and economic life of our country.

Notes

[1] U.S., Commission on Civil Rights, *The Mexican-American,* 1968, pp. 3–4.
[2] Ibid., p. 53.
[3] Marvin Karlins, Thomas L. Coffman, and Gary Walters, "On the Fading of Social Stereotypes: Studies in Three Generations of College Students," *Journal of Personality and Social Psychology,* Vol. 13, 1:1–16 (Sept. 1969). See also: Walter Lippmann, *Public Opinion* (New York: Harcourt Brace, 1922), and H. Cantrial, *How Nations See Each Other* (Urbana: University of Illinois Press. 1953).
[4] Daniel Katz and Kenneth W. Braly, "Verbal Stereotypes and Racial Prejudice," in *Readings in Social Psychology,* ed. Maccoby, Newcomb, and Hartley (New York: Holt Rinehart and Winston, 1958), pp. 40–46.
[5] See: F. P. Bishop, *The Ethics of Advertising* (London: 1949), pp. 139–140;

The Regulation of Advertising, 56 Col. L. Rev. 1018, 1089 (1956); and *Television Advertising*. Note: 72 Yale L.J. 145, 156 n. 46 (1962).
[6] Gordon Allport, *The Nature of Prejudice* (Cambridge: 1954), p. 159.
[7] Robert K. Merton, "The Self-Fulfilling Prophecy," *The Antioch Review*, 8:5–17 (August 1948).
[8] Ibid., p. 200.
[9] U.S., Statutes at Large, vol. 44, p. 1162.
[10] *Congressional Record*, 67 Cong., March 12, 1926, p. 5479.
[11] KFKB Broadcasting Assn. v. FRC, 47 F. 2d 670 (1931); Trinity Methodist Church, South v. FRC, 62 F. 2d 850 (1932), Cert. den. 288 U.S. 599.
[12] 48 Stat. 1081, as amended, 47 U.S.C. Sections 301–97 (1964). See 6 F.C.C. Ann. Rep. at 55 (1940).
[13] 8 F.C.C. at 333 (1941).
[14] 8 F.C.C. at 339–340 (1941).
[15] United Broadcasting Co., 10 F.C.C. 515 (1945); Robert H. Scott, 3 P&F Radio Reg. 259 (1946); Johnston Broadcasting Co., 12 F.C.C. 517 (1947); Lawrence W. Harry, 13 F.C.C. 23 (1948); WBNX Broadcasting Co., 12 F.C.C. 805 (1948).
[16] 12 F.C.C. at 517–524 (1947).
[17] Reprinted at 25 P&F Radio Reg. at 1901 (1963).
[18] 25 P&F Radio Reg. at 1907 (1963).
[19] 18 P&F Radio Reg. 238, affd. 18 P&F Radio Reg. 701 (1959).
[20] 47 USCA Section 315(a) (1969).
[21] 47 USCA Section 315(a) (1959).
[22] 395 U.S. 367, 89 S. Ct. 1794, 1801, 23 L. Ed. 2d 371 (1969).
[23] 89 S. Ct. at 1802.
[24] Times-Mirror Broadcasting Co., 24 P&F Radio Reg. 404 (1962); Billings Broadcasting Co., 23 P&F Radio Reg. 951 (1962); Clayton W. Mapoles, 23 P&F Radio Reg. 586 (1962).
[25] 25 P&F Radio Reg. at 1899 (1963).
[26] Ibid.
[27] 25 P&F Radio Reg. at 1900 (1963).
[28] 29 Fed. Reg. 10415 (1964).
[29] 29 Fed. Reg. 10416 (1964).
[30] Ibid.
[31] 29 Fed. Reg. at 10420–10421 (1964).
[32] 29 Fed. Reg. at 10415 (1964).
[33] 31 Fed. Reg. 5710 (1966).
[34] Ibid.
[35] 10 P&F Radio Reg. 2d 1901 (1967).
[36] 10 P&F Radio Reg. at 1908 (1967).
[37] 32 Fed. Reg. 10303 (1967). Twice amended, 32 Fed. Reg. 11531 (1967). 33 Fed. Reg. 5362 (1967).

The Collective Preconscious and Racism

Armando Morales

Commenting on recent urban riots, the 1968 *Report of the National Advisory Commission on Civil Disorders* confronted America with its painful finding that "white racism is essentially responsible for the explosive mixture which has been accumulating in our cities since the end of World War II." [1] Urban America, Inc., and the Urban Coalition, reporting on America's racial crisis one year after the commission's report, stated that blacks and whites remained deeply divided in their perceptions and experiences in American society. At that time blacks and whites were found to be closer to being two societies, increasingly separate and no more equal. [2] Louis L. Knowles and Kenneth Prewitt believe that institutional racism is deeply embedded in American society. They maintain that individual racism consists of overt acts by individuals that may cause death, injury, or the violent destruction of property, but that institutional racism originates in the operation of established

This article is based on a paper at the "Conference on Mental Health and the Mexican-American," sponsored by the Sacramento area chapter, National Association of Social Workers, Sacramento, June 1970.

and respected forces in the society and therefore receives little condemnation from the public.[3]

> To detect institutional racism, especially when it is unintentional or when it is disguised, is a very different task. And even when institutional racism is detected, it is seldom clear who is at fault. How can we say who is responsible for residential segregation, for poor education in ghetto schools, for extraordinarily high unemployment among black men, for racial stereotypes in history textbooks, for the concentration of political power in white society?[4]

Knowles and Prewitt approach the problem by analyzing the ideological patterns in American society that historically and presently sustain practices they label institutionally racist. This article will focus on individual and institutional racism found in racial stereotypes affecting Mexican Americans that might be considered unintentional, disguised, and on an unconscious level.[5] The concept of the collective preconscious will be introduced as fundamental for an understanding of the stubborn persistence of white racism in America. An example of racism involving the media will be presented, and a few recommendations will be made about the interventive role that social workers might adopt in combating racism.

Conscious or unconscious?

It is a difficult task to determine how much racism is conscious and how much is unconscious. Charles Lamb once said that each of us is unconsciously a "bundle of prejudice."[6] Many writers believe that racism is rooted in the unconscious of individuals who are therefore unaware of these feelings.[7]

Whether racism is a deliberate device used to attain specific goals or an unconscious, unintentional reaction is irrelevant. In either case it has the same effect, and unrecognized, unconscious racism may actually be more injurious to minority group members than the deliberate kind.[8] For example, a deliberate remark, such as "We don't want dumb Mexicans and niggers to become medical doctors and social workers," produces the same results as "We recognize the disadvantage at which black and brown applicants have been placed by historical injustices—but those who cannot meet requirements will not be admitted. We have to maintain a certain quality and standard." Ethnicity and color cease to be used as factors for filtering out the "outgroup," and "objective" criteria are effectively substituted to accomplish the same goals. Racism? Class prejudice? Discrimination? Indeed, these are complex problems that only the minority group militants wish to confront—quite possibly because they do not view them as complex problems.

Herbert Blumer maintains that the vast literature on race prejudice is dominated by the idea that prejudice exists fundamentally as a feeling or set of feelings lodged in the individual. These feelings are usually depicted as antipathy, hostility, hatred, intolerance, and aggressiveness.[9] Blumer believes, however, that race prejudice is a defensive reaction that functions to preserve the integrity and the position of the dominant group.[10] He does not specify whether the defensive reaction functions on a conscious or an unconscious level, but a conscious defensive reaction is implied. "Race prejudice has a history," says Blumer, and "the history is *collective* [italics added]."[11] For the purposes of this article, the term *collective* will be understood to mean the simultaneity, uniformity, or similarity of a response to a stimulus among many members of a group or society.

The collective psychological experience

Although one might find general agreement about the definitions and operationalizations of the concepts of consciousness, preconscious, and unconscious as they pertain to individuals, the literature reflects inconsistencies in defining and applying these concepts on a collective level, that is, on the levels of the collective unconscious, the collective preconscious, and collective consciousness. The first writer to formulate an initial conception of a collective feeling, collective awareness, or collective consciousness was George Henry Lewes in 1874 in *Problems of Life and Mind*. Sociologist Franklin Henry Giddings quotes Lewes as calling this phenomenon a "general mind," defined as "the residual store of experiences common to all." [12] Lewes suggests that the "collective experience of the race" fashioned the experience of the individual and that:

> It makes a man accept what he cannot understand, and obey
> what he does not believe. His thoughts are only partly his own;
> they are also the thoughts of others. His actions are guided
> by the will of others; even in rebellion he has them in his
> mind. His standard is outside.[13]

Emile Durkheim viewed sociology as a study of social facts or social currents. In social life there are some facts, Durkheim maintained, that are inexplicable in physical or psychological analytical terms, and there are ways of acting, thinking, and feeling external to the individual that are endowed with a power of coercion over him. Durkheim's treatment of social facts is related closely to his discussions of collective consciousness, which he defined as the sum total of beliefs and sentiments common to most members of society, forming a system in its own right.[14]

In 1896 Giddings himself advanced the social theory of consciousness of kind, which is a state of consciousness in which any being recognizes another conscious being as of like kind. United through consciousness of kind, individual minds affect one another in such a manner that "they simultaneously feel the same sensation or emotion, arrive at one judgment, and perhaps act in concert."[15] Giddings saw consciousness of kind "acting on" social conduct in many different ways.

> Within racial lines the consciousness of kind underlies the more definite ethnical and political groupings, it is the basis of class distinctions, of enumerable forms of alliance, of rules of intercourse, and of peculiarities of society. Our conduct towards those whom we feel to be most like ourselves is *instinctively* and rationally different from our conduct towards others, whom we believe to be less like ourselves [italics added].[16]

Defining "instinct," he says that it is "knowledge which is *consciously* imparted to the young by their elders."[17] All of these sociopsychological processes seem to be, for Giddings, entirely on a conscious level.

Eduard von Hartmann, the nineteenth-century German philosopher, was one of the first persons to introduce into the literature the concept of the unconscious. In *The Philosophy of the Unconscious,* he maintained that conscious life was not the only existence.[18] Nevertheless, his theories were primarily metaphysical. Friedrich Nietzsche, in *The Dawn of Day,* anticipated Sigmund Freud's theories of the unconscious when he suggested that "all our so-called consciousness is a more or less fantastic commentary on an unknown text, one which is perhaps unknowable but yet felt."[19] Freud and Josef Breuer made the discovery of the unconscious—the realization of the important role played by unconscious processes in the determination of behavior—and in 1893 published their joint paper, "On The Psychical Mechanisms of Hysterical Phenomena," which constituted a great milestone in understanding the unconscious.[20]

In 1923 Freud distinguished two kinds of unconscious: "one which is easily, under frequently occurring circumstances, transformed into something conscious, and another with which this transformation is difficult and takes place only subject to a considerable expenditure of effort or possibly never at all." [21] To avoid ambiguity in the concept, Freud said, "We call the unconscious which is only latent, and thus easily becomes conscious, the 'preconscious' and retain 'unconscious' for the other." [22] There is evidence to show that Freud was attempting to broaden these concepts to a collective level.

In *Group Psychology and the Analysis of the Ego,* published in 1921, Freud appeared to be interested in Gustave Le Bon's concept of the group mind. Freud quoted Le Bon as saying:

> The most striking peculiarity presented by a psychological group (mass or crowd) is the following. Whoever be the individuals that compose it, however like or unlike be their mode of life, their occupations, their character, or their intelligence, the fact that they have been transformed in a group puts them in possession of a sort of collective mind which makes them feel, think, and act in a manner quite different from that in which each individual of them would feel, think, and act were he in a state of isolation.[23]

According to Freud, Le Bon believed that the particular acquirements of individuals become obliterated in a group and their distinctiveness vanishes. The racial (inherited, handed down from generation to generation) unconscious emerges, and what is heterogeneous is submerged in what is homogeneous. A mental superstructure develops (group mind) out of the unconscious foundations. In this way individuals in a group show an average character that at times is contrary to the character presented by the isolated individual.[24] Although the group phenomenon described by Le Bon appears similar to what might be called group contagion, his "group mind" and "racial unconscious" approach a concept of collective unconscious.

Carl Gustav Jung is credited with introducing the concept of the collective unconscious in 1934. Jung defined the term as follows:

> The collective unconscious is a part of the psyche which can be negatively distinguished from a personal unconscious by the fact that it does not, like the latter, owe its existence to personal experience and consequently is not a personal acquisition. While the personal unconscious is made up essentially of contents which have at one time been conscious but which have disappeared from consciousness through having been forgotten or repressed, the contents of the collective unconscious have never been individually acquired, but owe their existence exclusively to heredity. Whereas the personal unconscious consists for the most part of *complexes,* the content of the collective unconscious is made up essentially of archetypes.[25]

In addition to a person's immediate consciousness, which is of a thoroughly personal nature, Jung believed that there is a second psychic system of a collective, universal, and impersonal nature that is identical in all individuals. This collective unconscious does not develop individually, according to Jung, but is biologically inherited. It consists of preexistent forms (the archetypes), which can only become conscious secondarily and which give definite form to certain psychic contents.[26]

Le Bon's 1920 concepts of group mind and racial (inherited) unconscious seem similar to Jung's 1934 concept of the collective unconscious which is also inherited. Their collective unconscious biological inheritance, however, assumes a vertical generational collective process rather than an unconscious, nonbiological horizontal group inheritance. In other words, Jung and Le Bon suggest that the racial and collective unconscious are biologically inherited rather than acquired from others through some psychosocial process.

More recently, J. L. Moreno has attempted to clarify these concepts in his efforts toward understanding complex group psychodynamics. He states:

> Neither the concept of unconscious states (Freud) nor that of collective unconscious states (Jung) can be easily applied to these problems without stretching the meaning of the terms. The free associations of A may be a path to the unconscious states of A; the free associations of B may be a path to the unconscious states of B; but can the unconscious material of A ever link naturally and directly with the unconscious material of B unless they *share* in unconscious states? [27]

Moreno suggests that one must look for a concept that is so constructed that the objective indication for the existence of this two-way process does not come from a single psyche but from a still deeper reality in which the unconscious states of two or several individuals are interlocked with a system of "co-unconscious states."

Freud maintained that it was not easy to translate the concepts of individual psychology into mass psychology;[28] he would have agreed with Moreno that difficulties arise when one attempts to stretch the meaning of these concepts. Considering these limitations, however, continuing efforts have to be made to clarify, refine, and test these concepts in practice. Within the framework of these goals and constraints, this writer will attempt to build a concept utilizing some of the theoretical formulations advanced by the authors quoted in this article, who have endeavored to conceptualize some of the psychological processes—conscious and unconscious—that lead to collective behavior. The concept of the collective preconscious is therefore introduced.

Racism and the collective preconscious

The term *preconscious* is preferable to *unconscious* because it refers to thoughts that are unconscious at a particular moment but are not repressed, that is, unacceptable impulses or ideas rendered unconscious. These thoughts are therefore capable of becoming conscious, or available to recall.[29] Because racism offers an element of psychological advantage or reward to the dominant group,[30] it would appear inconsistent to conclude that these feelings would be unpleasant and unacceptable and therefore repressed to the unconscious.

To summarize, the collective preconscious will denote the simultaneity, uniformity, or similarity of a response to a stimulus perceived on a preconscious psychological level among many members of a group or society. It will include some of the beliefs and sentiments common to many members of society (Durkheim), including white racism, which may exist on a preconscious level. People unconsciously (substituting Giddings's "instinctively") learn to discriminate in their social conduct with others who are different. The act of discriminating may be of a positive (discriminating in favor of "ingroup") or negative (discriminating against "outgroup") nature.

It is theorized, therefore, that the collective preconscious acts in concert toward outgroups. Its actions are based on beliefs, norms, and values acquired through the acculturation process of formal and informal education. Racist attitudes may be absorbed from parents and important others on a conscious as well as on a preconscious level, as, for instance, through subtle racist advertising. The United States Commission on Civil Rights asserts that television has devastatingly confirmed the distorted perception that makes white people feel "normal" and superior in relation to ethnic minority groups. Whereas the ethnic minority group is made to feel inferior, the dominant white group is made to feel superior.[31] Dore Schary, playwright and producer, maintains that the media accommodate themselves to reflecting the culture rather than leading it. He believes that the media may "unwittingly be nourishing prejudice." [32]

> Indeed, the media may be as unknowingly accommodating to today's prejudices as they were to the prejudices of the past. So, for example, just as our society is nearly silent on the subject of Mexican-Americans, Puerto Ricans, and American Indians, the media too are silent. By this silence the media obviously do not intend to condone prejudice against these groups. But such, of course, is the indirect result. For where prejudice is not directly engaged, it is in effect sustained.[33]

By and large, the media are silent in regard to the economic, educational, and political suppression of ethnic groups by the dominant society. On the other hand, they are active in fostering racial prejudice toward Mexican Americans—a group of nearly ten million persons.

Thomas M. Martinez declares that advertisers exhibiting racist thinking at the expense of persons of Mexican descent are also creating unfavorable racial and cultural stereotypes in minds that previously did not harbor them. "Even unprejudiced parents," he asserts, "are not equipped to counter the steady and subtle bombardment of prejudicial suggestions that advertisers conveniently communicate to their children." [34] Table 1 was developed by Martinez to demonstrate how advertisers promote racism.

Some of Martinez's students wrote critical letters to firms whose commercials and advertisements communicated racism. Schary's viewpoint that the media may unknowingly be accommodating today's prejudices is negated by the following reply received from the Frito-Lay Corporation:

> In response to your letter dated February 25, we did not and never have had any racist intentions in presenting the Frito-Bandito cartoon character. It was meant to be a simple character which is intended to make you laugh, in turn we hope

that this laughter will leave our trademark implanted in your memory.[35]

Martinez suggests that the seeds of prejudice against Mexicans and Mexican Americans are "implanted in your memory." Would it not be possible for the collective preconscious to be affected in this manner? The viewers "incorporate" the entire product. "Incorporate" is used in the psychoanalytical (oral, eye, and ear) sense; that is, the viewers have "swallowed" the product. What is incorporated,

Table 1. Advertisers promoting racism: a partial listing

Name of advertiser	Context or content of ad	Racist message
Granny Goose	*Fat Mexican toting guns, ammunition	Mexicans=overweight, carry deadly weapons
Frito-Lay	†*"Frito-Bandito"	Mexicans=sneaky, thieves
Liggett & Meyers	*"Paco" never "feenishes" anything, not even revolution	Mexicans=too lazy to improve selves
R. J. Reynolds Camel Cigarettes	*Mexican bandito *"Typical" Mexican village, all sleeping or bored	Mexicans=bandits Mexicans=do nothings, irresponsible
General Motors	†*White, rustic man holding three Mexicans at gunpoint	Mexicans=should be and can be arrested by superior white man
Lark (Liggett & Meyers)	†Mexican house painter covered with paint	Mexicans=sloppy workers, undependable
Philco-Ford	†*Mexican sleeping next to TV set	Mexicans=always sleeping
Frigidaire	*Mexican banditos interested in freezer	Mexicans=thieves, seeking Anglo artifacts
Arrid	*Mexican bandito sprays underarm, voice says, "If it works for him it will work for you."	Mexicans=stink the most

†=newspaper or magazine ad
*=television commercial

Author's note: It is possible that some of these promotions are not appearing in some parts of the United States; it is also possible that some have already been discontinued. (Reprinted, by permission, from Martinez, Advertising and Racism, *El Grito,* 2:13 [Summer 1969].)

therefore, is an association of the pleasantness of the product, a psychological reward (I'm superior), and a projection of badness onto others (ethnic minority groups).

Mary Ellen Goodman and others affirm that standardized ideas and feelings about race are "transmitted" from one generation of Americans to the next.[36] She sees this "transmission process" affecting very young children and, in a study of 103 children, found it shocking to observe four-year-olds manifesting unmistakable signs of the onset of racial bigotry.[37]

It is theorized that not only is the collective preconscious of white children unknowingly affected by white racist ideology but also the minds of the oppressed targets—minority group children. In a study of 229 Philadelphia first- and third-graders of diverse ages, races, school abilities, and socioeconomic backgrounds, Raymond G. Taylor, Jr. found that children between the ages of six and ten possess negatively valued stereotypes of blacks and that white children held more of them than did black children. Black children were found to accept to a high degree the stereotypes of "dirty" and "dumb" as applied to their race.[38]

Considering the number of hours that children watch television, the impact of racist messages would appear astounding in relation to future white racism in America. Masses of people sharing racist beliefs in collective preconscious states would continue unknowingly to act in concert to exploit, oppress, and subordinate ethnic minorities to their will. Ethnic minority group children would unconsciously adopt and act out the roles that the media create for them and that society reinforces.

Possible approaches to intervention

If one can begin to conceptualize racism as existing for many persons in a collective preconscious state, then interventive modes on a large scale will have to be considered. Three possible approaches will be suggested.

Before social workers can confront collective preconscious racism "out there," they must discover and painfully probe their own preconscious feelings. White people must overcome their habitual exclusion of minority group members in this process of self-examination because they themselves are not likely to discover all the forms of subordination they impose on others without the help of those others.[39] For example, the Race Relations Institute sponsored by the National Association of Social Workers (NASW) at Warrenton, Virginia, August 13–16, 1967, did not include Mexican Americans among its participants.[40] Similarly, excluding ethnic minorities from the schools of social work for reasons of "academic standards," "no quotas," and "quality" has the net result of not disturbing collective preconscious feelings. The profession, in effect, unconsciously blinds itself to racist actions. Minority group students, who have been—and still are—its victims, are so sensitive to indications of racism that their presence in graduate schools of social work and their participation in professional policy making would certainly enhance the quality of the profession.

A second approach to the problem would be to promote social action through social work organizations, such as NASW, as a mode of intervention against forces in the media that influence the collective preconscious. Minority group members are at the mercy of the advertising media, which, by and large, ignore their pleas. Organized social workers operating on local and national levels could lend support and bargaining power to groups concerned with the damaging implications of certain commercials. Professional organizations and minority group members together could confront industry and the media in an attempt to put an end to one phenomenon that influences the collective preconscious and helps perpetuate the problem of white racism in America.

A third approach calls for additional research studies of the impact of televised racist stereotypes on Mexican-American children and the children of other ethnic minorities. Goodman and Taylor have done some pioneering work in this area.

Summary

This article has addressed itself to the problem of white racism in America with a special emphasis on its manifestations in relation to an ethnic minority rarely discussed in the current literature— persons of Mexican descent residing in the United States. The concept of the collective preconscious was developed from the works of Blumer, Lewes, Giddings, Durkheim, Le Bon, Freud, Jung, and Moreno as a beginning concept for an understanding of some of the collective, social-psychological dynamics that might be found in white racism, a phenomenon that is apparently passed on from generation to generation. Examples of the media's portrayal of Mexican Americans were presented to demonstrate how the media may unintentionally be contributing to white racism by implanting a superior racist message in the mind of the white child and an inferior message in the mind of the minority group child.

Three approaches to combating racism were suggested in the article. Certainly there are more. Briefly restated, ethnic minority students and faculty make a contribution to social work by helping it become more conscious of racism *in* and *out of* the profession. Through increased consciousness of the various manifestations of white racism, social work can approach the task of effectively influencing, by means of social action, those forces that become part of the collective preconscious. Finally, more research is needed to understand the impact of white racism on minority group children.

Notes

[1] National Advisory Commission on Civil Disorders, *Report of the National Advisory Commission on Civil Disorders* (New York: Grosset and Dunlap, Bantam Books, 1968), p. 10.
  For the purposes of this article, the definition of racism found in *Webster's Third New International Dictionary* will be adopted: "the assumption that psychocultural traits and capacities are determined by biological race and that races differ decisively from one another which is usually coupled with a belief in the inherent superiority of a particular race and its right to domination over others"; see *Webster's Third New International Dictionary,* s.v. "racism."
[2] Urban America, Inc. and The Urban Coalition, *One Year Later* (New York: Frederick A. Praeger, Publishers, 1969), p. 116.
[3] Louis L. Knowles and Kenneth Prewitt, *Institutional Racism in America* (Englewood Cliffs, N.J.: Prentice-Hall, 1969), p. 1.
[4] Ibid., p. 6.
[5] The literature is practically devoid of material on white racism and its impact on Mexican Americans—a group consisting of ten million persons of Mexican descent residing mostly in the southwestern part of the United States. The 1960 census showed a fairly large number also residing in Illinois, Indiana, Kansas, Michigan, Missouri, Nebraska, New York, Ohio, Utah, Washington, and Wisconsin. Over 80 percent of Mexican Americans are found living in the cities and, like blacks, are the objects of racial prejudice and discrimination, which are reflected in their median family income of $4,165 and in their education—7.1 years of school completed compared with 12.1 school years completed for Anglos and 9.0 for blacks. For further information, see U.S., Department of Commerce, Bureau of the Census, *We The Mexican Americans: Nosotros, Los México Americanos* (Washington, D.C.: Government Printing Office, 1970), and for a community perspective of these problems, see *La Raza,* 1 (July 1970), 3571 City Terrace Drive, Los Angeles, California 90063.
[6] Charles Y. Glock and Ellen Siegelman, eds., *Prejudice U.S.A.* (New York: Frederick A. Praeger, Publishers, 1969), p. vii.
[7] George D. Kelsey, *Racism and the Christian Understanding of Man* (New York: Charles Scribner's Sons, 1965), pp. 58–59; U. S., Commission on Civil Rights, *Racism in America and How to Combat It,* Clearinghouse Publication, Urban Series No. 1 (Washington, D.C.: Government Printing Office, 1970), p. 5; Erbin Crowell, Jr., "Anti-Racism: The New Movement," *Civil Rights Di-*

gest, 2:26 (Winter 1969); Mary Ellen Goodman, *Race Awareness in Young Children* (New York: Collier Books, 1952), p. 265; Arnold M. Rose, ed., *Mental Health and Mental Disorder* (New York: W. W. Norton & Co., 1955), p. 388; William I. Thomas, "The Psychology of Race Prejudice," in *Race Prejudice and Discrimination,* ed. Arnold M. Rose (New York: Alfred A. Knopf, 1953), p. 466; Marie Jahoda, *Race Relations and Mental Health* (Paris: UNESCO Publications, 1960), p. 16; Eugene B. Brody, "Psychiatry and Prejudice," *American Handbook of Psychiatry,* ed. Silvano Arieti (New York: Basic Books, 1966), 3:633–34.

[8] U. S., Commission on Civil Rights, *Racism in America,* p. 5.

[9] Herbert Blumer, "Race Prejudice as a Sense of Group Position," in *Race Relations: Problems and Theory,* ed. Jitsuichi Masuoka and Preston Valien (Chapel Hill: University of North Carolina Press, 1961), p. 217.

[10] Ibid., p. 222.

[11] Ibid., p. 227.

[12] George Henry Lewes, *Problems of Life and Mind,* quoted in Franklin Henry Giddings, *The Principles of Sociology* (New York: Macmillan Co., 1896), pp. 132–33.

[13] Ibid.

[14] Nicholas Timasheff, *Sociological Theory: Its Nature and Growth* (New York: Random House, 1955), pp. 106–109.

[15] Giddings, *Principles of Sociology,* p. 134.

[16] Ibid., p. 18.

[17] Ibid., pp. 142–43.

[18] Eduard von Hartmann, *The Philosophy of the Unconscious,* trans. William Chatterton Coupland (London: Kegan Paul, Trench, Trübner & Co., 1893).

[19] Friedrich Nietzsche, *The Dawn of Day,* quoted in Felix Marti-Ibanez, ed., "Dreams in History," *MD Medical Newsmagazine,* 9:173–74 (December 1965).

[20] James C. Coleman, *Abnormal Psychology and Modern Life* (New York: Scott, Foresman & Company, 1950), p. 49.

[21] Sigmund Freud, "The Dissection of the Psychical Personality," in *The Complete Introductory Lectures on Psychoanalysis,* ed. and trans. James Strachey (New York: W. W. Norton & Company, 1923), p. 535.

[22] Ibid.

[23] Sigmund Freud, *Group Psychology and the Analysis of the Ego,* trans. James Strachey (London: Hogarth Press, 1948), pp. 6–7.

[24] Ibid., p. 9.

[25] Carl Gustav Jung, *The Archetypes and the Collective Unconscious* (Princeton, N.J.: Princeton University Press, 1959), p. 42.

[26] Ibid., p. 43.

[27] J. L. Moreno, "Psychodrama," in *American Handbook of Psychiatry,* ed. Silvano Arieti (New York: Basic Books, 1959), 2:1389.

[28] Sigmund Freud, *Moses and Monotheism* (New York: Random House, 1955), p. 170.

[29] Charles Rycroft, *A Critical Dictionary of Psychoanalysis* (New York: Basic Books, 1968), p. 122.

[30] See Arnold M. Rose, *The Roots of Prejudice* (Paris: UNESCO Publications, 1951), p. 7; Barbara E. Shannon, "Implications of White Racism for Social Work Practice," *Social Casework,* 51:274 (May 1970); James P. Comer, "White Racism: Its Root, Form and Function," *The American Journal of Psychiatry,* 126:802–806 (December 1969).

[31] U. S., Commission on Civil Rights, *Racism in America,* p. 11.

[32] Glock and Siegelman, *Prejudice U.S.A.,* p. 104.

[33] Ibid., p. 105.

[34] Thomas M. Martinez, "Advertising and Racism: The Case of the Mexican-American," *El Grito,* 2:6 (Summer 1969).

[35] Ibid., p. 8.

[36] Goodman, *Race Awareness,* p. 244; Shannon, "Implications of White Racism," p. 274; Comer, "White Racism," p. 805.

[37] Goodman, *Race Awareness,* p. 245.

[38] Raymond G. Taylor, Jr., "Racial Stereotypes in Young Children," *Journal of Psychology,* 64:137–42 (November 1966).

[39] U. S., Commission on Civil Rights, *Racism in America,* p. 26.

[40] Roger R. Miller, ed., *Race, Research, and Reason: Social Work Perspectives* (New York: National Association of Social Workers, 1969), pp. 189–190.

Individual
Involvement
in the
Chicano Movement

Grace Burruel and Nelba Chavez

For many decades, Mexican Americans have been subservient to the dominant ethnic group. Recently, however, some Mexican Americans have been speaking up collectively. They are saying *Basta* to racism, social inequality, and discrimination. They want to be seen and heard; they are proud of their heritage; and they are attempting to revive their culture.

This attitudinal change has triggered many events throughout the Southwest, giving birth to a social movement—the Chicano movement—that may be viewed as the emergence of the new self-image and self-determination of the Mexican American. For the purpose of this study, the Chicano movement was defined as a collectivity of Mexican Americans who identify themselves as Chicano, as opposed to other labels, to promote new dignity and pride and to bring about social change for the betterment of *La Raza*.

Current literature merely describes the actions and characteristics of the new Chicano. For example, Edward Simmen points out:

> Tired of being the new "nigger"—tired of being the new minority target, the real Mexican-American is standing up and speaking—speaking sense. Tired of being exploited by manage-

ment, ignored by labor, and quickly forgotten by "promising" politicians, the real Mexican-American is standing up and demanding—demanding attention, recognition.[1]

Mario Compean speaking about Chicano power, says:

For many years people spoke of the passivity of *La Raza*. Well, in 1963 there was an awakening. There was an awakening of what the sociologist and people in general had called a sleeping giant. In 1963 in Crystal City Chicanos took over the city government and inspired people elsewhere to become active. . . . As a result of all this activity, this awakening we have had—especially in Texas—a concerted effort to make the Mexicano visible in every aspect of society—economically, politically, and otherwise.[2]

Ralph Guzman further asserts:

The new Chicano is telling the Anglo that things have changed. He's young, tough, smart and has a deep anger at injustice. . . . The goals of Brown Power may yet be confused but the Brown groups are not confused about their desire for action—direct action. They want confrontation and meaningful results.[3]

As with the literature, existing studies pertaining to Mexican Americans do not explain this change in attitude or other observable behavior. On the contrary, according to these interpretations, Mexican Americans would never be expected to speak up or initiate any social action.

Any attempt to analyze what is happening to the Mexican American today by examining what has been written requires critical evaluation of the perspective, approach, and thinking of the writers. It is contended that much that has been written about the Mexican American has been based on the concept of "traditional culture" to explain the conditions or characteristics of Mexican Americans. Observations, analyses, and conclusions of these writers are therefore distorted. Many writers begin with preconceived notions of Mexicans and merely perpetuate the already existing stereotypes. Cultural traits are perceived as the cause of the social conditions and attitudes of Mexican Americans with no consideration of the possibility that these may be the effect of having to live as a minority. From this point of view, the problems facing Mexican Americans are inherent in the nature of the people; thus, there is little hope for change.

For example, Ruth Tuck, Lyle Saunders, and William Madsen studied Mexican Americans to determine their cultural attributes by searching specifically for behavior, beliefs, and values that were supposed to be characteristic of Mexican Americans.[4] They never entertained the idea that many of these attributes might be the result of poverty or oppressive conditions rather than of ethnicity.

Along the same line, other authors, who have studied the social and attitudinal characteristics that inhibit acculteration and assimilation, also ascribe causation to the Mexican American per se rather than to the social context in which he lives. Hence, according to many writers, the Mexican American is an ahistorical person and what is happening today is without precedent.

Carey McWilliams is one of the few writers who attempts to analyze the social conditions of Mexican Americans by exploring the forces which may explain their attitudes or manner of coping. In his book *North From Mexico,* he describes the exploitation of Mexican Americans and their attempts to rebel against their subordinate status. In relating the struggle of Mexican Americans, he writes: "Once they had become conscious, however, of the way in which they were being subordinated in the social structure, the immigrant attempted to rebel. Dating from the late 'twenties,' this rebellion was most decisively crushed." [5] Today, through the Chicano movement, Mexican Americans are reviving the efforts of their antecedents, but with greater force and in greater numbers.

The Chicano movement represented a highly complex phenomenon to study. It could have been studied from any of several parameters. The focus could have been on ideology, leadership, structure, and process. It could have been studied from the viewpoint of the individual and the factors that impel him to participate in the movement. In general, social movements have been analyzed within the context of a deviant or threatening force; however, in this project, the Chicano movement was considered advantageous to the Mexican-American community.

Purpose of the study

The purpose of the study was to begin to understand and conceptualize the meaning of the Chicano movement in relation to the process of individual involvement. The major task was to determine why and how individuals become involved and to learn about their views, feelings, and attitudes regarding the movement.

Because of the present dearth of information, the goal was not to test scientific hypothesis. Instead, an attempt was made to gain new insights into the complicated phenomenon of why and how people become involved in the Chicano movement. The data were obtained from lengthy, unstructured interviews with eighteen Chicanos, ranging from twenty-four to seventy years of age, who were known to have various relationships with the movement.

Affecting Factors

Examining those factors that affected an individual and motivated him to join the Chicano movement, it was postulated that involvement was the result of accumulated experiences rather than of an isolated experience, and it was not discontinuous with previous life experiences. The questions to be answered were how individuals become involved in the Chicano movement and what constitutes the process of individual involvement. It was speculated also that there were different levels of involvement because of the variation among individuals and the heterogeneity of the Mexican-American community.

Rationale

Not only do theories concerning the Chicano movement seem to be nonexistent, but systematic investigation has also been limited. Therefore, rather than having broad-based expertise to serve as a guide, our beginning notions about the movement were foreshadowed by personal experience and knowledge about the movement.

This lack of a theoretical base necessitated a methodology that could produce information and insight leading to a refinement of concepts that might begin to explain observable behavior. The use of unstructured techniques afforded the opportunity of "developing the analytical, conceptual, and categorical components of explanations from the data itself—rather than from . . . preconceived, rigidly structured and highly quantified techniques. . . ."[6] As a result, this study was exploratory and based on participant observation methods.

Selection of study population

The study population consisted of eighteen Mexican Americans from the Southwest, purposely selected to include individuals whose involvement ranged from noninvolved to actively involved. The initial intent was to use individuals about whom nothing was known; however, the disturbance following the moratorium in East Los Angeles coincided with the schedule for data collection. Because of the existing tension, it was decided to limit the contacts to those individuals whom we knew personally or through a mutual acquaintance.

Method of observation

The assumption that involvement is a process and is continuous with previous life experiences led to selecting case studies as a major method of investigation. A self-characterization was sought, tracing the development of involvement. The areas explored were present situation, past circumstances, and feelings and attitudes toward the movement.

Because the motivation that prompts an individual to join a social movement is often unclear to him, it is even less likely to be understood by an outside observer. This fact became particularly clear during the pretest part of the study when it was learned that the questions were too structured. Instead, it was necessary to permit each individual candid discussion and expression of feelings and ideas about the movement and his involvement. Because of the subtleties implicit in the attitudes and feelings being studied, the open-ended, intensive interview was selected as the best method of acquiring data.

Although the interviews were unstructured, there were five general areas discussed with all respondents. The first—social-personal situation—included age, sex, marital status, educational level, and occupation. The second area explored was the individual's perception of the Chicano movement in relation to goals and means. The third general area pertained to perception of the Mexican-American situation in the United States, particularly the Southwest, and personal adjustment to the dominant Anglo society. Each individual's declared perception of himself in relation to the movement was the fourth general area. Finally, development of involvement in the movement, including description of life experiences, influence of other significant persons, and motivating factors, was discussed.

Data analysis

From the data, a typology of the Chicano movement evolved. The involvement of the individuals interviewed ranged along a continuum from those opposed to the movement to those actively involved. The classification was based on each individual's declared perception of himself in relation to the movement. Those who were opposed presented no classification problems. This situation, however, was not true for the other individuals. Although their responses also ranged along a continuum, the divisions or categories were necessarily arbitrary.

Four dimensions of involvement emerged: negatively affectively involved, positively affectively involved, indirectly behaviorally involved, and directly behaviorally involved. It should be noted that movement was not restricted to one direction, as it can be forward or backward. Furthermore, it was not possible to state how much more or less involved any given individual was than the other. (See table 1.)

1. *Negatively affectively involved.* This category included those individuals (two) who denounced the efforts of the movement and viewed it as a destructive force or a series of disturbances led by trouble-makers. They stated they wanted no part of it.

2. *Positively affectively involved.* In this category were those individuals (five) who expressed a positive feeling toward the movement but did not participate actively. Their involvement was primarily on a verbal level.

3. *Indirectly behaviorally involved.* This group included those individuals (three) who believed in the cause of the movement (betterment of the Mexican-American situation in the United States) but have some conflict about the means. They devoted time to the movement on an individual level within the profession or other established means.

4. *Directly behaviorally involved.* The largest category included those individuals (eight) who strongly believed in the cause and the means and were active participants in movement activities. They organized, took part in, or led protest and other group activities.

Table 1. Demographic data

Level of involvement		Age	Sex	Occupation	Education	Marital status	Generation
Negatively affectively involved	1.	49	F	Assistant in public agency	High school	M	First
	2.	46	M	Laborer in factory	Elementary school	M	Immigrant
Positively affectively involved	3.	45	M	Certified public accountant	College graduate	M	Immigrant
	4.	29	M	Mechanic	One year college	D	Third
	5.	27	M	Graduate student		M	First
	6.	28	M	Captain in Air Force	College graduate	M	Third
	7.	70	M	Retired business manager	Seventh grade	M	Second
Indirectly behaviorally involved	8.	29	F	Graduate student		S	Third
	9.	36	F	Social worker	Master's degree (MSW)	S	Third
	10.	62	F	Counselor in school	Master's degree (Education)	S	Second
Directly behaviorally involved	11.	24	M	Student in junior college	Master's degree (MSW)	S	Third
	12.	36	F	Graduate student		S	First
	13.	31	M	Social worker		M	Third
	14.	22	F	Store operator	High school	M	Third
	15.	70	M	Retired mine worker	Fourth grade	M	Immigrant
	16.	34	M	Collector for credit union	High school	M	Third
	17.	29	M	Director of social program	Graduate student	M	Third
	18.	27	M	Social work paraprofessional	Eighth grade	M	First

This typology is not exhaustive of the levels of involvement. For example, it is believed that a higher level—more revolutionary-oriented individuals—exist. It was not possible, however, to interview any of these individuals.

Analysis of the various levels of involvement

The responses were analyzed to determine if there were any factors that characterized all of the individuals categorized at a particular level of involvement. In each group similarities and differences were sought in relation to (1) social-personal situation, (2) adjustment to living in an Anglo society, (3) perception of the Mexican-American situation, and (4) perception of the movement. These general categories emerged during the pretesting of the interview schedule.

Those individuals who were negatively affectively involved expressed no explicit awareness of Mexican-American problems. They were primarily concerned with their own socioeconomic status and the rewards of the Anglo economic system. They considered the movement a threat to their own personal achievements.

The next two groups, the positively affectively involved and the indirectly behaviorally involved, both expressed an awareness and concern about the problems of Mexican Americans; however, they viewed Mexican Americans as the generators of their own problems. With some of these individuals, this perception was the result of having "made it" themselves and the belief that other Mexican Americans could do it also if they worked hard and took advantage of available opportunities. With others, it was related to their strong belief in American ideals and close association with the American way of life.

Prior to becoming involved in the movement, it was necessary for the individuals in the indirectly behaviorally involved group to resolve an internal conflict in relation to explicit identification as Chicanos. Subsequently, external pressures induced them to identify with the broader ethnic group. Although they came to accept the ideals and goals of the movement, participation was primarily on an individual basis and through established channels for effecting change.

Within the directly behaviorally involved group, there were two distinct subgroups—those who openly denied their ethnicity in order to "make it" in the dominant society and those who experienced difficulties in adjusting to the Anglo society and retained a closer identification with their ethnic group.

In the first subgroup, the influence of a close associate was responsible for two of the three individuals' becoming involved in the movement. With the third, it was her own internal turmoil and a desire to compensate for having denied her identity. All of these individuals, however, reacted to earlier experiences as Mexican Americans by becoming actively involved in movement activities. The individuals in the second subgroup struggled to maintain a close identification with their ethnic group. Direct, active involvement in the movement was the culmination of accumulated anger and frustration.

Motivation, such as individual discontent, thwarted personal goals, or dissatisfaction with their own personal life, was not revealed by any of the individuals interviewed. Involvement emanated more from their perception of the conditions of the broader ethnic group than from individual discontent. The involvement was more sensing a problem and wanting to do something about it themselves.

The level of involvement was influenced by the individual's perception of the reason for the group's inferior socioeconomic position. For example, if it was believed that Mexican Americans themselves were responsible for their status, involvement was on an individual level within established means, as in the cases of those who were indirectly behaviorally involved.

Those who were convinced that outside forces were the cause, such as the directly behaviorally involved, chose to participate on a higher level, as a group, to attempt to change the system. However, they also devoted time to the movement on an individual level. This group seemed more aware of the forces that operate to maintain a group of people in an inferior position. They also demonstrated awareness of the realities of the present power structure that influenced their decision to work at both levels.

From the data, a predictive model of the process of involvement was developed. It is based on the concept of "value-added" or aggregate conditions, which, in complete or partial combination, seem to account for the involvement or the level of involvement of the individuals interviewed.[7] Up to a point, the same factors that explained the directly behaviorally involved also explained the indirectly behaviorally involved and the affectively involved, both negatively and positively. For example, positive, affective involvement may be transformed into indirect or direct behavioral involvement.

The following conditions appear to be necessary before an individual becomes involved:

1. *Some degree of explicit awareness of the problems facing Mexican Americans.* If there is no conscious awareness of the problems facing Mexican Americans, there will be no involvement as seen in the negatively affectively involved. For the positively affectively involved, involvement stops at this level. These individuals have a positive feeling toward the movement because they recognize the problems encountered by the Mexican-American population. However, for one reason or another, they do not participate in the movement.

2. *Transition from identification as an individual to that of a member of the broader ethnic group experiencing problems.* This transition could create a conflictual situation, especially if the individual has been functioning at either extreme, by denying his identity or by identifying closely with Mexican Americans.

3. *Decision of the individual to do something about the problems facing Mexican Americans.* The individual becomes involved in the movement if he interacts with others who are already involved. The majority of the individuals who decided to become involved were pressured, influenced, or encouraged by some external force—either another involved person or direct exposure to the conditions under which the broader ethnic group lives. Thus, the conflictual situation, coupled with external pressures, produces involvement.

It may be speculated that the degree or level of involvement is related to a perception of the Mexican-American situation and to a perception of the movement in relation to the means of involvement. Those persons who are positively affectively or indirectly behaviorally involved perceived the Mexican American as responsible for his inferior position. Hence, they chose to work on an individual level within established means. On the other hand, those who are directly behaviorally involved perceived outside forces as the cause. The indirectly behaviorally involved did not relate to the movement until they recognized that it was possible to contribute on an individual level within the system rather than by "demonstrating in the streets."

Because these formulations are based on a selective group, there are few factors that can be generalized. It was not the intention of the project, however, to offer generalizations. Instead, it was hoped that this study could provide a basis or starting point for additional studies related to the Chicano movement. It was also hoped that the knowledge gained from exploring the reasons and the means by which individuals become involved might prove useful in encouraging others to contribute at the level at which they feel most comfortable.

In the final analysis, the movement should be the concern of every Chicano. As exemplified by the individuals interviewed, there is a place for everyone in the movement—the young, the old, the educated, the skilled, the unskilled, the professional, and even entire families. If every Chicano would offer some time and effort toward the cause, perhaps someday the status of Mexican Americans in this country will be appropriately elevated.

The process of involvement of these individuals could be compared to the evolvement of the movement. As many of these individuals realized the cost of becoming assimilated into a nonaccepting dominant system—the rejection of their own identity—they attempted to liberate themselves through a process of self-examination. Thereafter, they were no longer willing to "accept what was given to them in the past." [8] The Chicano movement is "the manifestation of a people's coming of age." [9] It is also a struggle to obtain a "surrendered identity." [10]

Summary

The analysis suggests that individual involvement was preceded by the following necessary conditions: (1) an explicit awareness of the problems facing Mexican Americans, (2) the transition from identification as an individual to that of a member of the broader ethnic group, and (3) a decision to want to do something about these problems. The level of involvement was related to the individual's perception of the movement and the factors responsible for the problems facing Mexican Americans as well as external and internal pressures impinging upon him. Furthermore, the analysis suggests that there may be a wide range of levels and a complexity of types of involvement that would tend to contraindicate any notion of involvement as a simple process, readily dichotomized.

Notes

1 Edward Simmen, ed., Introduction, *The Chicano: From Caricature To Self-Portrait* (New York: New American Library, 1971), p. 15.

2 Mario Compean, "The Road to Chicano Power," *La Raza*, Vol. 1, No. 2, pp. 25–26.

3 Ralph Guzman, "The Gentle Revolutionaries: Brown Power," Reprint. Source Unknown, pp. 1–4.

4 Ruth Tuck, *Not With The Fist* (New York: Harcourt, Brace and Company, 1946); Lyle Saunders, "Spanish Speaking People of the Southwest," in *Social Perspectives on Behavior,* ed. Herrie Stein and Richard Cloward (New York: The Free Press, 1966); and William Madsen, *The Mexican-Americans of South Texas* (New York: Holt, Rinehart & Winston, 1964).

5 Carey McWilliams, *North From Mexico: The Spanish-Speaking People of the United States* (New York: Greenwood Press, 1968), p. 189.

6 William J. Filstead, ed., "Introduction," *Qualitative Methodology: Firsthand Involvement With the Social World* (Chicago: Markham Publishing Company, 1970), p. 6.

7 Neil J. Smelser, *Theory of Collective Behavior* (New York: Free Press, 1965).

8 Robert Pena, Book review, Stan Steiner, *La Raza: The Mexican Americans* (New York: Harper & Row, 1969), *Social Casework,* 52:333 (May 1971).

9 Philip Ortego, "The Chicano Renaissance," *Social Casework,* 52:307 (May 1971).

10 Erik H. Erikson, *Identity, Youth and Crisis* (New York: W. W. Norton & Co., 1968), p. 297, quoting Vann Woodward.

The Chicano Renaissance

Philip D. Ortego

In *Understanding Media,* Marshall McLuhan explains that "the medium is the message . . . that the personal and social consequences of any medium—that is, of any extension of ourselves—result from the new scale that is introduced into our affairs by each extension of ourselves." [1] Applying McLuhan's proposition to the Chicano movement, for example, we can see that the Chicano movement is the medium for extending ourselves (Chicanos) in American society, and, as such, the Chicano movement becomes the message. Such slogans as *Ya Basta, Venceremos,* and *Chicano Power* are only elements of the total message; they are simply part of the new scale introduced into Chicano affairs by each of our individual thrusts toward greater participation in American society. Indeed, the personal and social consequences of our extensions into American society have been the result of a new scale of values and aspirations that we have created with each extension of ourselves.

In particular, these extensions appeared first in the form of beneficial societies, then social clubs, and, after World War II, as political organizations. Our extension into the arts—generically including painting, sculpture, architecture, music, dance, literature, drama, and film—is a more recent phenomenon, although there were, of course, Mexican-American artists at various times since 1848.

These artists, however, did not reflect any significant thrust by Mexican Americans into artistic endeavors. They represented only individual successes in penetrating the artistic iron curtain because the animosities engendered by the Mexican-American War created Anglo-American resistance to Mexican-American participation in most spheres of American life except at the lower rungs of the societal ladder. Consequently, Mexican Americans became the backbone of such American enterprises as the cattle industry, the railroad, the cotton industry of the Southwest, mining, and, of course, the fruit and produce industry. The Mexican-American way of life paralleled the black-American way of life, although for the former there was no Emancipation Proclamation.

Nevertheless, the Mexican American was nurtured and sustained in spirit and soul by his music, dance, *cuentos* (folktales), and remembrance of things past—all contributing to the maintenance and development of Mexican-American folk music, folk art, and folklore. Unlike other peoples of the United States—except groups with English-speaking backgrounds, such as the Irish, Scotch, and English —Mexican Americans were reinforced continuously in their language, culture, and heritage by their very proximity to Mexico and the almost uninterrupted flow of immigration (legal and otherwise) from Mexico.

There are no accurate or reliable population figures from 1848 to 1900, but the census reports for those years indicate a steady and consistent growth of Americans of Mexican descent. Recorded Mexican immigration from 1900 to the present indicates that, because there was no quota on Mexican immigration until 1965, well over one million Mexicans have come to the United States. The actual figure may be closer to one and one-half million if other means of entry into the United States employed by Mexican nationals are considered. It is clear from these statistics and from the fact that now more than ten million Mexican Americans are living in this country that Mexican Americans are essentially a native group, most of whom were born in the United States.

Mexican Americans have always been "Americans" in the true sense of the word because they were very much a part of the landscape when the Anglo Americans arrived in the Southwest. Despite their early settlement and their large numbers, Mexican Americans have been the most shamefully neglected minority in the United States. In the Southwest, where approximately seven of the ten million live, they subsist on levels of survival far below the national norms. The reason for this low subsistence level, many Mexican Americans argue, is that they are victims of the Treaty of Guadalupe Hidalgo—a treaty that identified those who came with the conquered lands of the Southwest as defeated people. Those who came afterwards in the great migrations of the first three decades of the twentieth century have been equally victimized by stereotypes engendered by the Mexican-American War.

In recent years there has been an increasing social and political consciousness, leading to demands for reformation of the socioeconomic structure that has kept Mexican Americans subordinated these many years. With this increasing social and political consciousness has come the awareness of their artistic and literary heritage. Throughout the Southwest the sleeping Mexican-American giant has begun to flex his dormant muscles.

Redefining American literature

The decade of the 1970s promises to be one in which this awakening, this renaissance, will be manifested by a growing desire of Mexican Americans not only to attain status in sociopolitical and economic areas but to seek a more substantial literary identity in the ever-widening mainstream of American literature. In the 1970s Mexican-American writers, scholars, and teachers will attempt to redefine American literature as a fabric woven not exclusively on the Atlantic frontier by the descendants of New England Puritans and Southern Cavaliers, but as one woven also in the American Southwest with marvelous Hispanic threads that extend not only to the literary heritage of the European continent but also to the very heart of the Mediterranean world.

Like the British roots in the new American soil, the Hispanic roots have yielded a vigorous and dynamic body of literature that, unfortunately for us, has been studied historically as part of a foreign contribution rather than as part and parcel of our American heritage. Moreover, we seldom learn about the extent to which the Hispanic literary tradition has influenced American literature. The works dealing with the southern and southwestern parts of the United States, therefore, have become the neglected aspect of the American experience; the implication is that such works are not properly within the traditional definition of American literature because they were not written in English.

Language, however, is hardly a logical reason for not recognizing non-English material as American literature, although it was written in the United States—as in the case of Isaac Bashevis Singer —or what has become the United States—as in the case of the chronicles of the South and Southwest by the Spanish and their progeny. In the pluralistic cultural and linguistic context of contemporary America, we can no longer consent to the suggestions of American literary historians that American literature properly begins with the arrival of British colonials in America.

American literature actually begins with the formation of the United States as a political entity. Thus, the literary period from the founding of the first permanent British settlement in Jamestown, Virginia, in 1607, to the formation of the American union represents only the British period of American literature. So, too, the literary period from the first permanent Spanish settlement at Saint Augustine, Florida, in 1565, to the dates of acquisition of these Spanish and Mexican lands by the United States should, in fact, represent the Hispanic period of American literature. More appropriately, the British and Spanish periods should both be listed under the rubric "Colonial American Literature." The Mexican period of the Southwest should simply be labeled "The Mexican Period."

Loss of a literary birthright

The neglect of the Spanish and Mexican literature of the Southwest has produced unfortunate literary consequences for Mexican Americans because they have come to see themselves and their Mexican kinsmen portrayed in our national literature by means of racial clichés and distorted caricatures. Like other minority groups, Mexican Americans were and continue to be inaccurately and superficially represented in literature, movies, television, and other mass media. This situation sometimes has been caused by prejudice, but it has also been caused by those well-meaning romanticists who have seriously distorted the image of the Mexican American for the sake of their art.

Mexican Americans have been characterized at both ends of the spectrum of human behavior (seldom in the middle) as untrustworthy, villainous, ruthless, tequila-drinking, and philandering *machos* or else as courteous, devout, and fatalistic peasants who are to be treated more as pets than as people. More often than not Mexican Americans have been cast either as bandits or as lovable rogues; as hot-blooded, sexually animated creatures or as passive, humble servants. The pejorations and generalizations are to be deplored, and Mexican Americans today are beginning to rise up against the perpetuation of such racial clichés.

Whatever the reasons for deliberately or inadvertently neglecting the Hispanic aspect of American literature, the fact remains that not only have Mexican Americans been deprived of their literary birthright but all other Americans have been deprived of an important part of a literary heritage that is also rightfully theirs. Mexican Americans actually have a rich literary heritage. That they have been kept from it bespeaks a shameful and tragic oppression of a people whose origins antedate the establishment of Jamestown by well over a century (and even more, considering their Indian ancestry). Moreover, the shame and tragedy are compounded when Mexican-American youngsters learn about their Puritan forebears but not about their Hispanic forebears about whom they have as much right—if not more—to be proud.

Heretofore, Mexican Americans have been a marginal people in a sort of no man's land, caught between the polarizing forces of their cultural-linguistic Indo-Hispanic heritage and their political-linguistic American context. They have become frustrated and alienated by the struggle between the system that seeks to refashion them in its own image and the knowledge of who and what they really are. As a result, this cultural conflict has debilitated many Mexican Americans.

Mexican-American youngsters are taught about the cruelty of their Spanish forebears and the savagery of their Mexican-Indian forebears; they have been taught about the Spanish greed for gold, of the infamous Spanish Inquisition, of Aztec human sacrifices, of Mexican bandits, and of the massacre at the Alamo. They seldom, if ever, learn of the other men at the Alamo, their Mexican forebears— unknown and unsung in American history—who were killed fighting on the Texas side. American children probably have never heard of such men as Juan Abamillo, Juan Badillo, Carlos Espalier, Gegorio Esparza, Antonio Fuentes, José Maria Guerrero, Toribio Losoya, Andres Nava, and other Texas Mexicans at the Alamo.

In order to be fully comprehended, the ethnic phenomenon of

Mexican Americans since World War II must be viewed in the more personal context of their literature. What we have seen instead has been the myriad educational, sociopolitical, and socioeconomic accounts by Anglo investigators and researchers who have pursued the phenomenological chimeras of the queer, the curious, and the quaint. To understand the significance of human movements, we must assess the evidence from the arts. There is little doubt that the contributions to the American experience by Mexican Americans and their forebears have yet to be understood and measured.

In the Southwest the relationship between Mexican Americans and Anglo Americans is similar to that of a legally adopted child and adoptive parents. The analogy describes the circumstances of Spanish-speaking peoples in all the Hispanic territories acquired by the United States. To pursue the analogy to its proper conclusion, we must ask whether, in trying to educate the child about his proper past, we talk about the heritage of the adoptive parents or the *actual* heritage of the adopted child. To indoctrinate the child with the heritage of his new parents as if it were his own is to perpetrate the grossest kind of fraud at the expense of the child.

Information about the literary accomplishments of Mexican Americans during the period from the end of the Mexican-American War to the turn of the century, for example, has been negligible. As Américo Paredes has pointed out, "With few exceptions, documents available for study of the region are in English, being for the most part reports made by officals who were, to put it mildly, prejudiced against the people they were trying to pacify." [2]

American writers have tended to minimize the literary achievements of Mexican Americans in the Southwest for reasons ranging from jingoism to ignorance. It should be noted, however, that no sooner had the Spanish established their hold on Mexico than they started a printing press in Mexico City in 1529, more than a century earlier than any established in the British colonies of North America. Indeed, there was a substantial Spanish-reading public in New Spain and Mexico, including the North Mexican states, until the lands were ceded to the United States in 1848. Spanish literature was read and written in both the Spanish peninsula and in the New World. Such Spanish playwrights as Pedro Calderón de la Barca and Lope de Vega extended their literary influence to Spanish America just as the Mexican-born playwright Juan Ruiz de Alarcón extended his literary influence to Spain.

Oral transmission of heritage

In the Southwest the people who had come with the land continued to tell and retell the tales that their forebears had brought from the Old World and from Mexico. These folktales had been passed on from generation to generation until they became a decidedly strong oral tradition. Mexican Americans were therefore not "absorbed" into the American "culture" without a literary past and heritage of their own, as so many Americans believe.

To be sure, much of what they knew about that literary heritage had been acquired orally. Folk drama, for example, was immensely popular among the Mexican Americans, who continued to stage the old plays in much the same fashion as the early English folk dramatists had staged their plays in town squares, churches, or courtyards. In the Mexican Southwest, liturgical pastorals depicting the creation and fall of man and of Christ's resurrection evolved into "cycle plays" similar to those of Spain and England. Like the developing culture on the Atlantic frontier, the Southwest brought forth a new literature by New World men.

By the time of the Mexican-American War, the Mexican Southwest had been thoroughly nurtured on drama, poetry, and folktales of a literary tradition of several hundred years. Mexicans who became Americans continued the Indo-Hispanic literary tradition not only by preserving the old literary materials but also by creating new ones in the superimposed American political ambiance. To cite only one sphere of literary activity, by 1860 there were a number of Mexican Americans engaged in newspaper work. In New Mexico alone, ten out of eighty journalists of the period were Mexican Americans because most Anglo-American papers published bilingual editions for the vast numbers of Spanish readers in the Southwest. Moreover, Mexican Americans were employed to translate the English-language news into Spanish.

Disparaging images of Mexican Americans

Nevertheless, Mexican Americans were poorly regarded by the vast majority of Anglo Americans who came in contact with them, and many of the literary portraits of Mexican Americans by Anglo-American writers exerted undue influence on generations of Americans down to our own time. The disparaging images of Mexican Americans were drawn by such American writers as Richard Henry Dana, who, in *Two Years Before the Mast,* described Mexican Americans as "an idle, thriftless people" who could "make nothing for themselves." [3] In 1852 Colonel John Monroe reported in Washington:

> The New Mexicans are thoroughly debased and totally incapable of self-government, and there is no latent quality about them that can ever make them respectable. They have more Indian blood than Spanish, and in some respects are below the Pueblo Indians, for they are not as honest or as industrious.[4]

Four years later W. W. H. Davis, United States Attorney for the Territory of New Mexico, writing of his experiences with Mexican Americans, said that "they possess the cunning and deceit of the Indian, the politeness and the spirit of revenge of the Spaniard, and the imaginative temperament and fiery impulses of the Moor." He described them as smart and quick but lacking the "stability and character and soundness of intellect that give such vast superiority to the Anglo-Saxon race over every other people." He ascribed to them the "cruelty, bigotry, and superstition" of the Spaniard, "a marked characteristic from earliest times." Moreover, he saw these traits as "constitutional and innate in the race." In a moment of kindness, however, Davis suggested that the fault probably lay with their "spiritual teachers," the Spaniards, who never taught them "that beautiful doctrine which teaches us to love our neighbors as ourselves." [5]

In 1868 the *Overland Monthly* published an article by William V. Wells, "The French in Mexico," in which he wrote that "in the open field, a charge of disciplined troops usually sufficed to put to flight the collection of frowzy-headed mestizos, leperos, mulattoes, Indians, Samboes, and other mongrels now, as in the time of our own war with them, composing a Mexican Army." [6] In our time Walter Prescott Webb characterizes the Mexicans as possessing "a cruel streak" that he believes was inherited partly from the Spanish of the Inquisition and partly from their Indian forebears. Webb asserts:

> On the whole, the Mexican warrior . . . was inferior to the Comanche and wholly unequal to Texans. The whine of the

leaden slugs stirred in him an irresistible impulse to travel
with, rather than against, the music. He won more victories
over the Texans partly by parley than by force of arms. For
making promises and for breaking them he had no peer.[7]

Even John Steinbeck in *Tortilla Flat* portrayed Mexican Americans
as lovable carousers claiming Spanish blood in the face of their
color, "like that of a well-browned meerschaum pipe." [8]

That the defenders of the besieged Alamo were flying the Mexican
flag of 1824, not the Texas flag, had been forgotten by the time of
the Civil War. Forgotten too is the great heroic effort of Mexican
Americans in the Union Army during the Civil War. In Texas, the
fact that José Antonio Navarro's "Memoirs" are part of Mexican-
American literature has been obscured by time and ethnic myopia.[9]
Most Americans probably are unaware that Navarro, a Mexican
American, was a member of the first Texas State Senate or that
his son Angel III was graduated from Harvard in 1849. In the
commemoration of the Texas heroes, we hear little about Lorenzo
de Zavala, another Mexican American, who served as the first vice-
president (ad interim) of the Texas Republic. Instead we hear
about the "outrages" of Juan Cortina and his revolt of 1859, despite
the fact that Cortina was actually a Union-inspired guerrilla fighting
both the Texas Confederates and the French Mexicans.

Neglected writers

There were many Mexican-American writers in the last half of
the nineteenth century, but they have remained as neglected as
the people they represent. In New Mexico, for example, Donaciano
Vigil, editor of the newspaper *Verdad,* compiled a *History of New
Mexico to 1851;* [10] and in 1859 Miguel Antonio Otero wrote *The
Indian Depredations in the Territory of New Mexico.*[11] In California,
Juan Bautista Alvarado completed a "History of California." [12]
In northern California, Mariano Guadalupe Vallejo wrote prolifically
on a number of topics, composing sonnets for his children and for
special occasions. He culminated his literary activities with a five-
volume "History of California" that Herbert E. Bancroft hailed as
standing without rival among its predecessors in thoroughness and
interest.[13] Many Mexican Americans kept diaries (a major type
of Hispanic literature) and wrote letters to each other about their

day-to-day activities. These letters—most of them unpublished—reveal as much about the Mexican-American experience as the letters of John Winthrop and Roger Williams reveal about the Puritan experience in America.

Historical background

Quest for statehood

What most characterized the post-Civil War period in the Southwest was the quest for statehood by the territories of Colorado, Utah, Oklahoma, Nevada, Arizona, and New Mexico. The admission of Texas into the Union had of course precipitated the Mexican-American War, but the *fact* of statehood allowed Texas a measure of "progress" that was not realized in the other territories until later in the nineteenth and twentieth centuries. California became a state in 1850; Colorado, in 1876; Utah, in 1896; and Oklahoma, in 1907. Arizona and New Mexico, however, did not become states until 1912. The delay has been attributed to the fact that the preponderance of Mexican Americans made statehood unpalatable to the rest of the nation.

Although Mexican Americans had proved their loyalty to the United States in both the Civil War and the Spanish-American War (more than half of the Rough Riders in Cuba were Mexican Americans), ethnic hostilities toward Mexican Americans did not lessen. For example, Senator Albert J. Beveridge of Indiana, an outright anti-Hispano, led the resistance against statehood for Arizona and New Mexico on the grounds that Mexican Americans were unaspiring, easily influenced, and totally ignorant of American ways and mores and that, although fifty years had passed since the Mexican-American War, Mexican Americans were still aliens in the United States, most of them having made no effort to learn English.[14] According to Beveridge, such linguistic resistance was treasonous, to say the least, despite the fact that for part of the first decade of the twentieth century Miguel Antonio Otero, a Mexican American, was governor of the Territory of New Mexico (1897–1906), having been appointed by President McKinley and then reconfirmed by President Roosevelt after the assassination of McKinley in 1901.

Mexican Americans strove to become part of the United States in their own way, but they were regarded with disdain by a sizable segment of the Anglo-American population of the Southwest. Ironically, although Mexican Americans were being rejected by American society, the turn of the century saw the creation of "Spanish heritage and landmark" societies that vigorously espoused the restoration of "Spanish" missions in the Southwest. Mexican Americans were the butt of injustice after injustice while their lands, goods, properties, and persons were craftily secured by squatters, unscrupulous lawyers, and con artists who shamelessly bilked them because of their language handicap. Despite the fact that Mexican Americans constituted the majority of the population in the Southwest at first, they were quickly eased down the social rung with the increase of Anglo Americans in the area. By 1870 Mexican Americans ceased to be the majority in California. They had become a minority very early in Texas, although in New Mexico they held on until after the turn of the century. Nonetheless, Mexican Americans were slowly but surely reduced to conditions of peonage approximating the level of servitude into which the blacks had been forced.

Rags-to-riches mystique

Against this background emerged the rags-to-riches mystique that was to influence American life well into the twentieth century. Horatio Alger's characters, Tattered Tom, Ragged Dick, and Phil the Fiddler, became the American standard for success through hard work. A Mexican American's "wealth," however, was judged as the product of connivance rather than of fortitude and application. For instance, when the Mexican-American Lugo family of southern California lost its wealth in 1865, Benjamin Hayes quickly suggested that the finger of Providence was responsible for the decay of the Mexican Americans.[15]

Not even Mariano Vallejo's "true history of California," which was meant to show Anglo Americans that Mexican Americans were not as they were caricatured in conversation and literature, could counteract the firmly lodged prejudices of Anglo Americans toward Mexican Americans.[16] Perhaps Leonard Pitt best summarizes the situation of Mexican Americans at the end of the nineteenth century when he writes, "By emphasizing injustice, violence, and broken promises in their memoirs, the Californians [Mexican Americans] came closer to a meaningful truth than the Yankees who spoke of Providence."[17]

Indeed, the providence of the Yankee was fraught with peril for the Mexican Americans, despite the fact that the Yankees had guaranteed them full citizenship and had agreed to regard them as equals rather than as conquered people. The Yankee rationalization for broken promises that Vallejo bemoaned was simply that "progress has its price" or that the Mexican Americans were "culturally unsuited to the new order" or else that the Mexican Americans had "brought it on themselves." The American pretense at ethical behavior appears all the more reprehensible because of blatant bigotry.

By 1900 Anglo Americans in the Southwest had so taken over the Mexican Southwest that what had once been Mexican and Spanish had been neatly appropriated and transformed into an American "tradition." Mexican water and mining laws were retained in toto by Anglo-American settlers and governments. Spanish words were transformed into English equivalents. *La riata* became *lariat; juzgado* became *hoosegow; calabozo* became *calaboose; chiapas* became *chaps,* and so forth. The American *cowboy* became simply an altered reflection of the Mexican *vaquero,* saddle, ten-gallon hat, and all. The language of America had absorbed a considerable number of expressions, but Mexican Americans themselves were kept at arm's length as "outsiders," to be forgotten for another fifty years.

Resistance to Anglo aggression

It would, however, be an egregious error to conclude that Mexican Americans were passive in defending themselves against Anglo-American "aggressions." In 1883, for example, Mexican-American agricultural workers went on strike for better wages and working conditions in the Panhandle; in 1903, Mexican-American sugar beet workers went on strike for similar reasons in Ventura, California.

To counter their exclusion from Anglo-American schools, many Mexican Americans formed private and parochial schools, such as El Colegio Altamiro, founded in Texas in 1897. To overcome rural depredations, Mexican Americans in New Mexico formed the Knights of Labor in 1890, a mutual assistance and protective organization. Some Mexican-American organizations, such as Los Gorras Blancos (the White Caps) of New Mexico, were called marauders by Anglo Americans, but their purpose was primarily to protect themselves from such violent repressions as that which in 1904 took the life of Colonel Francisco J. Chaves, a surgeon and Civil War veteran who had become a Mexican-American spokesman, leader, and territorial superintendent of public instruction.

Migration from Mexico

As has already been noted, La Raza in the United States was to be culturally and linguistically renourished as no other group—save English-speaking—had been. In the decades between 1880 and 1940, almost three-quarters of one million Mexicans officially migrated to the United States. Mexican migration to the United States was one of the truly major mass movements of people in the Western Hemisphere. The phenomenon reflects "the failure of roots," as Ernesto Galarza explains.[18]

At the same time, however, Mexican migration to the United States reflects the growth of technology in North America. From 1880 to 1910, for instance, President Porfirio Díaz sped the construction of 15,000 miles of railroad lines linking the mineral wealth of Mexico to American smelters just north of the border. Mexicans not only worked the rails but were caught by the mystique of something better at the end of the tracks. Unquestionably the railroad provided the best escape for Mexicans in their exodus from war-torn Mexico. "Al norte!" was frequently the best alternative for Mexican refugees. Although the "depopulation" of Mexico was of great concern to the Liberal Party of Mexico, which had effectively brought Porfirismo's administration to an end and had promised to repatriate Mexicans in *el destierro,* the political and socioeconomic situation worsened in Mexico, thereby swelling instead of diminishing the ranks of fleeing Mexicans.

Travel either way across the Mexican-American border was relatively easy until the 1920s. It was not until 1924 that the Border Patrol was established to curb the illegal entry of Mexicans into the United States. Devoid of really natural barriers, the Mexican-American border is no more than a line staked out by markers from the Pacific to El Paso, or a barbed wire fence in places, or, during certain seasons, an almost dry river bed from El Paso to the Gulf of Mexico supporting the ubiquitous undergrowth of chapparal and mesquite. Mexicans settled easily in the Southwest, for, unlike European immigrants, Mexicans were really migrating to an area similar to that from which they came and that was peopled by their kinsmen. Indeed, there was *mucha raza en el norte.*

Significance of the renaissance

Perhaps the significance of the Chicano renaissance lies in the identification of Chicanos with their Indian past. It matters not what etymologies are ascribed to the word *Chicano;* the distinction is not in whether the word is a denigration but in that it has been consciously and deliberately chosen over all other words to identify Mexican Americans who regard themselves as Montezuma's children. They have thus cast off the sometimes meretricious identification with the Spanish templar tradition foisted on them by Anglo-American society because of its preference for things European. To reinforce their identification with their Indian past, Chicano writers have appropriated for their literary symbols Aztec and Mayan figures, including the great Aztec calendar stone.

Significantly, a literature draws from the history and myths of its people's past. Those of Mexican-Indian ancestry are well aware of the extent to which the myths and history of their Indian past are operating in the Mexican-American ethos. Understandably, it is to the Mexican-Indian past that the Chicano renaissance has turned for its most meaningful literary symbols and metaphors. The selection of Quinto Sol as the name of a publishing group is itself a manifestation of the Chicano writers' deliberate identification with their Indian past, for the Aztecs were the people of the Fifth Sun (*Quinto Sol*). According to their mythology, there had been four previous epochs, each governed by a sun. The first epoch ended with the inhabitants of earth devoured by ocelots; the second world and sun were destroyed by wind; the third, by a rain of fire; and the fourth, by water. According to the Aztecs, the sun and world in which they lived—the fifth sun—was destined to perish as a result of earthquakes and famine and terror.

Chicano publications

Mexican Americans have been struggling within the predominantly Anglo-American culture of the United States for over 122 years. Although Mexican Americans have been writing all that time, the realization of Mexican-American literature as the *élan vital* in the life styles of the people themselves has happened only within recent years. In the fall of 1967, a cohort of Mexican-American writers at Berkeley, California, formed Quinto Sol Publications in a tiny office over a candy store. Their purpose was "to provide a forum for Mexican American self definition and expression on . . . issues of relevance to Mexican Americans in American society today." [19]

Alternatives is the key word in what has since blossomed into the Chicano renaissance. Mexican Americans had been completely disenchanted with the plethora of writings about them, writings that depicted them in a variety of literary contexts resorting to the most blatant stereotypes and racial clichés, all of them by "intellectual mercenaries" as the Quinto Sol group called them in the first issue of their literary quarterly magazine, *El Grito: A Journal of Contemporary Mexican American Thought*.[20] The promise of *El Grito* was that it would be the forum for Mexican Americans to articulate their own sense of identity. Even more important, the printed word was seen as a very important medium in the Chicano struggle for equality.

To compound the problem, Mexican Americans have not only been deprived of their literary birthright but they have effectively been kept from articulating their experiences in American literary outlets. In the last twenty years, for example, few Mexican Americans have published in the "leading" American literary quarterlies. In 1947 Mario Suarez published two sketches entitled "El Hoyo" and "El Señor" in the *Arizona Quarterly,* a literary journal that published the fiction of such other Mexican-American writers as Arnulfo D. Trejo and Amado Jesús Muro and the prose works of such Mexican-American scholars as Rafael Jesús Gonzalez.

Some Mexican-American writers have managed to find literary outlets, but at the expense of their art as Mexican Americans. Understandably, the greatest outpouring of Mexican-American writing since 1900 has been in prose, all of it essential in laying the foundation for what was to erupt as the Chicano renaissance in the last years of the 1960s. The prose (much of it cast as polemics and rhetoric) helped to refashion first their psychological image and then their literary image. Mexican-American writers who sought to break the long-standing and readily accepted stereotypes about Mexican Americans in print found little or no favor with magazine editors because the images of the "Mexican" in American literature were hard to put aside.

As recently as 1968 an editor of a high school multiethnic text who was looking for material on Mexican Americans rejected a "nonfolk story" by this writer and suggested that the ninth-year reader in which J. Frank Dobie's popular "Squaw Man" appeared would provide an idea of the kind of material he was seeking for the reader. Of course, what he really wanted was the "queer," the "curious," and the "quaint" kind of "folksy" stories most editors have come to expect about Mexican Americans.

At another time, this writer suggested to the editor of a prestigious midwest literary quarterly the idea of publishing an issue on Mexican-American literature because he had just devoted an issue to American-Indian literature. The response betrayed the editor's lack of knowledge about Mexican Americans and their literary achievements, for he indicated he had heard that Quinto Sol Publications had published an anthology of Mexican-American writing but that he had not seen it. Because this writer had indicated he was working on an anthology also, the editor wondered if there would be anything of special significance left over for a special issue with two anthologies available.

Until the 1960s, fiction, such as Floyd Salas's *Tattoo the Wicked Cross* and John Rechy's *City of Night,* was rare.[21] Both authors are Mexican-American writers who have penetrated the literary iron curtain not as ethnic writers but just as writers. This success simply attests to the fact that, like black writers who have written nonblack works, Mexican-American writers are capable of writing non-Mexican-American works. Like the market for black works, the market for Mexican-American works was limited to those who wrote what most editors expected; and what most editors had come to expect was the image of the Mexican American as an indolent, passive, humble servant who lived for *fiestas* and *mañana.* Chicano writers, however, are no longer struggling to penetrate the literary iron curtain; they have come to realize that the only viable outlets for their works are those that they create for themselves. In this way was born the Chicano renaissance and hundreds of literary outlets, from mimeographed magazines to such slick publications as *El Grito* and the Los Angeles-based *Con Safos.*[22]

El Grito has become to the Chicano renaissance what *Partisan Review,* for example, became to the New Criticism. It has published a variety of fiction, poetry, and prose appealing to the wider Mexican-American community. Principally, however, it has sought to show the patent falsity of Anglo-American works that purport to "explain" the Mexican American in terms of debilitating profiles and criteria. From the beginning, Octavio Romano and Nick Vaca, founders and editors of *El Grito,* have attempted to rearticulate the identity of Mexican Americans from the perspective of Mexican Americans. They have taken American social scientists, in particular, to task for perpetrating false images of Mexican-American culture. In addition, *El Grito* has provided an outlet for emerging Mexican-American writers.

Perhaps *Con Safos* best articulates Chicano life in the barrio. (Most Mexican Americans are still in the barrios or have come from them.) *Con Safos* has a slick news magazine format and, like *El Grito,* runs first-rate exposé pieces. Although *Con Safos* is more pictorial, *El Grito* regularly has provided space for portfolios of Mexican-American artists. Both magazines are essentially experimental in approach; they publish what reflects the Chicano community however it may be written—in Spanish or English or both—and rely heavily on striking covers employing Mexican-Indian motifs. There is no question of which magazine better articulates the Chicano experience, for both magazines articulate the essential problems of Chicanos everywhere.

Other Chicano magazines are springing up as Chicanos become increasingly aware of the power of the pen and the persuasiveness of print. For several years Francisca Flores, a fiery and undaunted Chicana from Los Angeles, published *Carta Editorial* by herself and at her own expense, commenting on the ills besieging Mexican Americans. What the Anglo-dominated mass media failed to cover in the Chicano community, Francisca Flores reported fearlessly in her small four-page newsletter. To be properly informed on what was happening in Mexican-American affairs, one had to read *Carta Editorial.* In 1970, *Carta Editorial* was absorbed into *Regeneración,* still edited by Francisca Flores but with a news magazine appearance and an expanded core of commentators and contributors.[23] What makes the venture of *Regeneración* significant is that the "new" magazine is really a revival of the journal that Ricardo Flores Magon, the Mexican exile, published in the United States while keeping clear of Porfirio Díaz's secret police. Magon started out by publishing *Liberación* in Mexico until he was forced to flee Díaz's wrath.

In the United States, Magon found refuge first in the Mexican-

American community of San Antonio, Texas, and then in St. Louis, Missouri, where he founded *Regeneración.* Later, forced to leave St. Louis, he made his way to Los Angeles, where he continued his attack on Porfirisomo. He was finally taken into custody by American federal agents on the charge of having violated American neutrality laws. He was imprisoned at San Quentin, where his health failed and where he died. There is no doubt that *Regeneración* was instrumental in the downfall of Díaz.

There has been a special literary relationship between Mexicans and Mexican Americans, for when Mexican intellectuals and writers have fled from Mexico, they invariably have come to the United States and to Mexican-American communities. Many successful and abortive plans involving Mexico have been hatched in Mexican-American homes and communities. Benito Juarez's successful recapture of Mexico from the French was made possible by Mexican-American assistance in the form of money and material—and sometimes men. Porfirio Díaz himself launched his political career from Texas. During the Mexican Revolution of the twentieth century the Mexican-American Southwest provided asylum for many revolutionaries. It is little wonder that the heroes of the Chicano movement are Pancho Villa and Emiliano Zapata and that the Mexican revolutionary writers, Mariano Azuela, José Vasconcellos, and Martin Guzman, are read voraciously by Mexican Americans seeking their own liberation. No contemporary Mexican writers have influenced the Chicano movement so much as has Octavio Paz and his *Labyrinth of Solitude,* a work that goes far in exploring the Mexican mind and thought, not in its Hispanic origins so much but in relation to the Indian origins of Mexico.[24]

The Chicano theater

El Teatro Campesino, the Chicano migrant theater that grew out of the *Huelga* at Delano in 1965, has transformed the ancient Aztec myths for the *campesino* stage to Chicano relevancy. In one magnificent *acto* entitled "Bernabe," the Chicano link to the ancient Indian heritage is strengthened and articulated masterfully. This message is being carried everywhere in the United States (and abroad) by El Teatro Campesino in its various annual tours. Luis Valdez, director of the company, describes Chicano theater as "beautiful, *rasquachi,* human, cosmic, broad, deep, tragic, comic, as the life of

La Raza itself." [25] The consequence of El Teatro Campesino has been the creation of similar theatrical companies elsewhere, including universities with as few as a dozen Chicano students.

The distinctive character of Chicano theater lies in its seeming "artlessness." There is no attempt to create setting or atmosphere or character. Valdez, for example, employs *calavera* (skull) masks to create the illusion of temporality. All the skull masks are identical. Only the actions, dress, and voices of the actors differentiate them as characters. The end result is a kind of stylized theater resembling the Japanese Kabuki theater or the Greek mask plays.

In 1969, El Teatro Campesino filmed Rodolfo "Corky" González's stirring epic poem, "I Am Joaquín." Although the poem created considerable impact on the Chicano community, the film version has elevated it to a new dimension. Few, if any, Chicanos who view it are left unstirred because González has skillfully woven myth and memory and desire into a masterwork of poetry. Joaquín becomes the enduring spirit of the Chicano soul and spirit buffeted by alien winds in the country of his forebears where he walks as if he were a stranger. Joaquín's final words are not an empty incantation but a promise that he will endure.[26]

Chicano poetry

The heart of Chicano poetry lies in the imperative cry of Joaquín. The works of such other Mexican-American poets as Luis Omar Salinas, Abelardo Delgado, Miguel Ponce, and José Montoya reflect the existential problems of survival that Chicanos face day in and day out. There is anguish and frustration in the vision of Chicano poets, but there is also determination bred from the knowledge of who they are. In "Aztec Angel," for example, Salinas glorifies the beauty of the Aztec mother and child, thus encouraging pride in the heritage of the Chicano.[27] In the poem "The Chicano Manifesto," Delgado writes of the impatient *raza,* but tempers that impatience with an appeal for brotherhood.[28]

The message from Chicano poets for change is loud and clear. There is no mistaking the insistent plea for reformation. Although the spirit of Chicano poetry may be considered revolutionary, its intellectual emphasis, however, is on reason as it attempts to move the hearts and minds of men by appealing to their better natures.

The Chicano novel

The Chicano novel is a post-World War II phenomenon. José Antonio Villarreal's novel, *Pocho*, was published in 1959.[29] At that time it received scant attention and quickly went out of print. Although it appeared a decade too early, it stands in the vanguard of the Chicano novel for depicting the Chicano experience in the United States. Villarreal's style was influenced by the American "pop" novel of the 1950s, and his portrayal of the linguistic characteristics of Chicanos was clearly influenced by the work of Ernest Hemingway and Steinbeck. The novel's strength, however, is in the author's skillful presentation of the Mexican background of the Chicano migration to the United States.

Two recent novels by Chicanos represent the nexus between the Chicano and Anglo worlds at this time and indicate the direction the Chicano novel will probably take. Richard Vasquez's novel, *Chicano,* will be of special interest to Chicano readers because, in a manner similar to that of *Pocho,* it deals with the substance of their lives and experiences.[30]

Chicano details the odyssey of Hector Sandoval from Mexico to the United States during the Mexican Revolution and the travails of his children, Neftali, Jilda, and Hortencia, and their heirs in California. *Chicano* is an important novel for its portrayal of the Chicano migration, although some critics contend that the values of the novel have been misplaced in a rendition of the traditional fictions about Chicanos.

On the other hand, Raymond Barrio's *The Plum Plum Pickers* is a more exciting work, not because it is experimentally in the same mold as *Cane*—a novel that figured prominently in the Negro Renaissance of the 1920s—but because Barrio has been concerned less with presenting a panorama of Chicano life than with dealing entirely with the contemporary situation of the migrant couple, Manuel and Lupe, caught in the grip of agricultural exploitation.[31]

Essentially, *The Plum Plum Pickers* focuses on the proletarian view of life. Lupe is drawn as a significant figure in the novel, not as a female trifle caught at the edges of that fictive *machismo* so dominant in *Pocho* and *Chicano*. Barrio has gone beyond the form of the "pop" novel to create a significant work of American literature.

The linguistic aspect

Another important aspect of the Chicano literary renaissance to consider is the linguistic aspect. Chicano writers are expressing themselves on the printed page in their Chicano language, evolved from Spanish and English, and their particular experiences in American barrios, *colonias,* and ghettos. Like black English, the Chicano language is at the heart of the Chicano experience; but unlike black English, the Chicano language deals not only with dialects of American English but with dialects of American and Mexican Spanish. Moreover, it has produced a mixture of the two languages resulting in a unique kind of *binary phenomenon,* in which the linguistic symbols of two languages are mixed in utterances using either language's syntactic structure.

For the bilingual (Spanish-English, for instance) writer, this structure involves using either his English or Spanish idiolect at will to produce a "stereolect." For example, Alberto Alurista's poetry in *El Espejo-The Mirror: Selected Mexican American Literature* (published by Quinto Sol) reads as follows:

> Mis ojos hinchados
>   flooded with lagrimas
> de bronce
> melting on the cheek bones
> of my concern
>   razgos indigenes
> the scars of history on my face
>   and the veins of my body
> that aches
>   vomito sangre
> y lloro libertad
>   I do not ask for freedom
> I am freedom.[32]

In order to understand contemporary Mexican-American literature, it is important to understand the function of binary phenomena in Chicano communication and expression. It is equally important, however, to understand that these phenomena are not of Mexican-American origin, for binary phenomena occur wherever there is linguistic contact and coexistence. In New York, for example, binary phenomena ("stereolecticism") occur among American speakers of Yiddish. In literature, such contemporary American writers as Philip Roth and Saul Bellow use many Yiddish expressions in their works.

Linguistically, it is important to keep in mind the primacy of language in the life of an individual or of a society or culture because the language we speak shapes our particular view of the world. Thus, to comprehend the Chicano experience, one must critically examine the language of Chicanos, not with preconceived notions of what is correct or standard in language usage in Spanish or English but with knowledge of the role language plays in human intercourse. We can no longer tag the Chicano language as "poor Spanish" or "poor English" or as "Mex-Tex," "Spanglish," "Pachuco," or other such denigrations. We must guard against stupidities that suggest that Mexican Americans are nonlingual because they speak neither English nor Spanish. We must bear in mind that we do not depreciate the language of Chaucer's time by calling it "Frenglish," though more French than English was spoken by the upper classes.

Ironically, California proved to be the birthplace of the renaissance that Aurora Lucero had hoped New Mexico would produce. In 1953, she wrote optimistically:

> There now remains but one renaissance to be effected—the literary. With the happy accident that New Mexico possesses more traditional literary materials than any other Hispanic region it should be possible to bring about such a rebirth in the reenactment of the lovely old plays, in the keeping alive the lovely old folk dances and in the singing of the old traditional songs.[33]

The Chicano renaissance came into being not in relation to the traditional past but rather in the wake of growing awareness by Mexican Americans of their Indian, not Hispanic, identity. The Chicano renaissance is but the manifestation of a people's coming of age. It has been long overdue, and in another country, like Milton's unsightly root, it bore a bright and golden flower.

Notes

[1] Marshall McLuhan, *Understanding Media: The Extensions of Man,* 2d ed. (New York: New American Library, 1964), p. 23.
[2] Américo Paredes, "Folklore and History," in *Singers and Storytellers,* ed. Mody C. Boatright, Wilson M. Hudson, and Allen Maxwell (Dallas: Southern Methodist University Press, 1961), pp. 162–63.
[3] Richard Henry Dana, *Two Years Before the Mast* (New York: Bantam Books, 1959), p. 59.

4 U.S., Congress, *Congressional Globe*, 32d Cong., 2d sess., January 10, 1853, Appendix, p. 104.
5 W. W. H. Davis, *El Gringo: Or, New Mexico and Her People* (New York: Harper & Brothers, 1857), pp. 85–86.
6 William V. Wells, "The French in Mexico," *The Overland Monthly*, 1:232 (September 1868).
7 Walter Prescott Webb, *The Texas Rangers: A Century of Frontier Defense* (Austin: University of Texas Press, 1965), p. 14.
8 John Steinbeck, *Tortilla Flat* (New York: Bantam Books, 1965), p. 2.
9 José Antonio Navarro, "Memoirs," Archives Division of the Texas State Library.
10 Donaciano Vigil, *History of New Mexico to 1851*, New Mexico State Archives, Santa Fe, New Mex.
11 Miguel Antonio Otero, *The Indian Depredations in the Territory of New Mexico*, Library of Congress, Washington, D. C.
12 Juan Bautista Alverado, *Historia de California*, 1876, Bancroft Library, Berkeley, Calif.
13 Mariano Guadalupe Vallejo, *Recuerdos historicos y personales tocante a la Alta California: historia politica del pais, 1769–1849*, 1875. Translated as *History of California*, by Earl R. Hewitt, Bancroft Library, Berkeley, Calif.
14 In 1902 Beveridge filed a majority report for his committee investigating statehood for New Mexico and Arizona. The report objected to statehood.
15 Benjamin D. Hayes, *Pioneer Notes . . . 1849–1875*, ed. Marjorie Tisdale Walcott (Los Angeles: Marjorie Tisdale Walcott, 1929), p. 280.
16 In 1875 Vallejo wrote to his son, Platon, that he was completing his "true history of California" to serve as a guide for posterity. See Nadie Brown Emparan, *The Vallejos of California* (San Francisco: Gleeson Library Associates, University of San Francisco, 1968), p. 129.
17 Leonard Pitt, *The Decline of the Californios: A Social History of the Spanish-Speaking Californians, 1846–1890* (Berkeley and Los Angeles: University of California Press, 1970), p. 283.
18 Ernesto Galarza, *Merchants of Labor: The Mexican Bracero Story* (Santa Barbara, Calif.: McNally & Lofton, 1964), p. 17.
19 Editorial, *El Grito* 1:4 (Fall 1967).
20 Ibid.
21 Floyd Salas, *Tattoo the Wicked Cross* (New York: Grove Press, 1967); and John Rechy, *City of Night* (New York: Grove Press, 1963).
22 *Con Safos*, P.O. Box 31085, Los Angeles, Calif. (Published irregularly as sufficient material becomes available for an issue.)
23 *Regeneración*, P.O. Box 54624, T.A., Los Angeles, Calif. (Published monthly.)
24 Octavio Paz, *Labyrinth of Solitude* (New York: Grove Press, 1961).
25 Luis Valdez, "Notes on Chicano Theater," *El Teatro* (Official newspaper of El Teatro Campesino, published by El Centro Campesino Cultural, P.O. Box 2302, Fresno, Calif.), p. 4.
26 Rodolfo González, "I am Joaquín," *El Gallo* Newspaper, 1967.
27 Luis Omar Salinas, *Crazy Gypsy* (Fresno, Calif.: Origenes Publication, La Raza Studies, Fresno State College, 1970), p. 51.
28 Abelordo Delgado, *Chicano: 25 Pieces of a Chicano Mind* (Denver: Migrant Workers' Press, 1970), pp. 35–36.
29 José Antonio Villarreal, *Pocho* (Garden City, N.Y.: Doubleday and Co., 1959).
30 Richard Vasquez, *Chicano* (Garden City, N.Y.: Doubleday and Co., 1970).
31 Raymond Barrio, *The Plum Plum Pickers* (Sunnyvale, Calif.: Ventura Press, 1969).
32 Octavio I. Romano-V, ed., *El Espejo-The Mirror: Selected Mexican American Literature* (Berkeley, Calif.: Quinto Sol Publications, 1969), p. 172. Reprinted by permission of the poet.
33 Aurora Lucero, *Literary Folklore of the Hispanic Southwest* (San Antonio, Tex.: The Naylor Company, 1953), p. 210.

Psychological Research and the Mexican American

Amado M. Padilla

Psychology is the science directly concerned with behavioral and social processes. As practitioners of this science, psychologists have been looked to for guidance in providing new and better ways of promoting human welfare. However, psychologists thus far have contributed little in bringing their knowledge and resources to bear on the pressing social problems that exist today.[1]

It is true that there has been a group of psychologists who have argued for involvement in the issues confronting society. It is not to this group of psychologists that this article is addressed, but to that community of psychologists who seek to maintain the status quo by continuing to support a psychology that de-emphasizes the promotion of human well-being.

For example, these psychologists have been unable to deal with the significant social problems that affect the Mexican Americans and other minority groups because they have confined themselves to a laboratory model of psychology.[2] A laboratory-oriented approach to psychology assumes that only when one can control and manipulate variables in a laboratory can one study behavior scientifically. Such an approach fails to recognize all of the cultural, environmental, and social influences that motivate the Mexican American.

On those rare occasions when these psychologists leave the laboratory and attempt to implement their hypotheses of behavior on people culturally different from themselves, they often resort to ethnocentric interpretations of their observations. Ethnocentrism is the tendency to evaluate people and experiences from the viewpoint of one's own group. Such an approach, when employed by a psychologist, serves to cloud his objectivity and often to retard his understanding of culturally different people, such as the Mexican American.

The purpose of this article is: (1) to show how some psychologists, because of their rigidity in adhering to a laboratory model and their own ethnocentrism, have created a situation which is intolerable to today's Mexican American, (2) to show how such approaches have resulted in inadequate and irrelevant psychological services, and (3) to offer recommendations for change. These objectives will be approached through an examination of the psychological literature that relates to certain issues centering on family-child relationships, bilingualism and intelligence tests, and mental illness and mental health practices among Mexican Americans.

Family-child relationships

The psychological research community has not as yet dealt in depth with Chicano family-child relationships, but has relied on the writings of anthropologists and sociologists. Family-child relationships are described by these writers in overgeneralized statements. For example, the Chicano family is supposedly primarily authoritarian and patriarchal. The father maintains authority through tradition and force. He is aloof and inhibits his feelings of love and concern for his children. He is a poor model for his male children and consequently his children have difficulty in establishing adequate masculine identification.

The mother, in contrast, is submissive, quiet, obedient, and faithful to her husband. She is fatalistic in her philosophy of the world and dependent upon her husband and family. She is a good mother only because her children are an extension of her own dependency needs.[3]

Moreover, it is claimed that the Mexican American is not competitive, ambitious, or achievement oriented because these qualities have not been rewarded during his early childhood. What have been rewarded are dependence, obedience, compliance, and silence. He is not active, mobile, curious, or talkative. The Mexican-American child, because of his early childhood training, is forever expecting to have his dependency need fulfilled by the environment.

In summary, the stereotyped Mexican-American family has a high regard for authority, an adherence to tradition, a philosophy of acceptance and resignation, and a religious orientation. This view contrasts with the Anglo-American family, which values achievement and success, activity and work, efficiency and practicality, material comfort, equality of opportunity, freedom, science, democracy, and individual personality.[4]

For the sake of brevity, the important cultural differences in family-child relationships described by social scientists can be outlined as follows:

	Training	*Activity*	*Time Orientation*	*Man-Nature Relationship*
Mexican American	Dependence	Being	Present	Subjugation to Nature
Anglo American	Individualism	Doing	Future	Mastery over Nature

It should be pointed out again that these stereotypes have not originated from the writings of psychologists. However, they have been accepted by psychologists without concern for documentation. Inferences made about the Mexican American are made without concern for the cultural and ecological variability that exists among Chicanos. Chicanos occupy all positions on the social, economic, and educational ladder. Some persons are at the lowest step; others occupy positions at the top. Some Chicanos are rural, but most are urban dwellers. There are differences in cultural awareness; some Mexican Americans prefer total assimilation and acculturation, and others prefer a parallel system. Yet, to read the Anglo accounts of Chicanos, the numerous overgeneralizations that describe him are noticeable.

In addition, social scientists have studied the Mexican American from an assumption that total assimilation into the mainstream is desirable; therefore, because of the Chicano's resistance to assimilation, his family structure is at fault. This *modus operandi* has resulted in social scientists describing the Mexican-American family structure in negative terms with little or no concern given to the positive attributes of the Chicano family.

The achievement syndrome often found in the writings of Anglo social scientists offers a good example of the above discussion. Achievement motivation is a prized index often pointed to by Anglo researchers in drawing cross-cultural differences. Celia S. Heller states:

> Parents, as a whole, neither impose standards of excellence for tasks performed by their children nor do they communicate to them that they expect evidence of high achievement. . . . The home also fails to provide the kind of independence training that . . . is highly functional for achievement. . . . It is not surprising, therefore, that these children seldom show initiative or freely express their own ideas.[5]

It is the contention here that Mexican-American parents are no different in what they want for their children from their Anglo counterparts. Chicanos want the same educational and occupational opportunities for their children. However, they believe that these should be attainable without the loss of the Chicano value systems.

It is this kind of sensitivity to cultural values that social scientists and psychologists have failed to recognize in their study of the Mexican-American family. Only one study in the psychological literature has adequately recognized that the Mexican-American family orientation differs on many variables besides ethnicity. In this study, Ronald W. Henderson and C. B. Merritt showed that the potential for school success of Mexican-American children was dependent upon the number of intellectually stimulating experiences to be found in the home, rather than in a belief that the more "Americanized" the parents, the greater the potential for success. As Henderson and Merritt state, "The data seem to refute the common assumption that children from families that are 'most Mexican' in their behavior and outlook will have the most difficulty in school." [6]

The conclusion to be drawn from the above exposé on the family is that psychologists have allowed the misrepresentations and stereotypes of the Mexican-American family to persist because of their acceptance of these stereotypes. What is needed is a thorough examination of all the dynamic interactions that occur in the Chicano home situations. Only such an analysis will reveal how the Chicano family differs from the Anglo in child-rearing practices that result in different aspirational and achievement orientation. Such studies must include controls for socioeconomic status if the present state of knowledge about the Chicano family is to be clarified.

Bilingualism and tests of intelligence

Psychometrics is an area of psychology that until recently enjoyed a major role in the study of racial and ethnic differences. The philosophical belief underlying intelligence testing is that men are not created equal in their intellectual capabilities and that such differences can be measured.[7] It is in this area that Mexican Americans have been intensively investigated.

A bibliographic search by the writer has indicated that no less than forty-eight of slightly over one hundred studies in the psychological literature pertaining to the Mexican American have in some way involved the issue of test performance and bilingualism. Many of these studies have shown that the intellectual functioning of Mexican-American children is below that of Anglo-American children. These studies have, more importantly, shown that the gap in intellectual functioning increases with age. It has been suggested that the major reason for this difference is due to the Spanish-speaking background of the Mexican-American child.[8]

It has also been suggested that bilingualism results in cognitive confusion that limits the child's ability to learn concepts as rapidly as a monolingual child. The usual conclusion drawn by educators from such suggestions is that the bilingual child, or child who is monolingual in Spanish, is a poor educational risk. Such conclusions have had clear racist implications, yet psychologists have failed to recognize the social significance of such messages. In short, such findings have been taken by some persons to mean that there are fundamental hereditary differences in intellectual capability between English-speaking and Spanish-speaking people.

Only recently, and under great pressure, have educators been forced to change their policies on the outcomes of intelligence tests. For instance, Chicano residents in California and certain communities in Texas have discontinued the educational tracking of their children based on mental tests.

Pressure has not yet been applied to psychometricians for a proper reevaluation of their tests. It is true that they have engaged for years in a continuous dialogue about the importance of cultural variables on intelligence measuring instruments; however, little progress has been made in developing culture-free tests or even culture-sensitive tests for various ethnic groups other than the Anglo American.[9] The standard psychological tests employed have not taken into account the cultural and environmental background of Mexican Americans. Nor have they included Chicanos in their standardization procedures. To illustrate the importance of these two factors, consider the implications that would be drawn if psychologists speaking only English were tested for intelligence in Spanish, on instruments standardized with Mexican Americans!

Two avenues of research have shown that there is a need to reexamine the relationship of bilingualism to intellectual functioning. One of these directions focuses on neurological theorizing and the other on recent psychological findings that show how the learning of two languages at an early age facilitates cognitive development.

Wilder Penfield, a noted neurologist, has for many years advocated bilingualism as a way in which the cortex of the young child can be given additional stimulation. Of equal importance is the fact that at an early age the brain seems to possess a greater plasticity and capacity for acquiring languages. The secret lies in an action called the switch mechanism, a conditioned reflex that works automatically in the brain. This switch mechanism enables the child to switch from the vocabulary of one language to that of another language with ease, so that both languages are learned directly and without confusion.[10]

Further, it has been shown that in some situations bilingualism serves to facilitate intellectual performance and that in some cognitive areas knowledge of two languages might be advantageous.[11] Joshua A. Fishman believes that functions related to the labeling of objects at an early age are advanced by knowing two languages because the child is thus facilitated in his acquisition of a mature notion of the nature of labels. Labeling of objects is important because such an ability is the precursor to more elaborate cognitive skills involving the use of labels in sentences.[12]

A recent study using bilingual Mexican-American Head Start children showed these children to be superior to monolingual children in tasks involving the naming of objects and the use of names in sentences. These findings confirm Fishman's hypotheses about the importance of two-language learning. What has still to be determined is the import such research receives from the psychological community.[13]

What psychologists have failed to recognize is that the question of intellectual functioning is not one of bilingualism per se but is a matter of economic, cultural, and situational factors. One factor that has received little consideration is malnutrition. Because it is unfortunately true that many Mexican Americans exist from day to day in a condition of poverty, it is not hypothetical to assume that many children are chronically malnourished. And it is a well-established fact that dietary deficiencies in young children are related to retardation in intellectual development and mental functioning.[14]

An interesting hypothesis has recently been advanced by Michael C. Latham and Francisco Cobos that may explain the depressed intelligence test scores of Mexican-American children and the observations made by anthropologists of these children. According to Latham and Cobos, a caloric-deficient diet results in a physiologic response to conserve energy for purposes of growth and for essential activities only. Thus, the child spends long periods of time passively and quietly. The time spent playing with his peers, verbalizing with his mother, manipulating objects, and stimulating his senses is limited. His subsequent poor performance on tests may then be due to his inactivity. Moreover, reports from anthropologists suggesting that Chicano children are inactive, compliant, and silent may be observations of the effects of malnutrition, rather than of Mexican-American child-rearing practices.[15]

The result of the misuse of psychological tests by psychometricians is that many Mexican Americans have come to have a negative self-concept. The negative self-concept has taken the form of the Chicano child's perception of himself as a failure in the educational setting; this image has consequently resulted in his withdrawal, only to find increased negative stereotypes of himself as an illiterate and uneducated burden on society. For many Chicanos these feelings have been repeatedly reinforced and have been transmitted from parents to offspring.

Advantages of bilingual training

To summarize, psychologists and educators have very adequately programmed the Mexican American into a "self-fulfilling prophecy" of failure through the use of inappropriate psychological measuring instruments. This situation can no longer be tolerated, but only with a concerted effort by the Mexican-American community in general, and the Chicano psychologist in particular, will such practices be corrected. Toward this goal, all people who share a bilingual-bicultural heritage should become advocates of early bilingual training for the following reasons:

(1) Bilingual training increases the early stimulation of the child that is so vital in the early phases of the educational process.

(2) There is sufficient evidence to show that such training increases the overall cognitive development of the child.

(3) Such training reduces the emotional shock that children undergo when forced to participate in a monolingual, in this case English, educational process.

(4) Such training reduces the social discomforts and stigma of having to operate at only the level of a single culture and language.

(5) Bilingual-bicultural training enhances the social mobility of the person as he grows into adulthood because he can communicate with the older members of his family at home and in the Anglo world on an equal basis.

(6) Finally, such training serves to enhance the mental health of the person because there is no interfering problem of marginality that sociologists have documented so well in persons who have lost their cultural and lingual heritage.

Mental illness and mental health practices

Chicanos have been perceived as childlike in their beliefs of what constitutes mental illness and in their mental health care practices. According to some psychotherapists, the Mexican American views illness as a suffering imposed by God that is not to be questioned because the imposed illness is part of God's plan for the universe. Because mental illness is part of a grand plan, it is a family affair as well as a community concern. It is seen in a religious and social context, rather than in the medical-scientific context of the Anglo society.[16]

It is this conception of illness that the psychologist and related mental health workers employ when attempting to understand psychopathology among the Chicanos. The psychological and mental health literature on this topic is filled with anecdotes of such folk beliefs as: *susto* (fright), *embrujada* (bewitchment), *mal ojo* (evil eye), *caido de la mollera,* and *empacho* (food-blocked intestine). Moreover, accounts of the practices of *curanderas* (folk healers) fill the pages of psychiatric journals.[17] These accounts make fascinating reading for the non-Chicano clinicians because they are replete with mysticism and because they stir the reader to the belief that the Chicano is at a primitive stage of development, desperately in need of assistance.

It is known that urban Mexican Americans do not differ overall from Anglo Americans in their perceptions of mental illness. However, their are some intragroup differences among Chicanos in their perceptions of mental illness that must be clarified. Among older and less acculturated Chicanos, there is greater reliance on such beliefs as the inheritance of mental illness, the effectiveness of prayer as a cure of mental illness, and a familistic orientation which maintains that the mentally ill person will recover sooner by remaining at home. It should be emphasized, however, that as Mexican Americans have become more urbanized, their perceptions do not differ substantially from other ethnic groups.[18]

Little is known about the prevalence of mental illness among the Mexican Americans. Little epidemiological work has been conducted on the incidence and manifestations of mental illness among the Mexican Americans. The limited existing data suggest that Mexican Americans, at least in the state of Texas, have a lower incidence of mental illness than do Anglo Americans. E. Gartly Jaco has suggested that these findings are attributable to the existence of a warm, supportive, extended family with strong values of mutual acceptance, care, and responsibility, which tend to protect Mexican Americans against the development of major mental illness.[19]

Two studies supporting Jaco's observation that the family structure is vitally important in an understanding of mental disorders among the Chicano have been reported. In the first study, Horacio Fabrega found that hospitalized Mexican Americans appeared to be more severely disturbed than their Anglo counterparts. More important is the fact that the families of these Mexican-American patients may have been tolerant and willing to assist, and consequently delayed seeking help or hospitalization for their mentally ill family member. It is this delaying procedure that appears to be the causal agent for the severity of the disorders found among the Mexican-American patients.[20]

A second study employing standard projective techniques found that the family occupies a much more influential role in the cognitive structure of Mexican Americans than is true of Anglos or blacks. Responses on the Thematic Apperception Test pointed out differences between the Mexican Americans and the other two groups in themes of family unity and in their characterization, particularly of father-son and mother-son relationships.[21]

Taken together, these studies are indicative of the positive attributes of the Mexican-American family structure, contrary to the description in an early section of this paper. Because of the supportive family structure, the family offers an excellent entry into the psychotherapeutic situation. It is unfortunate that psychologists and related mental health practitioners have not as yet capitalized on the Chicano family structure in providing mental health services for the Chicano. What actually has occurred is that Mexican Americans have been forced to seek mental health care in settings that have discriminated against them and have offered services which are culturally and emotionally irrelevant.[22]

It should be emphasized that Mexican Americans require the same quality of mental health care as other Americans; but it is true that clinical psychology and many of the traditional psychotherapeutic techniques are geared toward the middle class values and standards of the non-Chicano suburbanite. Many avenues of mental health care have excluded not only the Chicano, but all groups who differ from the model. Only when therapists become sensitive to the social, economic, and political dynamics of the Chicano and the barrio will the mental health care of the Chicano become relevant and adequate.

Mental health care, to be adequate for the Mexican American, must be preventive. It must focus on the mental well-being of the Chicano child and on the positive coping mechanisms that are characteristic of the adult who has been able to survive in an often hostile environment. It must also have bilingual-bicultural components that are responsive to the needs of the Mexican American.

Recommendations for a responsive psychology

Psychology can only become relevant for the Chicano when psychologists realize that the barrio is a living entity consisting of the interplay of intragroup and intergroup relationships, ecological factors, cultural differences, and developmental forces that motivate the behavior of the Chicano. The existing psychological knowledge of the Chicano has been obtained in poorly conceived and inadequately controlled cross-cultural investigations. Until well-planned experimental studies that bear directly on the needs of the barrio, rather than on the proclivities of the non-Chicano investigator, are conceived, Chicanos should perhaps call a moratorium on research in which they are involved as subjects.

Psychologists, as well as other behavioral and social scientists, must begin to realize that a science of behavior cannot be limited to one segment of a population. There must be a concern for individual differences, both within a group of people as well as between culturally different peoples. This new psychology that is to incorporate all people—be they from the suburbs, ghetto, or barrio—must seek to enhance the psychological well-being of all people. This aspect of the profession has for too long been neglected.

Toward this goal, psychologists must desist in their arrogance, that is, in the belief that because psychology is the study of behavior they know what will be best for people. Chicanos, as well as other minorities, have suffered from this arrogance when research and service programs have been planned. It is becoming clearer that the community must be involved in all phases of planning. Only when full community participation is accepted will psychology be a viable force which can plan, research, provide, and promote the well-being of all Americans.

An extension of this community participation includes the increased training of Chicanos in psychology. With proper training these new Chicano psychologists will be able to utilize their skills in serving the needs of the barrio.[23]

The Chicano stands at the crossroads of decision concerning the kind of psychological research and services he wants and needs most. If he uses his power to his advantage, he can dictate to psychologists the direction that their investigations should take. He can call a halt to the use of time-worn hypotheses and models. He can demand that studies by psychologists become interdisciplinary and sensitive to his culture. He can be sure that mental health service programs become relevant through the inclusion of bilingual-bicultural components. The Chicano can shape a psychology that will be meaningful to him and from which Anglos will prosper in their proper understanding of him. Only this two-way concern will bring an end to the Chicano's case history of neglect at the hands of psychologists.

Notes

[1] George A. Miller, "Psychology as a Means of Promoting Human Welfare," *American Psychologist*, 24:1,063 (December 1969).

[2] In order to avoid confusion, Mexican American and Chicano will be used interchangeably in this article to encompass a group of people of Mexican descent who have been variously described by social scientists as Mexican, Mexican American, Spanish, Latin, Chicano, and so forth.

[3] Ari Kiev, *Curanderismo: Mexican-American Folk Psychiatry* (New York: The Free Press, 1968).

[4] Lyle Saunders, *Cultural Differences and Medical Care: The Case for the Spanish-Speaking People of the Southwest* (New York: Russell Sage Foundation, 1954).

[5] Celia S. Heller, *Mexican American Youth: Forgotten Youth at the Crossroads* (New York: Random House, 1967), pp. 37–39.

[6] Ronald W. Henderson and C. B. Merritt, "Environmental Backgrounds of Mexican American Children with Different Potentials for School Success," *Journal of Social Psychology*, 75:101 (June 1968).

[7] For a thorough examination of the reasoning of such a belief and the arguments that result, see Arthur R. Jensen, "How Much Can We Boost the I.Q. and Scholastic Achievement?" *Harvard Educational Review*, 39:1–123 (Winter 1969).

[8] Natalie T. Darcy, "Bilingualism and the Measurement of Intelligence: Review of a Decade of Research," *Journal of Genetic Psychology*, 103:259 (December 1963); and Hilding B. Carlson and Norman Henderson, "The Intelligence of American Children of Mexican Parentage," *Journal of Abnormal and Social Psychology*, 45:544 (July 1950).

[9] Anne Anastasi, *Differential Psychology* (New York: Macmillan, 1937).

[10] Wilder Penfield and Lamar Roberts, *Speech and Brain Mechanisms* (Princeton: Princeton University Press, 1959).

[11] Elizabeth Peal and Wallace E. Lambert, "The Relation of Bilingualism to Intelligence," *Psychological Monographs*, 76:1 (No. 27 1962).

[12] Joshua A. Fishman, "Bilingualism with and without Diglossia; Diglossia with and without Bilingualism," *Journal of Social Issues*, 23:29 (April 1967).

[13] Carol Feldman and Michael Shen, "Some Language-Related Cognitive Advantages of Bilingual Five-Year-Olds," *Journal of Genetic Psychology*, 118:235 (June 1971).

[14] Joaquin Cravioto, Elsa R. DeLicardie, and Herbert G. Birch, "Nutrition, Growth and Neuro-Integrative Development: An Experimental and Ecologic Study," *Pediatrics*, 38:319 (August 1966).

[15] Michael C. Latham and Francisco Cobos, "The Effects of Malnutrition on Intellectual Development and Learning," *American Journal of Public Health*, 61:1,307 (July 1971).

[16] Kiev, *Curanderismo*.

[17] John Gillin, "Magical Fright," *Psychiatry*, 11:387 (November 1948); Margaret Clark, *Health in the Mexican-American Culture* (Berkeley: University of California Press, 1959); James Galvin and Arnold Ludwig, "A Case of Witchcraft," *Journal of Nervous and Mental Disease*, 133:161 (August 1961); and William Madsen, "Value Conflicts and Folk Psychotherapy in South Texas," in Ari Kiev (ed.), *Magic, Faith, and Healing* (New York: The Free Press, 1964).

[18] Marvin Karno and Robert B. Edgerton, "Perception of Mental Illness in a Mexican-American Community," *Archives of General Psychiatry*, 20:233 (February 1969); and Robert B. Edgerton and Marvin Karno, "Mexican-American Bilingualism and the Perception of Mental Illness," *Archives of General Psychiatry*, 24:286 (March 1971).

[19] E. Gartly Jaco, *The Social Epidemiology of Mental Disorders* (New York: Russell Sage Foundation, 1960).

[20] Horacio Fabrega, Jon D. Swartz, and Carole A. Wallace, "Ethnic Differences in Psychopathology-II: Specific Differences with Emphasis on a Mexican-American Group," *Journal of Psychiatric Research*, 6:221 (July 1968).

[21] Dale L. Johnson and Melvin P. Sikes, "Rorschach and TAT Responses of

Negro, Mexican-American and Anglo Psychiatric Patients," *Journal of Projective Techniques*, 29:183 (June 1965).
[22] Marvin Karno, "The Enigma of Ethnicity in a Psychiatric Clinic," *Archives of General Psychiatry*, 14:516 (May 1966); Joe Yamamoto, Quinton C. James and Norman Palley, "Cultural Problems in Psychiatric Therapy," *Archives of General Psychiatry*, 19:45 (July 1968); Lawrence Y. Kline, "Some Factors in the Psychiatric Treatment of Spanish-Americans," *American Journal of Psychiatry*, 125:1,674 (June 1969); M. J. Philippus, "Successful and Unsuccessful Approaches to Mental Health Services for an Urban Hispano-American Population," *American Journal of Public Health*, 61:820 (April 1971); and E. Fuller Torrey, "The Irrelevancy of Traditional Mental Health Services for Urban Mexican-Americans," Paper presented at the Meetings of the American Orthopsychiatry Association, San Francisco (March 1970).
[23] Proof that such training programs are lacking can be seen when one compares the ratio of psychologists to the general population. Although there is one psychologist to approximately every 7,500 people, the ratio of psychologists to Chicanos is one to about every 160,000. These figures are based on a recent estimate of the number of Chicano psychologists by the Association of Psychologists for La Raza.

Chicanos and Coalitions as a Force for Social Change

John Florez

During the past decade this country experienced more attempts at social change than during any previous similar period. For the first time the federal government—through, for example, community action programs and the President's Committee on Juvenile Delinquency and Youth Crime—sanctioned the use of community organization strategies to change existing social institutions. Private foundations also became more active in funding projects aimed at social change, as evident in the Ford Foundation's "grey area" projects. During the decade of the 1960s, many people began to have great expectations and hopes for the future. For the first time we were going to improve the quality of living for many and conduct an all-out effort to eliminate poverty and to enfranchise those who previously had been disenfranchised.

In Chicano communities throughout the country we also saw hopes raised, although it was not readily acknowledged that we were having problems. In spite of the "benign neglect" we experienced, we made attempts to become involved. We attended board and committee meetings and tried to make the "maximum feasible participation" concept work. We told our people to talk about their problems and to participate in studies. As our own civil rights movement began to gather momentum and we realized that the established methods of causing change were ineffective, we began to employ other strategies and tactics to bring about change. More important, however, we renewed alliances with our traditional friends.

The old alliances

It is the purpose of this article to examine these old alliances as they pertain to the Chicano movement and to suggest new alliances through coalitions. It is important first to examine these old alliances, to know who they were and the position in which they have left us.

Liberals

When we reached out for allies to help us, we turned initially to our old liberal friends who were sympathetic listeners and more than eager to identify with our cause. Among them were those liberals who would identify with any new movement or any cause that involved oppressed people. There were other liberals who were more interested merely in attacking the establishment for its own sake, regardless of the consequences. They not only alienated the establishment but also exploited our cause for their own purposes. In addition, they frequently tried to enlist the Chicano in attempts to advance their own agenda. Many Chicanos equated strong rhetoric with genuine concern. The more antiestablishment the rhetoric, the greater their identification with our cause; however, when it actually came to enlisting their support on hard issues, they were nowhere to be found—*se volvían puro polvo* (they would turn to dust)!

The unfortunate outcome of forming these alliances with liberals was that it lulled us into complacency and prevented us from seeking other allies. They could neither provide our people with needed resources themselves nor influence others who possessed these resources.

Other liberals who expressed interest in helping the Chicano frequently hurt more than they helped. Their help was paternalistic and they tended to perpetuate the status quo. Among them were the do-gooders and social workers who adhered to the values of the predominant social system that has long maintained racist stereotypes of the Chicano.

Social workers

In the past, we also looked to social workers for assistance because they were the professionals who knew how to deal with social problems. Among them were some Chicano social workers who were supposed to be sensitive to our problems. The unfortunate outcome, however, was that they led us into dealing with our problems with traditional methods. They too had been victims of inadequate schools of social work. They practiced the archaic and crystallized social work concepts which had been long established in the social work profession.

These concepts included the need for cooperation, nonduplication of services, adherence to the worker-client relationship, assimilation, and allegiance to agency policy (field work evaluations included questions about how well the student supported and interpreted agency policy). They believed that men were basically of good will and would do the right thing if only they were told what needed to be done.

By their traditional practices, they frequently counseled our people into a state of deeper resignation and acceptance. They were the first to say we should go through channels and resign ourselves to administrative decisions. Consequently, social workers have frequently hurt our people more than they have helped. As the late Senator Robert F. Kennedy stated:

> We need to create new remedies to deal with the multitude of daily injuries that persons suffer in this complex society simply because it is complex.
> I am not talking about persons who injure others out of selfish or evil motives. I am talking about the injuries which result simply from administrative conveniences, injuries which may be done inadvertently by those endeavoring to help— teachers and social workers and urban planners.[1]

Many Chicano social workers frequently found themselves caught in the conflict between the traditional social work concepts they had learned and what they knew from personal experiences needed to be done. Some found themselves being oppressed; others found themselves seeking new employment; still others have become more effective as they developed clearer understanding of the roles they must play.

Middlemen

During the past decade we also saw a proliferation of new agencies and greater support given to old agencies with the understanding that they should seek greater citizen participation. We attempted to ally ourselves with these agencies and to participate in their boards and committees. For example, we saw more manpower programs to help minorities and United Funds to help the poor. The programs were funded and staffed, but there were no visible results. Housing programs for the poor were initiated, but somehow the poor seldom profited. More minority children appeared in United Fund posters, but there were no programs for minorities. Current United Fund policies, which exclude new groups from being funded, make it impossible for Chicano programs to be started. Those that have been initiated are frequently suppressed and meticulously monitored.

Our alliance with these middlemen has often given credibility to their projects and allowed them to demonstrate to the taxpayer that they are doing something for the Chicano. They are able to say that they are professional and have the public interest in mind. If the programs fail, they can blame the failure on the lack of adequate numbers of professionals and sufficient money.

Coalitions and Chicanos

It has become increasingly clear that if social change that will improve the living conditions of Chicanos is to occur, that change must be championed by Chicanos. Peter Marris and Martin Rein, after their study of the projects sponsored by the Ford Foundation and the President's Committee on Juvenile Delinquency, made the following statement.

> This is perhaps the most important general conclusion of our study: that no movement of reform in American society can hope to supplant the conflicts of interest from which policy evolves. It can only act as an advocate, not as judge. If it is to be persuasive, it must be singleminded about the interests it represents, and so willing to surrender any claim to universal authority.[2]

The issues of concern to the Chicano will never be articulated in the American democratic social arena that operates through pres-

sures of vested interests unless the Chicano does it himself. The social experiments of the past decade have demonstrated this point.
These experiments have proved that there must be a resolve and a
commitment to a cause. Liberals, middlemen, and disinterested re-
formers are too easily led into nonpartisan positions and collapse
for lack of a strong community base. Nonpartisan liberals are with us
one day if the cause is popular; the next day they are "turned on"
to something new. Four years ago they were concerned about the
poor; now they are concerned with the environment.

This statement does not imply, however, that we should *not* seek
the support of others, but simply that if we *ourselves* do not constantly press for the interests of our people, no one else will. As
Marris and Rein state:

> A reformer in American society faces three crucial tasks. He
> must recruit a coalition of power sufficient for his purpose;
> he must respect the democratic tradition which expects every
> citizen, not merely to be represented, but to play an autono-
> mous part in the determination of his own affairs; and his
> policies must be demonstrably rational. These criteria are not
> peculiar to the United States—nor irrelevant even to totali-
> tarian societies—but each gains in America a particular em-
> phasis. In the first place, the distribution of authority is
> uniquely complicated.[3]

It is this writer's contention that if change is to come about for the
improvement of the masses of our people, we must redefine our
strategies, our priorities, and our alliances. We must ask ourselves
the following questions: When do we sit in as members of a community committee? Which is more important—more Chicano social
work instructors and Chicano Studies or better health services for
our people? As one Chicano *tecáto* (an addict) said to a group of
Chicano college students, "You guys are more concerned with
Brown Studies than you are with us who are dying daily because of
an overdose of heroin."

Chicano coalitions

Today we are an aware group of people and are coming closer together to deal with the problems facing Chicanos. We are coming
closer together because of a new hope that flows not from being
accepted on an advisory board but rather from a sense of identifica-

tion with a cause. We are now aware enough to know that *no one* will express the concerns of Chicanos except Chicanos.

For some time we labored under the notion that "we needed to get ourselves together" and that when we were unified under one Mexican-American organization, our problems would be solved. Today we realize that, although we are a group of people—diversified in our concerns—who often differ in our methods of dealing with our problems, we have common threads that bind us together. In essence, within our own communities we have formed our own Chicano coalitions. We may not always agree on everything—for example, the youth as opposed to the elderly, the professional as opposed to the activist—nevertheless, we embrace a common philosophy based on self-determination and expressed through the following goals:

1. To bring to the Chicano individual all the resources available so that he can express his right of self-determination through the control of every phase of his life.
2. To identify all institutions and their agencies that prohibit the expression of our rights and potentialities. To identify avenues and methods of action to change such institutions.
3. To mobilize groups to advocate and articulate the need for change.
4. To develop communication networks at all levels of the Chicano social structure that will allow quick mobilization of groups to initiate change based on well-thought-out specific goals and expertise available to carry through such goals.[4]

More and more we are working together and minimizing the debate. We are utilizing the diverse skills we possess—including political know-how, technical skills, professional competence, program development, and activist strategies—toward *la Causa*. For example, in one community in the Southwest, all these skills were combined to develop a community-based organization that now is managing its own programs, competing with older established institutions for resources, and becoming an advocate for Chicanos. It required the activists to bring the need to the attention of the community, the professionals to package the idea, and those persons with political know-how finally to make the project a reality. Such examples are now becoming more frequent and are indicative of the Chicanos' ability to work with one another in common concerns.

Coalitions with new allies

Our past traditional alliances with other groups have at times hurt rather than helped our cause. We must, therefore, reevaluate our past alliances and redefine our relationships with them. Will the middleman consider himself as an all-benevolent but authoritarian *patron,* or will he see himself in a position of stewardship? Will the liberal sacrifice "doing his thing" for the sake of our people? More important, we must seek out those new allies who actually hold the power and resources to deal with our problems. We must learn to identify those "power blocs" and attempt to seek their support and with them form coalitions—temporary unions for a common purpose. In addition, we should identify those issues for which we can gain the support of those power blocs.

In the past, we have sacrificed action for debate over political philosophies (men often do the right thing for the wrong reasons). At times we failed to seek the support of key groups because we were told by our old allies that they would not support us, but we never bothered to find out for ourselves. We too were "hung up" about our stereotypes about the power structure. In *To Seek a Newer World,* Senator Kennedy said:

> Too often in the past we have been enmeshed in the traditional debate between liberals and conservatives over whether we should or should not spend more government funds on programs. What we have failed to examine with any thoroughness is the impact of these programs on those we sought to assist, indeed whether they have had any impact at all.[5]

Recent experiences in the coalition process with new allies have demonstrated some successes. In one city, for example, a Chicano tenant union, a bank president, and other members of the power structure coalesced to replace an old-time public housing authority director with a more responsive individual. In other cities, corporation presidents have supported Chicano issues and provided financial support. Although these are isolated examples, it is important to note that within the power structure of a community there are potential allies, but we have failed to seek their support. In the past we have allowed the middlemen professionals to tell those in power what needed to be done. The outcome was more of the same kind of programs and the same kind of attitudes being maintained by the public. This writer advocates the elimination of the middleman wherever possible.

Increasingly, we are seeing some changes in the leadership of the power structure. We should, however, be in a position to understand and define the nature of the relationship into which we enter with our new allies. We should realize that, although they may agree with us on certain issues, they may disagree completely on many others. In some instances the power structure may coalesce with us in wresting resources from the middlemen on such issues as welfare reform, school problems, and legal issues. In other instances they may provide resources from their own private sector for economic development and special projects. At the same time, however, this same group may not support us in *la huelga*. Does their lack of support in some areas mean that we will not work with them if they do not totally agree with us all the time? All too frequently some Chicanos have failed to recognize this difference· and consequently have been responsible for the denial of needed help to our people. In short, while some of us are "doing our thing" (as are the liberals), we use our own people in the process.

Too frequently we have heard, "I do not want to deal with the establishment because I'll lose my credibility with my people." This writer is not certain that the "people" who are unemployed and suffer from inadequate housing, ill health, inadequate courts, and a high rate of incarceration are concerned about anyone's credibility. Although these issues are not romantic and are not readily solved, they are, nevertheless, some of the problems with which we must cope if we are to help the masses of our people. Can we not find allies to help us deal with these problems without losing our integrity?

Finally, we must be sufficiently flexible to dissolve current relationships and form new ones as we define new objectives. If we understand and accept the terms of the relationship with these individuals or groups as being specific and for a definite objective, there is no loss of integrity.

Conclusion

Although there is no question that Chicanos must look after the interests of Chicanos, there are times when they can unite with other groups for a common purpose. We have failed in the past to

examine more closely the composition of those groups, and we have
failed to see that rhetoric does not always produce action. For too
long we have missed opportunities to relate directly to power blocs
and instead have related to middlemen and other "nice guys." If
we are to be successful in solving the great problems of our people,
we must have the ability to deal with them by using many kinds of
methods. The coalition process is only one of these methods but it is
one that we have not fully explored. Can we have the vision to use
this process in the interest of our people?

Notes

[1] Robert F. Kennedy, Address on Law Day, University of Chicago Law School,
Chicago, Illinois, May 1, 1964.
[2] Peter Marris and Martin Rein, *Dilemmas of Social Reform: Poverty and
Community Action in the United States* (New York: Atherton Press, 1967),
p. 230.
[3] Ibid., p. 7.
[4] Marta Sotomayor, "The Chicano Movement and Power Strategies" (Paper
delivered at the Urban Coalition Conference for Mexican-Americans, Denver,
Colorado, March 21, 1970).
[5] Robert F. Kennedy, *To Seek a Newer World* (New York: Doubleday & Co.,
1968), pp. 32–33.

The Status of
Religion Among
Mexican Americans

Jorge Lara-Braud

The status of religion among Mexican Ameri-
cans today fluctuates between routine and renaissance. Routine has
much to do with the legacy of missionary outreach; renaissance has
much to do with the people's new spirit of self-assertion.

From the beginning, Catholic and Protestant churches have shown
concern for the Mexican American in a manner that contrasts with
the rejection or neglect of other American institutions.[1] Both Catholic and Protestant churches early defined their missionary outreach
in relation not only to spiritual ministration, but also to deliberate
Americanization. After the military conquests of 1836 and of 1846
to 1848, the new citizens of Mexican extraction were considered
remnants of an alien, inferior, and hostile culture. Their well-being, it
was thought, would be largely dependent upon adequate acculturation to the language, traditions, and values of the new nation. Understandably, the churches made Americanization a top missionary
priority, not just for the sake of Mexicans, but also for the public

This article is based on a paper given at a meeting of the American
Academy of Religion and the Society of Biblical Literature–Southwest
Region, Texas Christian University, Fort Worth, March 1971.

acceptance of those church organizations that would develop in their midst.

Neither Catholic nor Protestant churches were even remotely equipped to carry out their two-fold task of spiritual care and cultural conversion. The Catholic Church was in virtual collapse in the Southwest when this huge piece of real estate became the property of the United States. No diocesan priests were available to take the churches. The missions of Texas and California were practically abandoned. It is a supreme irony that a missionary strategy, of which one of the chief goals was Americanization, was soon to rely heavily on religious orders imported primarily from France and Spain. Oblate Fathers of Mary Immaculate came from France to South Texas as early as 1847. Some time later, Spanish Claretians were dispatched to Texas and California, as were subsequently also Immaculate Heart Missionaries, Vincentians, and Piarists. Until the 1930s, it could be said that the majority of bishops in New Mexico and Texas had been French.

The experience of other Catholic communities undergoing the process of Americanization is in marked contrast to the experience of Mexican Americans. The Irish, the Italians, the Germans, the Czechs, and the Poles had their own priests from the beginning. Moreover, among those groups loyalty to priestly leadership and church membership was well developed. The traditions among Mexicans, however, of anticlericalism and noninstitutional Catholicism were deeply imbedded before they became citizens of the United States. Certain 1971 statistics dramatize the contrasting legacy. It is estimated that 17 percent of the Catholic population of the United States is of Irish extraction. Fifty-six percent of the 275 bishops of the Catholic Church are also of Irish extraction. Approximately 20 percent of Catholics in the United States are Mexican Americans. With the elevation of Patrick Flores in 1970 to the episcopacy as auxiliary bishop of the Archdiocese of San Antonio, it may be said that now there is *one* Mexican-American bishop in the nation. Of a total of about fifty-nine thousand Catholic priests, not quite two hundred are native Mexican Americans. In the Archdiocese of San Antonio, with an estimated constituency of half a million, of whom 75 percent are Mexican Americans, there are at present eleven Mexican-American diocesan priests, with seven more belonging to religious orders—a total of eighteen priests, not all of whom serve Mexican-American parishes.

Catholicism and Mexican Americans

The question remains, however, whether in the light of such massive legacy of lack of indigenous leadership, the Catholic Church has succeeded in effectively reaching Mexican Americans with her spiritual ministrations. The answer has to be a cautious yes. The Church's pastoral activity reaches now into every nook and cranny of the community. The response of the people, nevertheless, is ambiguous. Approximately 95 percent of the seven million Mexican Americans regard the Catholic Church as theirs, but they are either highly selective in the use of the Church services or seriously neglectful of them. If one qualifies as a practicing Catholic by taking communion at least once a year, then more than half of the Mexican Americans of the Southwest would be regarded as nonpracticing Catholics or "noncommunicants."

The other question is whether the Americanizing goal of the Catholic outreach has been achieved. To this question the answer is an unqualified no. Few Mexican Americans would lament this failure today. In fact, many consider it providential. The outcome has multiple causes. The community never ceased to be replenished by a heavy, constant influx of immigration from Mexico. Although today approximately 90 percent of the Mexican Americans of the Southwest are citizens of the United States and perhaps 85 percent are urban dwellers, at least 65 percent still retain Spanish as the primary language spoken in the home. Furthermore, the Church for Mexican-American Catholics has not been the center of social or cultural life as it has been for the blacks or for other ethnic minorities. Perhaps the Church might have been such a center if it had been under indigenous leadership, but it is doubtful whether Mexican-American leadership would have made Americanization a prominent concern of missionary outreach.

Space will not permit tracing in as much detail the missionary legacy of Protestantism among Mexican Americans. A few highlights are in order, however. Anglo Protestant missionaries were busily at work among Mexican Americans as early as the 1840s. By the 1930s most of the missionary labor was being done by specialists who were either native Mexican Americans or Protestant nationals from Mexico and Latin America. At the present time, however, final decisions for mission policy, allocation of resources, deployment of personnel, and institutional administration are made primarily by Anglo executives.

Influence of Protestantism

It is estimated that about 5 percent of the present Mexican-American population belongs to some Protestant communion. Doctrine and practice among Mexican-American Protestants were considerably influenced by the patterns of missionary work developed by American Protestant churches in Latin America in the second half of the nineteenth century. At that time there was a wholesale transplantation of models of church life from New England and the Bible Belt, and those models became normative. There was heavy emphasis on Bible instruction, individual conversion, moral discipline, segregated social life, sectarian institutions, a Protestant ethic of work and upward mobility, and a complete rejection of anything Roman Catholic as pagan. Every missionary from the United States was in some way influenced by the anti-Catholic sentiment of the nativist movement and by the chauvinistic Manifest Destiny so characteristic of nineteenth-century American Protestantism.

Out of that apprenticeship emerged the Protestant passion for the conversion of Mexican Americans. This passion was a thoroughly Americanizing agent even before it arrived in the Southwest. The names of its converts may have been García, López, or González, but when they, in turn, became the evangelists among their people, north or south of the Rio Grande, their style of mission differed little, if any, from that of Smith, Jones, or Wilson except that Spanish was no longer hesitant, broken, or butchered!

Lest this discussion be interpreted as belittlement, some remarkable achievements deserve special mention. The greatest of them all is the pioneer work of Protestants in introducing illiterate and literate alike to the powerful impact of the Bible. One cannot be exposed to it without sharing in some way its passion for the poor, its proclamation of liberating grace, its call to abundant life, and its eagerness for a future rule of righteousness in opposition to the present rule of unrighteousness. Impelled by that vision, men and women were truly converted—turned around—to a newness of life that no religious propriety could ever contain. Thus, it is no coincidence that today in every hamlet, town, or metropolis in which the human rights of Mexican Americans are at stake, one finds a number of

Mexican-American Protestants playing decisive roles totally out of proportion to the size of their religious community and often despite the apathy or antagonism of their coreligionists.

There are probably in excess of two thousand Mexican-American Protestant congregations in the Southwest. About two-thirds belong to some kind of Baptist or Pentecostal group. The remaining one-third comprises so-called "historical" denominations, the largest number probably belonging to the United Methodist Church. There are more than one thousand active pastors, more than half of whom are probably natives of Mexico or another Latin American country. In contrast to the two hundred Mexican-American Catholic priests for the whole nation, the high number of Spanish-speaking pastors serving Protestant parishes in the Southwest suggests an advanced degree of indigenization. In practice, however, Anglo executives, as has been mentioned earlier, are still very much the important decision-makers. More significant is the marked loyalty of Spanish-speaking congregations to the religious ethos of nineteenth-century American Protestantism.

The road to renaissance for Mexican-American Catholics and Protestants lies unmistakably in their willingness and ability to insist on indigenous leadership and to make their forms of church life consonant with the spirit of self-assertion sweeping through the entire ethnic community. This spirit is one not of assimilation or of separatism, but of pluralism. It is nourished certainly by the example of the black liberation struggle, but it is nurtured also by the claims that the many other subcultures, such as Indians, Orientals, white ethnics, youth, women, hard-hats, suburbanites, and peace groups, are making upon society.

Diversity of culture

On the eve of the birth of a truly pluralistic society, the Mexican American is stirred by the richness of his own inner diversity. He is not only a Mexican—tough Mexicanhood lies at the core of his being. He is not only an American—tough Americanhood touches every particle of his life. He is a Mexican American—the human intersection of two histories, two nations, two cultures, and two languages converging, colliding, blending, and embracing, depending on one's location within the human geography evolved by one and one-half centuries of relentless interaction. The interaction is by no means over. Through dogged determination, more Mexican Americans carve out leadership roles in every public institution that was formerly closed to people of color or was open only to those who would disguise their difference. Here and there appear counter-institutions of, by, and for Mexican Americans. Paradoxically, their long-range strategy is to return their graduates to the traditional institutions, to reorient them toward the further empowerment of the ethnic community and the larger pluralization of the entire national citizenry. In words reminiscent of New Testament eschatology, the Mexican American is speaking of himself as a new man—a man for whom there is no historical parallel, at least not in the experience of the United States. He speaks of his ethnic family as *La Raza,* a new family of man, the first fruits of a new humanity in which the color range of Mexican-American skin, from darkest to fairest, will in itself be the visible sign of a new age of fraternity.

These are the large dreams and great visions that young and old Mexican Americans perceive as possible, with themselves in the vanguard to make them come true. Can these dreams be called *Messianism?* Can they be termed *Utopianism?* Most certainly so! Don Quixote lives again. He walks through barrios and colonias. This collective Don Quixote, however, is a community reviving and revived by Christian ideals kept alive by French Oblates, New England missionary ladies, authoritarian Spanish Claretians, scholastic Presbyterians, humble Franciscans, unlettered Pentecostals, and the myriad of their unsung successors.

Spiritual leadership

Religion lives among church and unchurched Mexican Americans as a pervasive spirituality. One does not have to be a theologian or a professor of religion to know that spirituality can easily become superstition instead of enlightenment, repression instead of liberation. Much depends on the forces that lead it. It is at this point that one can be optimistic about the consonance of the new spirituality and the role of Mexican-American churches. "Indigenization" is the key factor. By indigenization is meant the embodiment of the new spirituality in leadership and structures, which themselves correspond to it. Perhaps the best example that can be offered here is the forces that led to the elevation of Patrick Flores as the first native-born Mexican-American bishop of the Roman Catholic

Church in May 1970. A nationwide association of Mexican-American priests, *Padres Asociados para Derechos Religiosos, Educativos y Sociales* (PADRES), had come into being in October 1969. One of the chief concerns of PADRES has been the participation of Mexican Americans on all levels of decision making in the life of Catholicism in the United States. PADRES is also the strongest voice in the Catholic Church for overall Mexican-American advancement.

The Church heard that voice. Patrick Flores stands today as the best loved and most respected church charismatic among Spanish-speaking Catholics. The Archdiocese of San Antonio, as a result, is in full renaissance. Many apathetic or even hostile Mexican-American Catholics have thronged back into the Church, following with enthusiasm the pastoral direction of the new auxiliary bishop. An archdiocesan Office for Mexican-American Affairs has been established. The marketplace and the church are thereby made responsive to each other in every area of human endeavor. The diocesan seminary, lately decimated of teachers and students, is on its way to full recovery, with new church vocations and the possibility of becoming a national center for the study of the pastoral apostolate among Mexican Americans. Other dioceses in the Southwest are pressing for similar developments. A compromise concession has been made in the Archdiocese of Los Angeles, where an Ecuadorean educated in England and in the United States has been made auxiliary bishop.

Movements parallel to PADRES are to be found now in Mexican-American Protestant caucuses among United Methodists, American Baptists, United Presbyterians, and Southern Presbyterians. Mexican-American Protestants are being employed in key positions of those same churches, and foreign and domestic boards and agencies search diligently for new Mexican-American members. Candidates for the ordained ministry are trickling back to denominational seminaries, which just three years ago were seriously questioning whether Mexican-American students would stop enrolling altogether.

Ecumenical cooperation

Much of the renaissance of religion among Mexican Americans is the result of ecumenical cooperation by Catholics and Protestants in a common apostolate of redress for a long-suffering community. Illustrations abound, none of which is more dramatic than the struggle of César Chávez and the United Farm Workers Organizing Committee to secure the right of collective bargaining for farm workers. Chávez's own genuine religious piety, his commitment to nonviolence, and his passion for social justice have naturally attracted the support of churches. In the process, sectarian interests have been put aside.

The practice of ecumenical solidarity with the poor of one's own ethnic family has also advanced a common quest for more indigenous forms of witness and service. Here and there liturgy, sermon, religious instruction, theological formulations, church buildings, and leadership style genuinely reflect Chicano features. This quest involves more than the renaissance of religion. It involves rather the rebirth of a unique spirituality whose saints are the black Peruvian San Martín de Porres, the brown Indian Virgin of Guadalupe, and the blond European madonnas, and whose Lord is a *mestizo* Jew, Jesus of Nazareth.

Note

1 Some of the historical material related to the Roman Catholic Church is drawn from Leo Grabler, Joan W. Moore, and Ralph Guzman, *The Mexican American People: The Nation's Second Largest Minority* (New York: Free Press, 1970).

The Survival of La Raza Despite Social Services

Tomás C. Atencio

Had education and social services been effective, we would have no Chicanos today. Somebody failed, and this failure has impelled me—a Chicano social worker—to write this article.

Viva La Revolución!
Viva La Raza!
Viva La Causa!
Viva La Huelga!
Tierra O' Muerte!
Ay Chico! Calla! Guarda orden, Raza! You are a social worker.
Be professional, hombre!

Are these slogans the fabrications of white radicals, or could these cries represent the melting of frozen anger, gushing out in self-assertive expressions and even hostile *gritos?* What about those long marches of *campesinos?* What of their *huelgas?* Are those *teatros* ends unto themselves, or do they represent something about La

This article is based on a paper presented to the Southwest Council of La Raza at the conference "La Raza Challenges Health and Social Welfare Practices," Tucson, July 1969. The conference was funded under National Institute of Mental Health Contract HSM–42–69–83.

Raza? The boycotts—grapes, Coors beer, and lettuce—and that phenomenon in northern New Mexico where La Raza changed its priorities from powdered milk and surplus cheese to demands for the
return of stolen land—what do they mean? Has the time arrived
when even the Chicano, that antique of a misty past, will finally
speak out against a neocolonialist system that first vanquished, second occupied, third missionized, and finally perpetuated its oppression through its welfare system—an institution *que ni te engorda ni
te mata* (that neither fattens you nor kills you)?

La Raza movement—the Third World in the United States—
elicits a myriad of conflicting feelings in Chicano social workers. To
some of us this whole movement is embarrassing. To others it is in-
vigorating. Both emotions are natural, considering our background.
After all, our education prepared us to react with *vergüenza* (shame)
when our brother demands, and those who welcome the revolutionary
rhetoric and concomitant acts somehow emerged untarnished despite
social work education.

Others of our colleagues exclaim that the current approaches to
social change are ethnocentric and reflect a reverse racism. Unfortunately, the charge is accurate. We have learned only too well the
lessons of our masters, who feared to color the melting pot stew
with brown, red, or black. What is even more devastating is that not
only is the world in which we live separatist but that many Chicano
social workers, even now, find themselves on the other side, advocat-
ing racism against themselves. In truth, what alternative do we have,
having been trained and subsequently employed by institutions that
survive on racism?

At last, however, the Chicano client has spoken to all of us. In
his attack he charges, "Your casework! Your therapy! They have
only helped me to adjust to my *miseria*. You got my head straight
only so that I would accept your crumbs. . . . But now I have to
change the conditions that caused my sickness.

"Your community organization," he continues, "has wasted itself
getting together those do-gooders with power—those who hand out
the goodies—so they could find better ways to distribute your measly
crumbs. Yes, you organized the powerful; with your help they keep
the poor and powerless down.

"From now on," the Chicano warns us, "*te chingas sochel worquer,*
you and your *migajas*. No more *queso* and powdered milk. If you

say you help, help me be myself and change the conditions of the world—don't change me to fit into the world."

The attack is fierce, and it is real. What do we do, those of us who choose not to submerge ourselves in the polemics of professionalism or shield our status with ACSW certificates? My problem as a Chicano social worker is, if I believe that these *gritos* and vindictive acts are justified, what can I do as a social worker? If I deny the existence of the conditions that cause the cries, can I be a social worker? I hope you, the reader, are in the same quandary, whatever your skin color.

First, however, I must examine what social work intended for us, its agents, to do. If I search diligently enough, we may emerge clean —victims of a system we do not control; but, if together we ponder deeply, we may decide to establish a counter-community in which all human beings can live better and fuller lives. We may find *La Nueva Raza*.

How social work works

Educational systems aggregate events and experiences into a body of knowledge that is then transmitted to others. Social work education is no different. Through the years it has collected a body of knowledge derived from the experiences of individuals and agencies in social work or allied fields and from historical events. A philosophy and value system has been formulated to render some academic legitimacy upon which to base the teachings and actions of the profession. The following discussion analyzes some of the salient values undergirding social work education.

As a point of departure, questions germane to the issue of cultural and social plurality within a nation must be posed. Could I, trained in a United States school of social work that reflects United States values, practice social work in Cuba? Trained under the same conditions, can I practice within the Chicano community without superimposing the superordinate system's values? Can I practice within the community of the poor as an advocate of the poor? Some can probably answer these questions without further research and discussion. For those who question—and with respect for internal consistency and logic—I shall examine some of the philosophical foundations upon which social work and its training are based.

Social work philosophy mirrors the values imbedded in the American democratic tradition. More specifically, it reflects the ideas of "the inherent dignity of the human person, society's responsibility for individual welfare, and the individual's responsibility for contributing to the common good." [1] Fundamental to these ethereal, humanistic goals is the notion that man must be free to realize his own potential and to make his own choices. Theoreticians are quick to add that this freedom is not absolute but is relative to temporal events and to sociocultural conditions. Therefore, what is freedom today may not be freedom tomorrow, or, to use a worn-out cliché, your freedom ends where my nose begins.

Adding more weight to the value of freedom, Mary J. McCormick writes that the principle of autonomy in social work affords man self-determination and self-direction.[2] Members of allied helping disciplines have recognized that autonomy is not only important as an ethical consideration but is at the base of the helping process. A person must have the "capacity and freedom to be himself, to make his own decisions, and to work out his own problems." [3]

The principle of autonomy or freedom finds its way into the practical world of social work through the use of the concept of self-determination. With the application of this concept by the social worker, the client is afforded the choices upon which to base his behavior. However, self-determination is hastily redefined as a relative value—a means toward the greater end of human worth and the dignity of the individual. In pragmatic terms, it is viewed as limited because the client's unharnessed behavior may be manifested in asocial actions and in ambivalent decision making. Logically, one may deduce that self-determination is real only for those who have the capacity to make decisions—decisions that are in conformity with the dominant value structure and in harmony with the establishment's agenda. All other persons must receive assistance.

Can I practice in my barrio?

Another principle holds a position close to the throne of social work values—the principle of individualization, or the value of the individual. Throughout the social work literature this concept looms equally important as that of autonomy. Everything in the world exists for the enhancement of the individual. This concept implies, moreover, that one individual's behavior must enhance the individuality of another. Accordingly, the notion of the responsibility of one individual for another is harnessed with laws apparently intended to bring equality to all individuals. Equality may not be desirable for Chicanos. Who wants to be equal with the white masses? Never is brotherhood mentioned, however, nor is the meaningfulness of community or communalism ever suggested as a greater means for enhancing the person's dignity or worth.

For the client—especially the client from the Chicano community —the principle of individualization becomes a tool for his exploitation, for the separation of one brother from another. It is a burden that places a fraudulent concept of responsibility on one for the other. Responsibility, as duty, becomes a hurdle, a diagnostic tool, a yardstick to assess the person's behavior. As with self-determination, the value of the individual is employed to determine whether his behavior is in harmony with the dominant values.

Can I practice in rural villages?

Who can discern whether a person is capable of making his own choices? Who can decide whether a person is acting as a responsible individual, enhancing the individuality of another? The answer would probably be the professional behavioral science practitioners, the social worker who has learned how to diagnose his brother. Hence, another value emerges to top all values supporting social work education and practice—professionalism. With this crowning value, can I practice social work with the migrant?

At the risk of repetition, I shall summarize the analysis of autonomy, self-determination, and individualization. Until recently, most Chicanos in social work took for granted the values underlying the concept of autonomy. Seldom is autonomy questioned, and it is hardly ever practiced consciously. A closer scrutiny of the principles of autonomy and self-determination reveals the multiplicity of the meanings of these two terms. Similarly, the principle of individuality has rarely been examined critically. It is usually defined as a value that protects the worth, respect, and dignity of the individual person. If this definition is valid, the importance of the term is unquestionably accepted. With its concomitant de-emphasis of the importance of group and community, however, does it not create certain unfortunate results? Could the helpless, oppressed, dependent client or patient not find therapeutic company with his peers in his problem-solving efforts rather than in front of the social worker's desk or on a couch?

We may draw some parallels between individualism as accepted by social work and individualism as used by colonizers. In *The Wretched of the Earth,* Frantz Fanon describes the experiences of the colonized in the struggle for liberation.

> All the mediterranean values—the triumph of the human individual, of charity, and of beauty—becomes lifeless, colorless knickknacks . . . individualism is the first to disappear. . . . The very terms of organization of the struggle will suggest to him a different vocabulary. Brother, sister, friend are words outlawed by the colonist bourgeoisie, because for them my brother is my purse, my friend is part of my scheme for getting on. . . . Henceforward, the interests of one will be the interest of all.[4]

Could we Chicanos be looking for a community that has been dislocated, perhaps not through a conspiracy but through the imposition of the values of a society alien to our own? Are we now prepared to develop a new sense of community, or, by accepting the empty values of individualism and autonomy, shall we continue to allow our sense of community to decay?

The behavioral side of law and order

Although autonomy, self-determination, and individuality are accepted by social work philosophy as worthwhile values, they are not absolute values. They are limited by the responsibility that freedom itself implies. In relation to actual practice, limits are defined by the goals the discipline has placed for itself. A professed goal of social work is the prevention of social dysfunction and the restoration of social functioning. The person is viewed as a social being interacting with others in his adjustment to his environment. If an imbalance exists in this interacting relationship, social work provides the resources to restore the balance. Mary J. McCormick states that social functioning is a response to societal values, "a response that represents man's co-ordinated, directed reactions to those worthwhile commitments that are shared by all the members of a given social system." [5]

In view of these definitions, someone must police man's activities to insure harmony with societal values. In accordance with social work education, this task has become the responsibility of social work; it is labeled the "social control function."

The *Dictionary of Sociology* defines social control as "the sum total of the processes whereby society, or any sub-group within society, secures conformity to expectation on the part of its constituent units, individuals or groups." [6] According to this definition, this control can be either coercive or persuasive, and, in either case, it serves to enhance the helping process. We are further told that "social work treatment, whether casework or group work, is one of society's alternative ways of exercising social control of persons who manifest deviant behavior, although such services are not usually regarded in this way." [7]

Besides claiming the social control function, the Freudian policeman—the social worker—has armed himself with rightful authority.

> Authority, like responsibility, is intrinsic in the nature of social agencies and of social work as a profession. It derives from their assumption of a welfare role that is accepted as valid by the state and the community, to which they are accountable.[8]

Some claim that our authority to exercise our control function comes from our professional expertise; others say we receive it from our clients—the helpless coming to the strong for help.

Although we have all kinds of arguments in defense of social control, we have yet to question seriously the dominant values to which we bring conformity through our social control function. As a Chicano nation, could we have worthwhile commitments that we must preserve? Could we preserve them while being trained to defend and protect the worthwhile commitments of the dominant social order? Could we and our life styles contribute to that stronger system?

If there is hope for institutional change, the transition must begin with the reflection of different values and different world views that heretofore have been ignored. The seed must germinate from the centers of knowledge—schools and training institutions.

Anything short of a redefinition of the value structure undergirding our training and educational institutions will render us as Chicano social workers incapable and unqualified to work as agents of social change in our own Chicano nation. At best we are now accepting alien values, and, as agents of social control, we are bringing our people into conformity with those values. We cannot adhere to the values that led us to this condition; we must present those that are in harmony with our life styles and our goals. A discussion of these goals follows.

Multiple exposure

Although there is some talk of separatism, of establishing a Chicano nation, it is a fact that we are intertwined with the North American system and its institutions. We have become who we are because we have interacted with these institutions—subjects of them, yet, at the same time, Chicanos. To this date the Chicano nation still depends on the health, welfare, and educational institutions of this society. Nevertheless, despite our being subject to them, we have not received our due in relation to our culture and our life styles, and many conditions—that is, conformity with the agenda of the dominant structure—preclude our using any service.

We therefore have two clear alternatives in dealing with these institutions: (1) change them so they can better serve La Raza or (2) develop parallel systems and establish total independence. Clearly, the latter is the ideal solution because previous attempts at reforms have failed. Nevertheless, the former is the one that most of us would desire to try first.

If we choose the first alternative and there is evidence that change is occurring, we must insure that the reformed institutions respond to the natural cadence of La Raza. We must not assume that altered prose and memoranda will necessarily be manifested in deeds. For example, if in New Mexico the Chicano believes that the control of the land is basic to his life style and to his economic structure, the welfare institutions must support him. If in our culture the young still care for the elderly, let the system accept an alternative to its own policies and provide the resources that can cause a beautiful relationship to endure. May social policy no longer punish us for wanting to love. May institutions recognize and support the organization of the consumer into power groups.

If the first alternative is our choice, then the constituencies of health and social services must have meaningful influence on the agencies affecting their destiny; that is, they must have self-determination. Selection of the first alternative demands the devaluation of the social control function and the elevation of the freedom to make choices, even at the expense of deviations from normal standards.

Institutions must now enhance freedom by supporting client participation and control.

Assuming that we will work toward the first alternative and attempt to change the institutions, how can we accomplish our goals? First and foremost, we must cast overboard the value of professionalism, the byword of the entire social work education process. The conditions that prevail in the health and social welfare systems are evidence that "professionals" do not create radical change; we perpetuate our professionalism; professionals are "nice guys" to the agencies—those agencies that exercise the social control function.

Now one must be the advocate of the client. Rather than "keeping the natives down," we must organize clients to have a meaningful influence on our agencies. To accomplish these goals, we can no longer accept as values the empty rhetoric of democracy—individualization, self-determination, social control, law and order. These terms must be redefined. Individualization—yes—but the individual as a person interacting and transacting with brother, sister, friend— with a community that spells brotherhood, a brotherhood that means power. Not individualization that dislocates from the life-giving community of brother, sister, *compadre,* and *camarada.* Self-determination—yes—but not saddled with conditions that undermine man's humanity. Self-determination that affords self-help and creates power to participate in and control one's own destiny. No longer can we accept those values underlying the training that has made us agents of the status quo.

The new humanity

Some countries have revolutions to produce the climate for the emergence of the new man. I propose that we use the institutional framework to create that *person* who will end all revolutions. First, we begin by setting as our goal the evolvement of a counter-community —a community that finds a balance between technology and human values. We shall work with and within the established institutions to forge the conditions that will make this community a reality. Second, we adhere to a service-educational model, through which institutional agents will aid the consumer or potential client to develop an awareness of self through his culture and that portion of history that he has appropriated for himself. Simultaneously, they will raise the level of consciousness concerning the social-political-

economic conditions that impinge on the client's life, and they will
build a corresponding "respond-ability" to these conditions.[9] In
order to avoid the mistakes of our Anglo precursors, we shall assist
in evolving that capability to respond and create by adding to the
individual's own culture and self-appropriated history. Never should
agents of human service impose an alien system of values.

In the face of the prevailing attitudes reflected in social work
education, the recommendations made in this article will be difficult
to execute. Nevertheless, were I to have the liberty to execute such a
plan through the institutional structure, I would do it accordingly.
First, I would change social work philosophy from its neo-Freudian-
ism adjustment-adaptation model to an education-learning theory-
conservationist-ethicist model. In order to function in this framework,
social workers would have to shed their aura of professionalism and
don the spirit of brotherhood. We would no longer seek to help people
adjust to the world; rather, we would generate in people a thirst
for consciousness and for the technology to change conditions (education). The new social worker would seek to identify the world
view from which a person's behavior is produced, conserve it, and
build awareness and respond-ability from it; not, as has been the
case, deride and destroy that which people value (conservationist).
Ultimately, this new breed of social worker would seek the good
life for all people in place of the prevailing emphasis on adjustment
and effective management of people's affairs (ethicist). In the process
described, the social worker must emerge as a model of that new
man—aware, respondable, and capable of working with and within
the institutional framework to accomplish the goal of creating a new
humanity.

Unfortunately, this situation is merely hypothetical. These suggestions will not find realization in action. Therefore, the only alternative for some of us has been to devise and implement our own
educational plan. Founded to develop a body of knowledge meaningful to *La Raza,* La Academia de La Nueva Raza is an education-
action-research institute that has assumed a strong role in education
for community living. Learning material is derived from the individual's life experience, his culture, lore, and oral history, through
which he is made aware of the social, political, and economic conditions that affect his life. From this knowledge the individual develops a skill for coping with conditions—an experience that is
self-fulfilling—and a sensitivity for creative living. Although La Acad-

emia is not designed for social workers, its program enables some of us to resolve the conflict I have described.

We hear the cries of the oppressed. We believe they are based on reality. As human beings, we must respond; as social workers, we can utilize some of the technical skill we possess; as Chicanos, we act arrogantly and declare that from the wisdom of our culture we can aid in creating the *new man*.

Notes

1 Werner W. Boehm, *Objectives of the Social Work Curriculum of the Future,* The Comprehensive Report of the Curriculum Study, vol. 1 (New York: Council on Social Work Education, 1959), p. 43.
2 Mary J. McCormick, "The Role of Values in the Helping Process," *Social Casework,* 42:6 (January 1961).
3 Ibid., p. 9.
4 Frantz Fanon, *The Wretched of the Earth* (New York: Grove Press, 1968), p. 47.
5 Mary J. McCormick, "The Role of Values in Social Functioning," *Social Casework,* 42:71 (February 1961).
6 Henry Pratt Fairchild, ed., *Dictionary of Sociology* (New York: Philosophical Library, 1944), p. 279.
7 Irving Weisman and Jacob Chwast, "Control and Values in Social Work Treatment," *Social Casework,* 43:451 (November 1960).
8 Edna Wasser, "Responsibility, Self-Determination, and Authority in Casework Protection of Older Persons," *Social Casework,* 42:264 (May-June 1961).
9 This concept has been developed in greater detail by the writer in an article, "La Academia de La Nueva Raza: Su Historia," to be published by La Academia de la Nueva Raza.

The Chicano
and Social Work

Alejandro Garcia

It is the contention of the Chicano that the white social work practitioner is, for the most part, ignorant of Chicano culture, values, and aspirations and that this ignorance has contributed significantly to stifling the upward mobility potential of Chicanos in this country. It appears that social service agencies have also remained insensitive to the differences between the Chicano culture and the majority culture.

Part of the fault for these shortcomings lies with the schools of social work. For too long schools of social work have been either blind or indifferent to cultural differences of minority groups, especially Chicanos and blacks. Only in recent years have they begun to recognize this serious shortcoming in their curricula. This article is intended to introduce social work practitioners, agencies, and schools of social work to some of the needs, problems, and cultural differences of the Chicano and to offer some suggestions for the improvement of social services for the Chicano.

The Chicano's plight

To illustrate the plight of the Chicano, let us consider some of the problems he presently faces. A Chicano child rarely sees a Mexican hero on television or in a movie. He does, however, see Mexican bandits trying to kill the Anglo hero or burning down the Anglo's ranchhouse. He sees Mexican servants catering to the Anglo masters. In some schools, Chicano children are fined for speaking Spanish on school grounds. In others, Chicano children are given I.Q. tests without any concern for language and cultural barriers, and if their scores are low, they are placed in classes for mentally retarded children.

In schools in Texas, Chicano children are still taught that the Mexicans were the aggressors in the Texas war against Mexico and that the *gringo* revolutionaries were the heroes, that the Anglo men who died at the Alamo were great men, and that the Mexican soldiers who were fighting that aggression were ruthless savages. A monument perpetuating that myth still stands in San Antonio, Texas.

Chicano children start to feel the pain of prejudice when they first enter the educational system. The Anglo children are better dressed, better prepared for school, and better treated. It is during this time that Chicano children first begin to hear and recognize such racial insults as "greaser," "spic," "bean," and "wetback." These epithets usually precipitate a fight. Racial slurs, such as "honky," for the Anglo have come into use only recently; therefore, fists were the only responses from Chicano children.

The Chicano child's struggle for racial or ethnic identity is difficult indeed. A Chicano child, exposed both to the Chicano culture of his parents and to the Anglo culture, is subjected to external pressures forcing him to make a choice and causing considerable internal ambivalence. Should he reject his parents and accept the culture, ideals, and aspirations of the Anglo majority and, as a result, face possible rejection by his family? On the other hand, should he maintain his cultural identity and, as a result, eliminate the possibility of being admitted to the white controlled world that offers success and escape from the poverty cycle?

The temptation is to identify with the Anglo. The constant bombardment of abuse may cause the Chicano child to wish that he had blue eyes and blond hair and that his name were an Anglo one so that he would be better treated. Unfortunately, he eventually discovers that, regardless of whether he identifies with the Anglo majority, he is rejected because Anglos maintain and perpetuate numerous stereotypes about him. His name is foreign, his skin is often a different color, and he speaks a language that the Anglo does not (want to) understand. He soon realizes that despite his efforts to prove himself, he will still be considered inferior by the Anglo majority.

This writer contends that most Chicano children are subjected to these denigrating experiences. Although these experiences may be similar to those suffered by some other ethnic minority groups, such as Jews, Russians, Poles, and Italians, there are significant differences. These other groups immigrated to the United States to improve their economic conditions or to escape from a tyrannical and oppressive government. They were, however, Caucasians and were able to "pass" as subsequent generations overcame the language barriers. Too many people either do not know or have conveniently forgotten that many Chicanos were already located in what is now the southwestern part of the United States when this country devoured all land within its reach with its "manifest destiny" appetite. There is a difference between willingly submitting to a different culture in an attempt to improve one's fortune and already living in that land and being forced to change one's entire culture to accommodate the intruders.

The Anglo's stereotyped criticism of Chicanos is that Chicanos are not sufficiently ambitious. At the same time, the Chicanos have many stumbling blocks to overcome, such as having to attend inferior schools and being restricted to blue collar and agricultural employment that pay little and help perpetuate the poverty cycle. The Anglo prejudice creates a situation for Chicanos that is analogous to a person's being ordered to lift himself off the floor with an insurmountable weight on top of him. These kinds of contradictory and almost schizophrenic messages from the Anglo majority to the Chicanos constitute the major cause of many Chicanos' having developed inferiority complexes, which they later have had to overcome. The myth that the Chicano is inferior is perpetuated by constant and repetitive negative reinforcement by the Anglos.

Failure of social work

The social work profession has accomplished little to ease the burden of the Chicano. For example, bilingualism is not considered an advantage. On the other hand, if a person does not speak the dominant language, he is harrassed, punished, or ignored. A Chicano client who did not speak English explained to this writer during the initial interview that previous visits from non-Chicano social workers had been upsetting experiences for her. The social workers had not spoken Spanish and had made the client feel guilty and inferior because she knew no English. Whenever the social worker came, one of her small children had to be sent to a neighbor's home to ask for someone to serve as interpreter for her. She said she was distressed to have to answer questions through her neighbor because some of the questions the social worker asked were of a personal nature, and she did not care for her neighbor to hear her responses. She said, however, that she had no choice because she needed to have the assistance funds continued in order to feed her children.

The client was worried about what her neighbor might tell the social worker, and she feared that she and the worker were not really communicating with each other. She was concerned also about the numerous papers she had to sign and was fearful of the consequences of signing the forms. These reactions are typical of a non-English-speaking client who has been assigned a non-Spanish-speaking social worker.

Agencies generally have not encouraged their workers to learn to speak Spanish. To this writer's knowledge, only one county welfare agency places a premium on Spanish language fluency and awards a bonus to those social workers who can communicate fluently in Spanish. Most agencies, however, continue their punitive practice of helping only those clients who can communicate in English. Schools of social work now support the thesis that a social worker who has some ethnic background knowledge of a particular client is better able to work with that person, but they neither include in their curricula nor encourage language studies that would enhance the social worker's communication with Chicanos.

Practice problems

Although a great deal of a student's graduate social work education generally prepares him to help the Chicano client, there are several cultural factors that are unique to the Chicano and that must be considered in working effectively with the Chicano. The purpose of discussing these factors in this article is to encourage the non-Chicano practitioner to strengthen his knowledge of his Chicano clients.

Chicano life style

In the life style of the Chicano, the husband is the dominant figure in the household. The familial relationship, however, is more than a patriarchal one; it is a relationship in which the man of the house assumes full responsibility for managing his household, and his wife assumes a complementary role. Contrary to the popular misconception, the Chicana woman is anything but submissive, as has been proven by her participation in the Mexican Revolution and more recently in César Chávez's farmworkers' organizing movement. It is important, however, for the social worker to know that, in order to achieve positive results in working with the family, the man of the house must be involved in any plans made with the family. Although it is recognized that this aspect is a traditional one that applies to all client groups, particular effort must be exerted to involve the male parent in working with the Chicano family.

The Chicano male suffers excessive duress under societal racism and discrimination. The contrast between the position of the man in his own household and the subordinate, denigrating, and limiting position that he is allowed to hold in the Anglo society affects his own sense of adequacy and eventually the home situation. How can he be a man to his wife and a father to his children when societal prejudices and pressures have almost emasculated him? Moreover, having a female social worker to advise him on family matters may exacerbate the situation; therefore, a female social worker must be particularly sensitive to a Chicano's self-image.

Aware of the extended family pattern of the Chicano, the worker should not suggest out-of-home placement of an elderly or disabled relative. The Chicano has close family ties, and he assumes responsibility for those relatives who can no longer care for themselves. His training from early childhood has conditioned him to the tradition of the young and able person's assuming the responsibility for the elderly and disabled.

Religion

The fact that Catholicism is the dominant religion of the Chicano family should alert the social worker to the possibility that any suggestions of birth control measures might be vigorously rejected and might jeopardize the client-worker relationship. If the family is Catholic, the social worker should be aware of church attitudes toward the use of contraceptives, abortion, marital separations, and divorce.

Superstitions

The non-Chicano practitioner should also acquaint himself with such superstitions as *mal de susto* (a behavioral condition presumed to be caused by a bad fright) and *mal de ojo* (the evil eye). The worker should know that these are treated in a religio-superstitious manner and should differentiate between this practice and pathological behavior. He should also know about *curanderos* (faith healers), whose activities include those of social worker, doctor, and priest.

Suggested solutions

Chicano social workers would be more effective in working with Chicano clients than would white social workers. Without having to cope with communication and cultural barriers, worker and client can begin to work almost immediately on the presenting problem. In 1969, however, fewer than 2 percent of the students enrolled in schools of social work across the country were Chicanos.[1]

There are several factors contributing to the shortage of Chicano social workers. One is that schools of social work are not sufficiently aggressive in their recruitment programs. Few of them offer stipend awards specifically for Chicano students, and, considering the cultural pressures to support their families, the majority of Chicanos cannot attend graduate school without financial assistance. To prevent Chicanos from attending their schools, several institutions have insisted on the achievement of high scores on irrelevant entrance examinations. Unfortunately, those few Chicanos who may qualify for admission to graduate schools tend to select the more lucrative professions of law, medicine, or business rather than social work.

Until there are enough Chicano social workers to work with Chicano families, it is the responsibility of the schools of social work, the agencies, and the practitioner to become more sensitive to the Chicanos and to make renewed efforts to work more effectively with them. The schools can help improve the situation of the Chicano by reexamining themselves, their entrance requirements, and their relevancy to the Chicano. Are Chicano studies an integral part of the curriculum? Is conversational Spanish encouraged or required? What aggressive efforts are being made to attain ethnic diversity in their faculties and student bodies? Are special provisions for stipend awards made each year for Chicano students?

The delivery of social services for the Chicano client must be redesigned, and agencies must reevaluate their present practices and directions. Agencies should also encourage their professional staffs to improve their awareness of the Chicano through staff development programs and continuing education courses, and they should reward those staff members who have made special efforts to maximize their potential for working with this ethnic minority. Perhaps agencies could even work with nearby colleges to develop courses in conversational Spanish for social workers. Practitioners, too, should demand that their agencies afford them the opportunity to improve their knowledge base to work with the Chicano.

With such a shortage of Chicano social workers, one must call on other social workers to work with the Chicano community. With proper language and cultural training, they can be effective. To enhance the non-Chicano practitioner's relationship with the Chicano client, community workers who serve as barrio liaisons could be used to bridge the cultural and language gap. Although these workers do not have the formal education of the social worker, they have the language, the cultural background, and barrio education necessary to assist in working effectively with the Chicano client.

The National Association of Social Workers (NASW) has, with some exceptions, just begun to focus some of its efforts on "the forgotten minority." The support of the association's fifty-two thousand members could influence the present social welfare picture as it pertains to the Chicano. Its increased focus on the Chicano, from its local to its national level, could help bring desperately needed attention and help to the Chicano. The conference on Chicano mental health sponsored by NASW in the summer of 1970 in Sacramento, California, the increase in the number of Chicanos participating in the NASW leadership training program, and efforts in career recruitment of minorities are excellent initial steps; however, much more must still be done.

For example, the association also could insure that its new testing procedures for ACSW social worker certification would include a working knowledge of the Chicano in those areas of the country in which this kind of knowledge is essential. Local chapters across the country could insure that the testing connected with the licensing of social workers and certification legislation on which they are working require a working knowledge of the Chicano. The association should also give special attention to equal employment opportunities, pay differentials, and professional advancement for Chicanos. The association, in its continuing education program, could create workshops and institutes on the Chicano to educate members and improve their practice. It also could influence the federal lawmakers through its registered lobbyist and its legislative action program in regard to the creation and support of relevant social services for the Chicano and related issues. It could cooperate with Chicano efforts (1) to force an impartial investigation into the death of *Los Angeles Times* Chicano columnist Ruben Salazar, (2) to oust Judge Gerald Chargin of San José, California, who condemned Chicanos as animals, (3) to publicize the fact that the 1970 United States Census virtually ignored the existence of Chicanos in the United States, and (4) to support the nationwide lettuce boycott led by César Chávez. The NASW also should initiate national and chapter social action programs to deal with inequities in employment, civil rights, and related problems.

It is obvious to the Chicano that the social work profession has focused its attack on racism by dealing with the serious problems facing the blacks in America and that it has lumped the Chicano, the second largest minority in the United States, with "others." Because the Chicano social workers were frustrated by the present welfare system, *los Trabajadores de la Raza,* the national Chicano social worker organization, was created in 1969. In the few years of its existence, this association has significantly increased the relevancy of agencies and schools with which it has worked. It has confronted local, state, and national agencies, as well as schools of social work, in constructive attempts to make these institutions sensitive to the needs and problems of the Chicano.

With no money and few members, this group of dedicated Chicano social workers and community workers has attacked schools of social work on their institutional racism and agencies on their irrelevancy to the Chicano community. It also has assisted schools in recruiting Chicano faculty members and in involving Chicanos in curriculum planning. Considering that most of this work has been done during the members' free time, the accomplishments have been notable: from developing a Chicano statewide mental health conference in

California in 1970 to co-sponsoring with the University of California at Los Angeles and the University of Southern California a recruitment and training program for Chicano mental health workers.

Conclusion

This article has attempted to acquaint non-Chicano social workers with some of the cultural differences and the problems and the needs of the Chicano in order to initiate some action toward helping the Chicano. If the social work profession is indeed dedicated to the eradication of racism and is determined to be in the forefront of the battle against poverty, we professionals will have to demand of ourselves a continuing, critical examination of our relevancy in helping the Chicano with his plight.

Note

[1] Frank M. Loewenberg and Thomas H. Shey, *Statistics on Social Work Education, November 1, 1969 and Academic Year 1968–1969* (New York: Council on Social Work Education, 1969), pp. 26–27.

Utilizing Barrio Expertise in Social Work Education

Mateo R. Camarillo and Antonio Del Buono

The purpose of this article is to suggest that social work education could be vastly improved through the utilization of barrio experiences and the development of barrio perspectives in social work students. The barrio has been a neglected source for professors in schools of social work although barrio professors are essential to the education of professionals who are able to relate to Chicanos. Moreover, their contribution need not necessarily be confined to social work students; they are in a unique position to teach numerous faculty members about the barrio experience. Although these barrio professors do not have the standard credentials that attest to their expertise, they have credentials that attest to their familiarity with the barrio, its people, its systems, and its needs. Because social work education is part of the total higher education system, a brief analysis of that system may elucidate its effect on Chicanos.

The university and Chicano communities

The university plays a key role in perpetuating racism, academic colonialism, and cultural imperialism.[1] Anglo and Chicano communities live apart—physically, linguistically, and socially. These two groups inhabit social and cultural worlds that are farther apart than the barrio and the suburb. Generally speaking, even informed Anglos know little about *La Raza,* its historical and present-day experiences, situations, and aspirations. The typical citizen does not know that Chicanos are abused by the police, humiliated by the courts, exploited economically, dominated politically, raped culturally, and forgotten historically.[2]

As an institution, the university maintains and supports racism, academic colonialism, and cultural imperialism, and it is deeply implicated in acts that distort perceptions of Chicanos by professors the university employs.[3] The evidence is clear that assimilation- and acculturation-based theories, which form the basis of Anglo curricula, are culture distorting and destroying. These theories fail to account for Chicano values and perspectives. More significant, the university is recognized as having a virtual monopoly on social studies, most of which stereotype Chicanos. The impact of this practice is reinforced by the university's power to credential, certify, accredit, and sanction.

The university serves to legitimize a racist relationship between Chicano and *gabacho* communities. The university contributes to the oppression of Chicanos by its involvement in agri-business, urban dislocation, wars, racist admission, and employment policies. Questions must be raised about the validity of the university's policies and programs that are based on premises of assimilation and acculturation. Such policies and programs result in the projection of fault to Chicanos for failing to enter the mainstream of the "American way of life," while they exonerate the exclusiveness of the university. In its pursuit of "objective" knowledge and science, the university has ignored cultural and racial differences as if all differences will melt away.

Perhaps nowhere is racism, academic colonialism, and cultural imperialism toward Chicanos so evident as in the exclusion of meaningful input from nondegree Chicano barrio workers. For this reason, university graduates who serve the barrio return to the barrio and there are retrained by nondegree Chicano barrio workers.

The university must rearrange its priorities and redefine its functions in relation to broader constituencies. This redefinition must include recognition of Chicanos who refuse to be treated as unmelted Anglos; the growing emphasis on the principles of community participation; and the knowledge that the university must be accountable to a multilevel constituency including the barrio. The day is past when the university could move ahead without extensive inclusion of Chicanos in the decision-making process. A mutuality of participation must prevail throughout the university and the teaching-learning process.

The impact of racism, academic colonialism, and cultural imperialism on social work

Currently there are few social workers who can provide social services to Chicanos and very few agencies that meet the needs of Chicanos. Agency practices do not encourage Chicanos to go to agencies. The past and present patterns of services delivered by agencies alienate Chicanos. Moreover, social workers are not prepared to strengthen the barrio. Generally, social welfare agencies are also unprepared to train social workers to provide humanistic social services in the barrios. A sampling of social work agencies reveals that Chicanos are almost totally excluded from staffs and services. For example, a recent study of California state departments that frequently deal with Chicanos reveals startling information about the number of Chicanos as employees.[4]

In California where Chicanos constitute the largest ethnic minority group, Chicanos constitute less than 3 percent of the state employees, most of whom are in low-paying jobs.[5] California counties reflect the same picture. Los Angeles, with the largest barrio in the country, had fewer than eighty Chicano social workers in 1970. In that year the Los Angeles County Department of Social Services had a total of 11,358 employees, of whom 291 had Spanish surnames. Of these 291 employees with Spanish surnames, 175 were clerical workers, 35 were auxiliary aid workers, 77 were professional-technical workers, and 3 were executive-managerial workers.[6] In most California counties Chicanos constitute only a small percentage of those employed in public assistance programs.[7]

It is significant that prior to May 14, 1970, social welfare agencies did not recognize and compensate for bilingual and bicultural skills. The first agencies to implement such a policy were in the county of San Diego, California. That policy evolved from conflict, negotiation, and determination by Chicano organizations, spearheaded by *Trabajadores de la Raza.*

It is difficult to document the extent of exclusion of Chicanos from staffs and boards of voluntary social welfare agencies. Statistical information is not readily obtainable and in many cases is nonexistent.

The impact of racism, academic colonialism, and cultural imperialism on social work education

Social workers are college graduates. Increasingly they are receiving training in graduate schools of social work. Social workers are, therefore, systematically socialized for sixteen to eighteen years without

Table 1.   Number of Mexican Americans employed by California state departments.

Department	Number of Mexican-American employees	Total number of employees
Corrections	271	6,699
Mental Hygiene	491	20,451
Youth Authority	201	3,680
Public Health	48	1,585
Health Care Services	1	250
Rehabilitation	71	1,693
Social Welfare	64	1,767
Industrial Relations	52	1,607
Human Resources	817	10,860

Table 2.   Number of employees with Spanish surnames in California counties.

County	Employees with Spanish surnames	Total employees
Orange[a]	8	597
Riverside[a]	31	522
Sacramento[a]	32	1,379
San Bernardino[a]	48	785
San Diego[a]	18	1,418
San Francisco[a]	30	1,273
Santa Clara[a]	78	1,066
Fresno[b]	61	569
Santa Barbara[b]	14	247
Ventura[b]	23	239

[a] Standard metropolitan areas with total populations of 500,000 or more
[b] Standard metropolitan areas with total populations of less than 500,000

significant Chicano input into their education. The absence of Chicano perspectives affects professional social work education. The environment of social work education gives a lucid picture of the almost total exclusion of Chicano perspectives in higher education. There are seventy-five schools of social work in the United States. In the 1969-1970 academic year there were only 120 Chicano students (of 6,699) entering the schools and 17 Chicanos (of 3,068) teaching full time in all the graduate schools of social work.[8] If the social work profession were to limit all places for students at all its graduate and undergraduate educational institutions or schools to Chicanos, it would still take twenty years for the Chicano community to develop an adequate service delivery system in the United States.[9]

Chicano perspectives are humanistic and pluralistic. Social work needs to take into account the composition of its consumers, one of which is the Chicano community—students, social work practioners, faculty, community workers, and grass-root barrio-based agencies and programs. In general the social work profession does not provide for an understanding and acceptance of cultural pluralism. Most social work programs do not allow for self-determination or the cooperation as equals between professionals with degrees and community members without degrees in the delivery of social welfare services.

Social work needs a better understanding of the barrio. A barrio is a universal, as well as a provincial, conception for Chicanos. We conceive of a barrio as having many levels with varying degrees of geographical, emotional, ethnocentric, social, and identity facets. The universality of the barrio character binds together a population of almost ten million people in the United States—regardless of the name they choose by which to define themselves—Chicano, Mexican, Mexican American, Hispano, or Spanish American. Although it recognizes heterogeneity in socioeconomic, educational, political, regional, and religious characteristics of *La Raza,* the barrio considers the cultural, psychological, historical, and language and ethnic attributes that define Chicano experiences and perspectives and communicate the humanistic feeling embodied in the term *carnalismo.*

Another level of a barrio is state, county, and city populations bound by ties of organizations struggling to improve the welfare of Chicanos. The more common level of a barrio is an area or specific location that may or may not transcend the boundaries of a city.

The life styles and culture of a barrio protect Chicanos from the pressures imposed by agencies and institutions, such as law enforcement, welfare, and education, which are based outside the barrio. Chicanos are strengthened by a feeling of *familia* that enables many to withstand institutionalized pressures of acculturation and assimilation. These pressures should be eliminated, and more effective, humane, and responsive services and agency practices should be initiated.

Chicano perspectives are needed to develop humanistic social workers to work with Chicanos in order to understand the norms, standards, and values and to modify, change, and reform social conditions that are adversely affecting Chicanos. Chicano perspectives embody the concept of cultural democracy and focus on institutional changes that are necessary to achieve the basic social work goal of enhancing social functioning at all levels of Chicano experiences—individual, group, and community.

The current challenge in social work education

In the 1960s and 1970s, Chicanos have been vigorously confronting racism, academic colonialism, and cultural imperialism in schools of social work. Traditional approaches, existing guidelines, elitist conceptualizations, and racist behaviors are under attack.[10] Chicanos are fighting schools of social work that typically send their students to barrios to experiment on Chicanos.

The Council on Social Work Education (CSWE), the national accrediting body for schools of social work, is becoming aware of past inadequacies. CSWE is now committed to giving priority to the eradication of racism.

> Social work education has a special responsibility and challenge, for it must prepare social work personnel with the commitment, knowledge, and skills needed (1) to recognize and call attention to social needs, human injustices, and dysfunctional systems for service delivery, (2) to plan and to bring about needed changes, and (3) to provide and administer social services in a more humane and effective way. . . . We must find new and better ways to prepare future social workers for different and more complex roles to overcome poverty and racism and to deal meaningfully with other individual and social problems.[11]

Significant issues have been raised. A persistent need is to include Chicano perspectives in the curricula of schools of social work. In many instances, schools of social work leave the burden of injecting Chicano perspectives and realities to Chicano students. This task should not be the responsibility of students, but that of the schools, which therefore should recruit barrio residents for faculties.

A great source of teaching exists in the barrio. Persons without traditional academic credentials have a vast knowledge gained through intense life experiences. In a typical barrio, formal and informal teaching-learning is part of the socializing process. Knowledgeable persons, such as uncles, aunts, grandfathers, and neighbors, share their wisdom at informal gatherings. Barrio expertise cannot be surpassed nor should it be ignored any longer. Barrio perspectives in curricula are essential to counteract the traditional social work ideology with its primary concern for social control and system maintenance. A need for barrio input to challenge the monocular view of social problems reflecting individual rather than social deficit is vitally needed.

New role models must be developed for social work education and training. Such education must be based on humanistic principles and interdependent relationships between Anglos and *La Raza.*

There are several methods of infusing Chicano perspectives into the educational process. The range of possibilities includes utilizing barrio residents as professors, detaching departments, programs, field placements, and instructors from the campus of a school and locating them in barrios; eliminating racist admission restrictions and employment policies that prohibit Chicanos from entering campuses; and making available to Chicano communities the resources of the schools.

The employment of people without a master's degree in social work in responsible positions in social work is not a recent development.[12] Unfortunately, previous efforts in using community people in social work have taken the form of a master-slave, professional-nonprofessional relationship. The community person is relegated to a role of helper to the master and so has been given such titles as case aide, indigenous worker, nonprofessional, or social work associate. The message is clear—the barrio person is an extension of the professional social worker, an aide who should perform menial tasks to reduce the burden of the professional. This master-slave relationship can be altered by hiring barrio professors as full members of faculties.

The practice of social work occurs in agencies and barrios. Social work in barrios can evolve beyond a method of controlling Chicanos. With barrio professors involved in the teaching-learning process, Chicano attitudes, values, and beliefs can be recognized, respected, accepted, and applied. A second step is to develop an interdependent relationship between the barrio and the suburb by means of humanistic values. A third step is to have social workers develop a knowledge of and a feeling for barrio perspectives. This development is essential not only for their own effectiveness in working with barrio residents, but also for their need to work with institutions that should, but in fact do not, provide services to Chicanos.

Criteria for hiring barrio professors

A person hired as a barrio professor must act consistently with barrio values and attitudes so that barrio residents can perceive him as a person with their values and beliefs. A barrio professor must be sufficiently committed to advancing the Chicano cause that he is willing to be identified with the barrio. More than one value is relevant for any given situation. Another requirement of a potential barrio professor is his being a force in discerning Chicano values through interaction in the teaching-learning process. A barrio professor should also be willing to establish humanistic interrelationships with Anglos. In addition, a potential barrio professor must be able to bring to the teaching-learning process a complex of values to share with students for analysis and integration. The actual integration of Chicano and Anglo values may not be entirely harmonious. The potential exists for an organization of values that can result in a synthesis of a new value or a value complex of a higher order. A potential barrio professor must also bring to the teaching-learning process a knowledge of past and present ways and means by which Chicanos deal with specific issues.

Barrio historical antecedents, methods of inquiry, standards of judgment, and patterns of organization require analysis and evaluation. Social workers practicing in a barrio must know the criteria by which facts, principles, opinions, and behaviors are tested and judged by that barrio. This knowledge is essential in explaining, describing, predicting, or determining the most appropriate and relevant action or direction of social work practice in the barrio.

Barrios are complex. Barrios are urban. Barrios are rural. Barrios are neighborhoods. Barrios represent an ongoing pluralistic and heterogeneous synthesis of native American-Spanish-Mexican-Anglo. A potential barrio professor cannot be expected to know in depth all barrios or even one barrio. He should be expected to have general knowledge of some aspects and facets of barrios.

Summary

El plan de San José

At San José State College, School of Social Work, the necessity for social work education to be responsive to the needs of Chicanos is recognized. The school has a philosophy based on barrio control and a mission to capture the essence of the barrio and highlight the interdependence between barrio residents and social work practitioners.

Barrio professors certified by the barrio have been hired by the School of Social Work at San José. They are an essential part of the educational process, full members of the faculty with rights, salaries, and responsibilities comparable to those of other professors, including having a significant voice in the way they function within the school. The initial thrust is in field practice with priority given to the preparation of social workers who can strengthen the barrios.

Barrio professors work with accredited social work professors on a team basis. Each affects and learns from each other. Teaching and learning are facets of the same process. The environment for the teaching-learning process and the application of theory to practice is a teaching-learning center. The teaching-learning center is located in a barrio. Classes taught in the center are open to barrio residents. The purpose is to enable barrio residents to influence the way social workers are trained for the barrio.

The problem-solving approach is the means used to teach social work students humanistic social work practice in the barrio. Interdependent relationships are taught and practiced through the cooperation of barrio professors, certified social workers, and students with organizations, groups, and individuals. At San José, future professional social workers are learning directly from Chicano social service consumers. Students practice humanistic social work in a barrio with Chicanos.

Barrio professors

At San José, barrio perspectives are infused in the process of developing and refining knowledge, values, and skills with priority placed on the field practicum because approximately half of the training is devoted to the application of knowledge, values, and skills to specific situations. These specific situations require a comprehension of diverse social needs, aspirations, value systems, and patterns of behavior. Barrio expertise will be utilized throughout the curriculum so that barrio experiences can be the focus of research, expand social service delivery strategies, and deepen practice content.

Vital ingredients that barrio professors bring to the teaching-learning process include bilingualism, biculturalism, and pluralistic life styles. By using a problem-solving approach, the team of barrio professor and accredited social worker can present to students two perspectives in each situation. The two perspectives in each situation are analyzed—broken down into their constituent elements to make explicit the relationship between the ideas expressed. Such analyses are intended to clarify the communication and to indicate the organization of the communication and the way in which it manages to convey its effects. By analyses of relationships between perspectives and the connections and interactions between groups, it is hoped that multidimensional social workers who are able to provide social welfare services to pluralistic consumer groups will be developed.

At San José, it is recognized that extensive work from a Chicano perspective is necessary in such areas as (1) analyzing value system concepts; (2) comprehending and valuing the nature and impact of cultural heritage; (3) understanding the influence of life style environments, such as child-rearing patterns, familial associations, and psychological sets; and (4) detailing and analyzing differentiations influenced by class, culture, cross-culture, and regions. The inclusion of barrio experiences in social work education can result in a more sensitive, responsive, and effective social worker able to deliver critically needed services. Hopefully, students will be better equipped to work with Chicanos to strengthen barrios and to change institutions that have a detrimental effect upon Chicano communities. At San José these tasks will be undertaken on a team basis with barrio professors to educate social workers competent to effect systematic change.

Notes

1 *Academic Colonialism* is a term for higher education's virtual monopoly of social studies of minority groups. *Cultural Imperialism* is a term for the process in which Anglo writers interpret ethnic minority existence in terms of white middle-class standards and ideologies. See Robert Blauner, "The Chicano Sensibility," Book Review, *Transaction,* 8:56 (February 1971).
2 There are numerous examples of police practices vis-á-vis Chicanos, but one of the most recent immoral police acts was the killing of the Sanchez brothers by Los Angeles law enforcement officers. For scope of the problem, see U.S., Commission on Civil Rights, *Mexican American and the Administration of Justice in the Southwest,* a report by the U.S. Commission on Civil Rights to the President, March 1970; and Armando Morales, "Police Deployment Theories and the Mexican American Community," *El Grito,* 4:52–64 (Fall 1970). For a glimpse of the exclusion of Chicanos from juries, see Oscar Zeta Acosta, "The East L.A. 13 vs. the L.A. Superior Court," *El Grito,* 3:12–18 (Winter 1970). For an iceberg view of the attitude of judges toward Chicanos, see "Judge Gerald S. Chargin Speaks," *El Grito,* 3:4–5 (Fall 1969). For a vivid picture of how Chicanos are raped culturally by the educational system at the elementary level, see Theodore W. Parsons, "Ethnic Cleavage in a California School" (Ph.D. diss., Stanford University, 1965). For a more detailed report, see U.S., Commission on Civil Rights, *Mexican American Education Study, Report 1: Ethnic Isolation of Mexican Americans in the Public Schools of the Southwest* (Washington, D.C.: U.S. Commission on Civil Rights, 1971). For an excellent account of the distortion of Mexican-American history by university-based "scholars," see Octavio Romano, "The Anthropology and Sociology of the Mexican American," *El Grito,* 2:13–26 (Fall 1968).
3 Ibid.
4 Robert Keyes, *Report to Ronald Reagan, 1969 Ethnic Census of State Government* (State of California, Governor's Office), Table V.
5 Ibid. Table III.
6 Individual Unit Report, *Equal Opportunity Survey of Grant-aided State and Local Agencies,* California Department of Social Welfare, Los Angeles County Only, July 8, 1970, Table I.
7 State of California, State Department of Social Welfare, Research and Statistics, August 17, 1970, Table I.
8 Council on Social Work Education, *Statistics on Social Work Education 1970* (New York: Council on Social Work Education, 1970).
9 Council on Social Work Education, *Chicano Task Force Report* (New York: Council on Social Work Education, forthcoming).
10 Chicano students have filed a complaint against University of California to have the Council on Social Work Education investigate the School of Social Work at Berkeley for its racist policies and practices. Chicanos have also charged schools of social work with racism at the 1971 Program Meeting of the Council on Social Work Education.
11 Arnulf M. Pins, "Social Work Education in a Period of Change," *Social Work Education Reporter,* 14:30-A, 30-G (April-May 1971).
12 Frank Loewenberg, "Social Workers and Indigenous Nonprofessionals: Some Structural Dilemmas," *Social Work,* 13:65–71 (July 1968).

Casework Services for Mexican Americans

Faustina Ramirez Knoll

"She doesn't understand my problem; she's not one of us," a potential Mexican-American client told a field representative of a community agency. The representative was trying to refer him to a family agency for counseling. His response was not unusual for a Mexican American living in the barrio.

The writer is a Mexican American who has worked with these clients through a grass-roots project of the Catholic Social Services of Wayne County. The general objective of the project was the improvement of living conditions in the area, and the major goal was the involvement of its Spanish-speaking residents. The purpose of this article is to share some experiences and to attempt to define the role of the family service agency in offering casework services to a Mexican-American client population in the urban ghetto.

The Detroit barrio

The Mexican-American barrio of Detroit includes a mixture of European and Appalachian whites, Mexican Americans, Puerto Ricans, Spaniards, and a few blacks. The estimated number of Spanish-speaking people (including Mexican Americans, Spaniards, Puerto

Ricans, Cubans, and South Americans) living in the Detroit area is seventy thousand, making Detroit the second largest Spanish-speaking community in the Midwest. Approximately sixty thousand of these people live in the vicinity of St. Anne Parish, the community in which this writer has worked. This community is west of Detroit's central business district and is bounded by heavy industry on two sides. Within its boundaries, one finds a continuous string of retail establishments, several of which are owned and operated by Mexican Americans. The homes consist mainly of two-story, wood and brick dwellings whose physical conditions range from deteriorated to good. There are two public schools, two private high schools, four newly established community service agencies, and several active churches.[1]

Detroit's Mexican-American population includes people who have been living there for several years, recent immigrants from Mexico, and seasonal farm workers who have been living in such states as Texas, Ohio, and Illinois. Texas-born Mexican Americans decide to move to Detroit because employment opportunities appear promising or because family and friends are there. Some come as migrant workers and decide to settle in the city. Many Mexicans who are permanent residents or United States citizens speak of their home or country as Mexico and frequently return there to live or to visit with family and friends; then they go back to Detroit to earn more money. Similarly, transplanted Texans living in Detroit travel frequently between Michigan and Texas for psychological and cultural reasons. Many of these Mexican Americans live alone or with friends and work in Detroit. Frequently they send financial aid to families in Mexico and Texas and assist other newcomers into a quasi-assimilative process.

Once in Detroit, many Mexican Americans settle in the "Mexican barrio," where some surface characteristics of Mexican life and culture are in evidence. There are neighborhood stores that sell Mexican foods not easily available elsewhere, restaurants, bakeries, bars, dance halls, record shops, barbershops, tamale and tortilla factories, and a movie theater. Mexican-American orchestras, trios, and bands are frequently brought into the neighborhood recreational establishments, and there are several political, religious, and social organizations that provide for fraternal exchanges. In the past, little evidence of political and community leadership and cohesiveness existed. In recent years, however, a small number of residents have attempted to identify the community as an entity.

Not unlike other families, the Mexican family is embedded in a network of mutually interdependent relationships with its own cultural group as well as with the wider society. It includes within itself the several social subsystems of husband-wife, mother-son, mother-daughter, father-son, father-daughter, brother-sister, brother-brother, and sister-sister. Frequently there are grandparents living in the home. Although these families had generally been considered large, it has been learned that the average household has only three children.[2]

In most cases, Mexican Americans come from economically and socially deprived rural backgrounds where there is no preparation for a white middle-class society with middle-class values and mores. The rural subsystem is replete with primitive religious superstitions of which the most common are *el ojo* (the evil eye) and *susto* (an emotional reaction thought to be caused by a severe fright). These commonly accepted superstitions are culturally and closely intertwined in the basic personality makeup of the Mexican-American population. Great respect and faith are consequently accorded to the *curandera* (faith healer). Because scientifically trained medical personnel are scarce, there is a great deal of dependence on the *curandera* and on the midwife, both of whom practice with home-made remedies, such as burning candles and incense to ward off evil spirits.

The Mexican American who comes to the Midwest does so with the hope of improving his lot. He comes with the ability and willingness to work long hours at hard manual labor, but he comes unprepared and has tremendous social handicaps. These handicaps include little if any knowledge of the English language; limited education and formal training; inadequate knowledge and understanding of white, urban, middle-class America; a different set of values and attitudes; a possible disruption of his family structure; and, frequently, illegal entrance into this country.

Other factors exacerbating the Mexican American's adjustment include his deeply dependent ties to the mother country or state, which result in frequent trips between the Midwest and Mexico or Texas. This process disrupts the children's school adjustments, peer relationships, and identity with the community and affects the parents' job stability and housing situations. It feeds into denial, lack of personal responsibility, and feelings of hopelessness and alienation.

Alienation is further reinforced by the immigrant's subsequent rejection by both his state or country of origin and the local community.

In the past, there was a notable absence of established institutions that might assist with relocation, housing, and job placement in the barrio. In general, the new residents were dependent on previously transplanted friends or relatives. Presently, however, efforts are being made by several community agencies—including the agency in which the writer has worked—to relate to barrio residents and to prepare new immigrants for their lives in an urban setting. The following three case illustrations are presented with the hope that other family service agencies will be motivated to extend services to Mexican-American residents of their respective communities.

Family agency services

Mrs. M, a thirty-year-old Mexican American, was referred by a local Spanish-speaking priest for help with placement of a one-year-old child. She had three children and was separated from her husband whose whereabouts were unknown. Mrs. M's current problem resulted from her father's leaving for Mexico for an undetermined period of time and her having to move from the chicken farm that provided both housing and a small income. Her father had helped care for the children while Mrs. M worked. When he left for Mexico, Mrs. M found a job that paid fifty dollars weekly and a prospective apartment renting for approximately sixty-five dollars a month. She had no relatives in the city and few friends who were in a position to help.

Casework interviews focused on foster and institutional care facilities, the possibility of obtaining Aid to Families with Dependent Children, and possible aid from relatives, friends, and *comadres* (*comadres* or *compadres* are counterparts to extended family make-up). Services were offered also in an area that involved the older children. Helped to examine realistic alternatives and clarify her goals, Mrs. M decided not to place her child. She requested no further agency service until she again perceived a need for concrete help.

Two years later, Mrs. M called the agency and asked for help in obtaining furniture. She had found a better paying job in an automobile factory, had saved her money, and was in the process of buying a house. The family was faced with an immediate need to move. Mrs. M's father, who had returned from Mexico, had been working as a caretaker in a building in which a basement apartment was provided. When he asked for an increase in salary, he was dismissed. The family then moved into a high-crime area, close to the children's school, where the grandfather was assaulted. In panic, Mrs. M agreed to use her savings to buy a house in a suburban working-class neighborhood—closer to her work but where there was little likelihood of her father's finding work. Therefore, full financial responsibility for the family rested on Mrs. M. After discussion of her plans, the worker contacted a neighborhood agency that specialized in providing clients with various articles of furniture.

This case illustration offers several points that should be of interest for family service agencies: the sources of aid that clients use initially, their manner of handling parent-child relationships, the need for tangible rather than intangible services, and the effects of the extended family on the family unit. The fact that Mrs. M initially requested services from a Spanish-speaking priest in the community who was able to refer her to a family agency with child placement facilities helps to point out the need to communicate with clergymen to inform them of existing programs and the special skills of personnel. The cultural role stress found in this case example should be noted. As in other families, a predominant characteristic among Mexican Americans is the woman's responsibility for child rearing and domestic tasks. In this and similar instances, the client has tremendous responsibilities that include assuming the breadwinner's role. (It was learned several years later that Mrs. M was not a legal resident of the community. This fact undoubtedly explains her reluctance to seek public assistance. Social workers can benefit their clients by informing them of state and local residency requirements for financial aid where they exist.) Exacerbating Mrs. M's role conflict is her father's decision to go for an extended visit to his homeland. This decision means the immediate loss of a job, housing, child care help, and emotional support, as well as the destruction of the existing family unit. On the other hand, the close interdependence among Mrs. M, her children, and her father upon the father's return to Detroit is characteristic of the traditional extended family.

The second illustration is the case of a proud and independent client who is suffering from environmental stress. The client is helped through an extended casework treatment plan, which provides a strong contrast to the use of short-term crisis intervention so necessary in the previous example.

Miss L, in her late thirties, was unmarried and lived alone in the barrio. She had been referred to the agency by a Spanish-speaking community organization worker after she had been injured at work and could no longer receive unemployment compensation benefits. Miss L had emigrated from Mexico with her parents when she was a young girl, and she eventually settled in Detroit. Both parents had been dead several years. Her siblings manifested serious psychiatric problems, and one sister, diagnosed as schizophrenic, had long been hospitalized.

Miss L had devoted her early years to providing a livelihood for her younger siblings; now that they were all married or living away from home, she found herself alone. Her only outlet was a few church activities. She was frequently depressed and suffered from several psychosomatic illnesses. Underlying the depression was an unresolved oedipal conflict and rage toward her parents and siblings for responsibilities placed on her. Even when she recognized some of these feelings, Miss L continued symbolically to express rage against relatives and siblings who were still making emotional demands on her—demands that she provoked. She found herself responding through psychosomatic symptoms that tended to undermine her well-being.

The short-range goal was to establish a casework relationship and to attempt to diagnose her problems. Miss L accepted referral only because the referral came from a Spanish-speaking community organization worker whom she respected and who, in essence, depended on her for carrying out church-related social projects.

Miss L demonstrated a curious mixture of cultural traits. Although she identified with the Mexican culture, she also denied this connection by speaking only English, by seeking experiences beyond the Mexican community, and by desiring to be Anglicized and to participate in the "American way of life." Eventually she obtained some insight regarding the origin of this conflict, which resulted from her unresolved oedipal conflict. She even began to refer some family members to the agency for marital counseling and another to a psychiatric clinic, believing that they too could find relief from their problems.

Miss L was a fairly well motivated, sophisticated, and verbal client with middle-class values who was able to use the services of a family agency through the referral of the community organization worker. She went through a process of establishing a trusting relationship with a community organization worker that she was able to transfer to a caseworker who was working closely with the community. As a relationship developed, she began to commute to the main office (enabling the caseworker to spend time in the community with other clients who could not travel to the main office) and continued to make steady progress.

In working with Miss L, the identification phenomenon was the most dynamic aspect of the casework relationship. With another Mexican American, Miss L was able to identify quickly and resolve her basic conflict. She might not have been able to identify with an Anglo worker and thus would have been prevented from using casework services.

One of the more typical presenting problems for which clients seek help from family agencies is that of parent-child conflicts. Frequently, the generation gap is widened by ethnic value differences that seem irreconcilable.

Mr. and Mrs. C were referred by the community organization worker because their eleven-year-old son, Juan, was exhibiting a school phobia. Both parents were born, reared, and married in Mexico. Mr. C was trained as a shoemaker and barber and had worked in these capacities until shortly before his marriage, when he began to work as a *bracero* (a migrant worker who enters the United States to perform seasonal farm labor).

During Mr. C's periods of employment, his wife would remain in Mexico caring for the children. Mr. C attempted several times to emigrate to the United States but was unsuccessful. In 1952 he brought his wife to Texas to give birth to their fifth child so that the child could be an American citizen. Before giving birth to her seventh child, Juan, two years later, Mrs. C again crossed into Texas and had a traumatic experience on the bridge. Experiencing beginning pains of labor—she delivered the same day—she was subjected to intensive questioning by the border inspector. She became acutely anxious and began to fear *el ojo;* she believed someone had put the evil eye on her. The delivery by a midwife was difficult, exacerbating her underlying guilt and anger about her pregnancy. In 1956 Mr. C came to Detroit on a permanent basis, and the entire family followed two years later. Mr. C obtained a semiskilled job that gave him a net salary of ninety-six dollars every two weeks.

The C's purchased their home in the Mexican community where

they lived with their ten children. In addition to the difficulties with Juan, there were problems with some of the older children. One son was having marital difficulties; an eighteen-year-old son was living in a common law relationship with a woman; an older daughter who had no other employable skills did not want to work as a domestic; and a third son was in business school, but the parents did not know what he was studying.

Juan had been truant from school for two and one-half years, and the attendance officer was threatening to take the parents to court. Mrs. C alternately described him as stupid, lazy, mischievous, and serious. Juan was nonverbal and uncommunicative with adults but provocative with the younger children. He refused to wear his much needed glasses and had averaged Cs in school work and Ds in deportment. He consistently ran away from home when Mrs. C attempted to make him attend school or keep appointments for treatment. Mrs. C was unable or unwilling to control this behavior. Juan spoke only English although his parents spoke only Spanish.

Mr. C verbalized extensive conflict resulting from the children's expectations for freedom to be able to come and go as they pleased. Although Mr. C assumed financial responsibility for them, he believed that they should work and contribute to the home. Because they would not or could not, he became immobilized in handling their demands and conflicts and relinquished the authority to his wife. Mrs. C, in turn, could not set limits or discipline the children, "because they're my children and I won't hurt them." Mrs. C would often miss appointments at the church-affiliated neighborhood office of the agency, necessitating many home visits wherein she would attempt to personalize the relationship.

This case illustration shows the complex manner in which cultural stress and personality pathology are intertwined. Mr. C is originally seen as highly motivated toward legal entrance into the United States. He is unable to enter legally but uses quasi-legal means, such as having his children born in Texas, in an attempt to facilitate his goal. Mrs. C is consequently denied extended family support and familiar surroundings during childbirth, which intensifies her personal inadequacies and crystallizes her need to hold on to and use *el ojo*. Mrs. C's separation during childbirth further alienates a questionable marital relationship that later extends into the total area of family dysfunctioning.

Even after many years in Detroit, the family's security is threatened by the fact that they are not considered legal residents and are fearful of discovery, even though legal assistance is offered them. The family's dysfunctioning is further aggravated because Juan's poor school adjustment brings them into contact with school authorities and possibly into contact with the courts. In the minds of the parents, these contacts are threats to their very existence. Hostility and fear prevail in all of the family's interactions.

It is interesting to note the family's ambivalence toward becoming United States citizens. Taking this step would indicate a rejection of their original Mexican culture. That there is conflict in this regard is manifest in the gaps between the parents and the children and between the husband and the wife. It is also seen in Mrs. C's seductive attempts to make the worker a friend and align the worker with her against the outside world.

In subculture systems, there is frequent community support against such establishment agencies as the juvenile court, the schools, and social service agencies, whose work is neither known nor understood but is seen by the community as extensions of or part of the outside world. Therefore, there is a need for social service agencies to extend their lines of communication—to interpret and define their work, to extend concrete and counseling services, and to follow up their clients. Communication is particularly needed with schools, the juvenile courts, and mental health and medical settings. The worker must be available to interpret special problems, patterns, and concerns of the family to the authorities and to serve as a link between alienated families and institutions in which adults and children can easily be lost or rejected.

Implications for family agencies

The case examples presented have shown that there are strengths and pathologies in Mexican-American families that are basically no different from those of other clients who seek help from family agencies. In many respects this article suggests that working with these clients is not unlike working with other lower-class, multiproblem families. Nevertheless, this client population does differ in respect to many specific cultural patterns.

Language is the most obvious cultural characteristic specific to this client group; many barrio residents speak limited—if any— English. In addition, strong emotional ties to Mexico or Texas often result in frequent trips between these areas and Detroit, creating a general lack of stability and disruptions of the family structure. Various problems and stresses may have their sources in the process of assimilation. There is much ambivalence and guilt present in those who are undergoing the process; the clients' reactions range from an almost total refusal to incorporate new values and mores into their life styles to a rather drastic renunciation of Mexican cultural patterns. The cultural accommodation often seen may underlie strong conflicts among nonassimilated adults and their children, who are learning and accepting new values from their schools and peer groups. American attitudes toward adolescent behavior—especially for girls—are particularly in conflict with Mexican values. One also finds a high degree of passive alienation among barrio residents who have not assimilated into the American culture and bear considerable distrust for non-Mexicans, particularly those in authority. A final cultural pattern worthy of note is the emphasis on fate, mysticism, and superstition in attitudes toward problems and everyday functioning.

This writer's experiences have shown that the majority of Mexican-American barrio residents do not seek counseling help from family service agencies. When they do come to an agency, they request concrete services. Many social workers with master's degrees and clinical training would find little reward in working exclusively with this client group; those who try have little success. Part of the difficulty may be explained by Jona Michael Rosenfeld's finding that differences in basic value orientations between helpers and clients are related to clients' use of services.[3] Moreover, family agency policies and basic treatment approaches are frequently based on the assumption that all clients have a similar orientation of values.

Because this client population does not share middle-class American values and, in fact, has values that are unique to its particular culture, agencies would do well to make flexible use of a combined staff of community organization workers, trained and skilled caseworkers, and paraprofessional and community workers. Social workers with master's degrees could best be utilized as supervisors, coordinators, and consultants for community workers who not only speak the language but share the cultural values of the client population. The social workers must have a high degree of commitment and be flexible and available to the community, for it is the community that should determine the direction that their service takes. In addition, social workers must give top priority to reaching out and educating the population regarding social services.

Agencies serving Mexican-American clients should begin to utilize flexible intake procedures that do not require obtaining extensive data on the telephone. If a client is not a legal resident, he will hesitate to give personal data. Such agencies should give consideration to the provision of concrete services as well as to the flexibility allowed in agency-client relationships. The physical presence of the worker and his availability to handle emergencies and provide short-term treatment during times of crisis may well be considered as important as his provision of long-term supportive casework.

Notes

1 A recent study found that the number of children in grades eight to twelve attending public school is more than twice that attending private school. However, 83 percent of the respondents preferred private education because they believed that Catholic schools provide superior education and discipline. See Sharon Popp et al., "Exploratory Study of the Mexican-American Community in Detroit, Michigan" (Master's thesis, Wayne State University School of Social Work, Detroit, Mich., June 1970).
2 Ibid.
3 Jona Michael Rosenfeld, "Strangeness Between Helper and Client: A Possible Explanation of Non-Use of Available Professional Help," *Social Service Review*, 38:19 (March 1964).

Mexican Americans and Intelligence Testing

Manuel Ramirez III and Alex Gonzalez

      The argument presented in this article is that the misuse of intelligence tests with Mexican Americans has been a direct result of the exclusionist melting pot philosophy.[1] This philosophy, which could also be referred to as the Anglo cultural superiority philosophy, has been adopted by many educational institutions in this country with respect to certain of the ethnic groups (primarily the peoples of *La Raza,* blacks, native Americans, and Orientals). The belief is that the language and behaviors of these peoples are deviant and un-American and must be changed to conform to the image of the mainstream American middle class. Intelligence testing thus has been used as a tool to achieve this goal.

      The article also introduces a new philosophy in education—cultural democracy. Cultural democracy refers to the legal rights of an individual to be different while at the same time he is a responsible member of a larger society. More specifically, it states that the way a person communicates (communication style); seeks support, acceptance, and recognition (incentive-motivational style); and learns (learning style) is a product of the value system of his home and neighborhood. Furthermore, it considers that an educational environment that ignores or rejects these behaviors is culturally undemocratic because it rejects a person's right (as guaranteed by the Civil Rights Act of 1964) to remain identified with the culture and language of his ethnic group. Cultural democracy, then, advocates that the primary goal of assessment is to change the institution so that it creates culturally democratic educational environments (that is, to develop educational settings based on the individual's unique communication, human relational, incentive-motivational, and learning styles). Unlike the exclusionist melting pot philosophy, therefore, the goal of assessment under cultural democracy is not to change the individual to force him to fit the image of the institution, but to alter the institution's teaching strategies, curriculum materials, and assessment instruments to make them more consonant with the psychological dynamics of the individuals it serves.

Intelligence testing as a tool of the exclusionist melting pot

A review of the literature pertaining to assessment of intelligence of Mexican Americans indicates that there are at least six important areas on which to focus in order to understand the weaknesses of intelligence tests currently in use.

1. *Language.* Most Mexican-American children are unfamiliar with the language of intelligence tests. For some children, it is totally foreign because their primary language is Spanish. Even for those children whose primary language is English, their rearing in an environment of poverty precludes their exposure to the vocabulary found in most intelligence tests.

There are numerous articles that have dealt with the language issue.[2] Most of these articles have shown that the language of intelligence tests renders them invalid for assessing Mexican-American children. By far the most dramatic is the study by John Chandler and John Plakos conducted under the auspices of the California State Department of Education. A sample of Mexican-American pupils, who were enrolled in classes for the educable mentally retarded (EMR) in school districts in California, was retested in Spanish to determine if they had been incorrectly diagnosed because of inability to understand the English language when the test was first administered.

The children were retested with the *Escala de Inteligencia Wechsler Para Niños* (with some minor modifications), the Spanish equivalent of the Wechsler Intelligence Scale for Children (which is the test they had been given originally in English). The results showed that the average gain between the testing in English, which resulted in placing the children in the EMR classes, and the testing in Spanish was 13.15 I.Q. points. The mean score for testing in English was 68.61, and 81.76 for testing in Spanish. The conclusion of this study was that many Mexican-American pupils are being placed in EMR classes solely on the basis of their poor performance related to their unfamiliarity with the language in which the test is usually administered.

The fact that the language of most intelligence tests makes these instruments inappropriate to the Mexican-American child has rarely been questioned by educators or social scientists. The depressed performance of Mexican-American children on intelligence tests administered in English was accepted as proof for the assumption that Mexican Americans were inferior.

2. *Content.* Most intelligence tests require knowledge of information that is distinctive for persons belonging to the mainstream of American middle-class culture. Items of the Wechsler Intelligence Scale for Children ask the following questions: What does C.O.D. mean?; Why is it better to pay bills by check than by cash?; What is the color of rubies?; How far is it from New York to Chicago? Most Mexican-American children, and especially those from poor homes, have never been exposed to this information. To highlight this particular weakness of intellectual tests, Arthur R. Jensen developed a series of tasks that would assess ability to learn independently of culturally biased content and language. The tasks were administered to Anglo and Mexican-American students equated on I.Q. as measured by the California Test of Mental Maturity.[3]

The results of the study showed that Mexican-American children who had obtained low I.Q.'s on the California Test of Mental Maturity, which is culturally loaded, performed significantly better on the learning ability tasks than did the Anglo-American children with low I.Q.'s—an indication that the Mexican-American children had been misclassified. Furthermore, it was found that the Mexican-American children with low I.Q.'s performed as well on the learning tests as did children with high I.Q.'s in both the Mexican-American and Anglo-American groups. The author's central finding was that such tests as the California Test of Mental Maturity are adequate for assessing the intelligence of Anglos but their cultural bias renders them invalid for assessing Mexican Americans.

Educational institutions have usually not questioned why it is that Mexican Americans should be penalized for being unfamiliar with cultural information to which they have never been exposed. The mere fact that Mexican-American children do not know the color of rubies or what is meant by the initials, C.O.D., has been taken as an indication of their innate inferiority.

3. *Norms.* Most intelligence tests used in schools provide norms based only on the performance of Anglo middle-class children. Mexican-American children, therefore, are hurt not only by the inappropriate language and content of these tests but also by having their scores compared against norms on which they are not represented; and consequently, many Mexican-American children have been inaccurately classified as mentally retarded. Jane R. Mercer states:

> When we consider that Mexican-American children were not even included in the samples on which the norms of the Stanford-Binet and WISC were established, the inappropriateness of a direct comparison of scores of Anglo and Mexican-American children is even more evident.[4]

The solution to this problem, however, is not in changing the norms of tests in current use for Mexican Americans. Changing the norms ignores the fact that these instruments are still culturally inappropriate and does not alter the structure and content of these tests. It would merely indicate tacit agreement with the philosophy of Anglo cultural superiority.

4. *Testing phenomena and test atmosphere.* Most Mexican-American children, and particularly those from poor homes, have had little experience with the type of testing situation typical of most intelligence tests. Testing, however, is an integral part of Anglo middle-class culture. There are games and educational toys that prepare children for the typical intelligence testing situation—an adult asking a child questions, or giving him a timed task to perform.

Not only is this entire concept of testing foreign to most Mexican-American children, but it is particularly foreign to have a stranger conduct the testing. If there is any testing to be done in Mexican-American communities, it is usually done by authority figures who are well known and trusted by the child.

The character of most intelligence tests also creates in the test situation an atmosphere of individual competition that is foreign to many Mexican-American children. There is research evidence which shows, in fact, that an individually competitive approach tends to depress the performance of Mexican and Mexican-American children. Spencer Kagan and Millard C. Madsen have compared the performance of Anglo, Mexican, and Mexican-American children in cooperative and competitive settings.[5] When r :wards could be achieved only if two children participating in a task cooperated with each other, Mexican children achieved the greatest number of rewards, Mexican-American children rated second, and Anglo children achieved the least number of awards. When, in turn, rewards were offered for competitive performance between the subjects on the same task, Anglo children achieved more rewards than did Mexican or Mexican-American children.

It appears from the results of the study that Anglo children have been conditioned to behave competitively, whereas Mexican and Mexican-American children have been conditioned to behave cooperatively. More important, however, these findings suggest cultural differences in motivational styles. Anglo children are rewarded for competitive behavior, whereas the Mexican-American and Mexican children are rewarded more for cooperative behavior. It can be concluded, therefore, that the competitive atmosphere created by intelligence tests may be incompatible with the culturally unique incentive-motivational style of many Mexican Americans.

5. *Learning styles*. The intelligence tests presently in use are not appropriate for the Chicano because these tests are biased toward the learning style most typical of the Anglo middle-class culture. Most of these instruments have been developed with and for members of Anglo-European cultures.

Douglass Price-Williams observes that researchers who have been interested in the intellectual assessment of people of cultures other than Anglo-Western cultures, as well as those who have concerned themselves with the intelligence of subcultural groups in the United States, have consistently failed to apply a cross-cultural perspective in intelligence testing.[6] In failing to recognize different ethnic groups as different cultural groups, therefore, social scientists and educators have failed to change their investigatory methods, and consequently have erroneously concluded that members of minority groups are intellectually inferior. Price-Williams recognizes the fact that culturally unique learning styles exist, and he believes that there is a need for individually tailored intelligence test instruments because the present instruments are based on Anglo-Western criteria for measurement of intelligence.

There is research evidence which shows that cultural bias is also present in nonverbal intelligence tests. At the University of Pittsburgh, Rosalie Cohen has identified the analytic cognitive style as being most typical of middle-class children and the relational cognitive style as most characteristic of children from minority groups. She has found that nonverbal intelligence tests are heavily oriented in the direction of the analytic style. She states:

> It has been most commonly believed that it is the information (direct experience) components of these tests that carry their culture-bound characteristics. Nonverbal tests concentrate on the ability to reason "logically." However, it is in the very nature of these logical sequences that the most culture-bound aspects of the middle-class, or "analytic" way of thinking are carried. Even more critical than either the quantitative and qualitative information components of such tests are the analytic mode of abstraction and the field-articulation requirements they embody.
>
> Nonverbal tests of intelligence have not freed themselves, then, of their culture-bound characteristics. Instead, they have focused on one critical aspect of culture—its method of selecting and organizing relevant sense data.[7]

Learning environments for unique cognitive styles

It may be concluded from the foregoing review that the assessment orientation that schools have followed through the use of intelligence tests has been misguided. The most important role that assessment can play in educational environments is to assess the child's culturally unique cognitive style. Once obtained, this information can be used to develop a culturally democratic learning environment with teaching methods and curricula that are consonant with the child's learning, incentive-motivational, and human relational style. We refer to learning environments that are consonant with the child's culturally unique cognitive style as culturally democratic. This orientation to assessment is focused on changing the institution to make it more compatible with the child. It differs from the assessment approach based on the Anglo cultural superiority philosophy that is oriented toward assessing the child in order to determine how to best get him to adapt to the demands of the institution.

Culturally determined learning styles

Gerald S. Lesser and his colleagues tested first grade children of four cultural groups: Chinese, Jewish, black, and Puerto Rican.[8] The results showed that the intellectual patterns varied for each of the ethnic groups and that the patterns held across socioeconomic groups within the same culture. The findings showed, for example, that Jewish children performed best on tasks of verbal ability and had difficulty on tasks of space conceptualization, whereas the reverse was true for Chinese-American children. Furthermore, the results were the same for members of the differing socioeconomic classes within each ethnic group.

It appears that the ethnic differences in intellectual patterns observed by Lesser and later by Susan Stodolsky and Lesser are manifestations of culturally unique learning styles.[9] The Jewish children had had more experience with verbal tasks and had been more conditioned in this sphere of intellectual activity, whereas Chinese children had had more experience with and had been more conditioned to achieve spatial tasks. These results imply that different ethnic groups prize certain areas of intellectual achievement or ability more than others. Valuing particular forms of achievement, therefore, parents and other cultural representatives employ culturally sanctioned teaching styles to develop in their children specific interests and aptitudes and greater expertise in some areas than in others.

Cognitive styles

Cohen's research has shown that learning styles can be subsumed under either analytic or relational cognitive styles, which incorporate both intellectual and affective characteristics of the personality. Cohen describes these styles as follows:

> The analytic cognitive style is characterized by a formal or analytic mode of abstracting salient information from a stimulus or situation and by a stimulus-centered orientation to reality, and it is parts-specific (that is, parts or attributes of a given stimulus have meaning in themselves). The relational cognitive style, on the other hand, requires a descriptive mode of abstraction and is self-centered in its orientation to reality; only the global characteristics of a stimulus have meaning to its users, and these only in reference to some total context.
>
> In the literature, it was also possible to identify clear-cut social and psychological correlates of both analytic and rela-

tional cognitive styles. Marked distinctions between individuals using each of these two cognitive styles have been drawn using a wide variety of tests, as well as through consideration of many of their social and psychological characteristics. Many school related learning characteristics, such as length and intensity of attention, preferences of optional reading material, and the differential dependence upon primary groups, also distinguish between these two types of individuals.[10]

In a similar vein, Herman Witkin has also identified two types of cognitive styles, field-dependent and field-independent, which also have intellectual and affective correlates.[11] The concept of field dependence-independence has the additional advantage of relating the learning style to cultural factors. Furthermore, research indicates the value of this particular cognitive style in analyzing several important factors involved in teaching or educational styles. Witkin and his associates have devised a methodology that is applicable to a wide variety of different cultural groups, as well as to teachers and pupils. Their methodology permits predicting success or failure of the teacher-pupil relationship and suggesting different teaching techniques and curricula.

Prescription for institutional change

The concept of field dependence-independence has implications for change in both teaching methodology and curriculum development. For example, field-dependent individuals are more influenced by or are sensitive to the human element in the environment. This characteristic is shown in their tendency to perform better on measures of social expressiveness and recall of human faces and their advantage in learning material containing human content. The field-independent individuals, on the other hand, are characterized by their greater advantage in testing situations in which the material is relatively impersonal or abstract. They are more readily able to isolate parts from the whole and are less constrained by conventional uses of objects and materials; hence, they are able to find more novel uses for them.

Another major group of differences between field dependents and independents concerns the interpersonal dimension of rewards. Field-dependent individuals are more likely to be motivated by those forms of rewards that have personal content rather than by those that have impersonal content. For such persons, support, recognition, or acceptance must be mediated in a highly personalized manner. Related to this idea is the fact that field-dependent individuals appear to view authority figures as models with whom to identify, in contrast to field-independents who seem to view authority figures as sources of information.[12]

Research on the cognitive styles of Mexican-American and Anglo fourth-grade children of the same socioeconomic class revealed that Mexican Americans are significantly more field-dependent than are Anglos.[13] Preliminary research on teachers, curriculum, and other aspects of the learning environment in schools, however, indicates a strong bias toward field-independence. Preliminary testing of teachers in schools with high concentrations of Mexican-American students showed that most teachers are significantly more field-independent than are their students. Similarly, Cohen has found that the analytic style (similar to field-independence) is favored more by the schools than the relational (similar to field-dependence) styles. She states:

> A new observation that emerged from this study of the literature on cognitive styles was that not only test criteria but also the overall ideology and learning environment of the school embody requirements for many social and psychological correlates of the analytic style. This emphasis can be found, for example, in its cool, impersonal, outer-centered approach to reality organization . . . so discrepant are the analytic and relational frames of reference that a pupil whose preferred mode of cognitive organization is emphatically relational is unlikely to be rewarded in the school setting either socially or by grades regardless of his native abilities and even if his information repertoire and background of experience are adequate.[14]

Ramirez and Alfredo Castañeda are currently developing teacher training and curriculum development techniques that will help to achieve culturally democratic learning environments for Mexican-American children. These techniques will (1) provide teachers with guidelines to help them assess the cognitive styles of students, (2) help teachers assess their own cognitive styles, (3) assess the cognitive styles reflected by the curriculum and the learning environment of the school in general, and (4) demonstrate training procedures for helping teachers to make their teaching strategies and curriculum development functional in both styles.

Although the cognitive style approach to assessment in educational environments is still in its infancy, we believe that it is a step in the right direction with respect to assessment of the culturally different child. The primary concern of assessment in education should be with the method of achieving culturally democratic learning environments that reflect the child's culturally unique learning, incentive-motivational, and human relational styles. It is only this orientation that will help to eradicate the undemocratic educational practices which have been built upon the Anglo cultural-superiority philosophy.

Notes

[1] Alfredo Castañeda, "Melting Potters vs. Cultural Pluralists: Implications for Education," in *Mexican-Americans and Educational Change* (Riverside, Calif.: University of California, Mexican-American Studies, 1971).
[2] John T. Chandler and John Plakos, *Spanish-Speaking Pupils Classified as Educable Mentally Retarded* (Sacramento: California State Department of Education, 1969); Jack E. Kittell, "Intelligence Test Performance of Children from Bilingual Environments," *Elementary School Journal*, 64:76–88 (November 1963); William R. Holland, "Language Barrier as an Educational Problem of Spanish Speaking Children," *Exceptional Children*, 27:42–49 (September 1960); Morton J. Keston and Carmina Jimenez, "A Study of the Performance on English and Spanish Editions of the Stanford-Binet Intelligence Test by Spanish-American Children," *Journal of Genetic Psychology*, 85:263–69 (December 1954); Grace T. Altus, "W.I.S.C. Patterns of a Selective Sample of Bilingual School Children," ibid., 83:241–48 (December 1953); Charles Mahakian, "Measuring Intelligence and Reading Capacity of Spanish Speaking Children," *Elementary School Journal*, 39:760–68 (June 1939); George I. Sanchez, "Bilingualism and Mental Measures," *Journal of Applied Psychology*, 18:765–72 (1934); and Benjamin F. Haught, "The Language Difficulty of Spanish-American Children," *Journal of Applied Psychology*, 15:92 95 (February 1931).
[3] Arthur R. Jensen, "Learning Abilities of Mexican-American and Anglo-American Children," *California Journal of Educational Research*, 12:147–59 (September 1961).
[4] Jane R. Mercer, "Current Retardation Procedures and the Psychological and Social Implications on the Mexican-American" (Position paper prepared for the South-Western Cooperative Educational Laboratory, Albuquerque, New Mexico, April 1970), p. 8.
[5] Spencer Kagan and Millard C. Madson, "Cooperation and Competition of Mexican, Mexican-American, and Anglo-American Children of Two Ages under Four Instructional Sets," *Developmental Psychology*, 5:32–39 (July 1971).
[6] Douglass R. Price-Williams, "Human Intelligence: The Cross-Cultural Problem" (Paper presented at a symposium on perspectives on the nature of intelligence, Neuropsychiatric Institute, University of California at Los Angeles, Los Angeles, Calif., June 4–5, 1971); and Arthur R. Jensen, "How Much Can We Boost the I.Q. and Scholastic Achievement?," *Harvard Educational Review*, 39:1–123 (Winter 1969); and Discussion, ibid., 39:273–356 (Spring 1970).
[7] Rosalie Cohen, "Conceptual Style, Culture Conflict and Non-Verbal Tests of Intelligence," *American Anthropologist*, 71:840–41 (February 1969).
[8] Gerald S. Lesser, Gordon Fifer, and Donald H. Clark, "Mental Abilities of Children from Different Social-Class and Cultural Groups," Monograph of the Society for Research in Child Development, vol. 30, no. 4, serial no. 102, 1965.

[9] Lesser, Fifer, and Clark, "Mental Abilities"; and Susan S. Stodolsky and Gerald Lesser, "Learning Patterns in the Disadvantaged," *Harvard Educational Review*, 37:546–93 (Fall 1967).

[10] Cohen, "Conceptual Style," p. 830.

[11] Herman A. Witkin et al., *Psychological Differentiation* (New York: John Wiley & Sons, 1962).

[12] Manuel Ramirez and Alfredo Castañeda, *Cultural Democracy in Education: The Case of The Mexican-American Child* (New York: Seminar Press, forthcoming).

[13] Manuel Ramirez, Douglass R. Price-Williams, and Alma Beman, "The Relationship of Culture to Educational Attainment," Center for Research in Social Change and Economic Development, Rice University, Houston, Texas (research in progress).

[14] Cohen, "Conceptual Style," p. 830.

Mexican-American Interaction with Social Systems

Marta Sotomayor

It has been assumed that if we knew the cultural elements that determine the structure of the Mexican-American family, we could be effective in the problem-solving process in this particular aspect of the life experience of the Mexican American. A number of descriptive articles have been written that summarily dismiss the issue of the Mexican-American family by presenting the structure of the so-called traditional patriarchal family with an authoritarian father, a submissive mother, and children lost somewhere between these two opposing forces.

This simplistic, descriptive approach is acceptable in scientific research literature. The rationale is that by applying this approach the major characteristics of the sample can be determined, thus enabling us to judge the extent to which the sample is representative of the entire population, and that "by utilizing some elementary techniques of empirical social research one learns to pose a hypothesis and second, how to organize the data necessary to test that hypothesis." [1]

If the prevalent hypothesis has been that all Mexican-American families follow the patriarchal model, then the data can be organized and manipulated to prove this hypothesis. This writer questions such methodology, the exclusive use of one hypothesis that predetermines a definition of all Mexican-American families, as well as the selection for study of a few familial issues isolated from a total view of these families.

Not only is the description of the patriarchal model of the Mexican-American families in the existing literature inaccurate, but the assumption that such structural patterns alone determine the value orientation of its individual members is also misleading. A recent article by Miguel Montiel clearly explains how such assumptions have influenced the method of studying the Mexican-American family in a variety of relationships.[2] Montiel also points out how the psychoanalytic model has been used exclusively in the definition of the Mexican-American family, emphasizing the themes of "inferiority and machismo." [3]

Issues to be considered

The issues under question here are (1) the hypothesis that Mexican-American families follow only the patriarchal model, one that is frowned upon by a democratic society that accords equal power to both spouses (possibly another myth); (2) the methodology of study that manipulates data to prove this hypothesis; (3) the sole use of the psychoanalytical model based on a concept of pathology that is unable to tolerate "differentness" and thus values conformity; and (4) the selectivity for study of such issues as inferiority and machismo, elements that are certainly not valued in this society.

There exist in the status arrangements of the members of the Mexican-American family the same variations that exist in any other ethnic group, and many factors can cause these structures to vary and change. Although it is important to understand the arrangements of roles in order to understand the specific functions of the family unit and its individual members, it is more important to understand the depth, subtlety, and complexity of familial relationships and the economic, political, social, and cultural variations that determine the Mexican-American family experiences.

Social work practice certainly has considered these factors; however, in working with Mexican Americans and other minorities, the profession has been ineffective. It is, therefore, necessary to analyze critically and systematically those factors that have been ignored in attempts to understand the life conditions of minorities in this country and other countries, in which members of the majority society have been intolerant of those who are different in their actions, speech, and skin color.

In practically all cultures, considerable importance is attached to the family as a social unit regulated by law and custom. Different approaches have been used in trying to acquire workable knowledge of all the forces that affect the family as a unit and its individual members. As many divergent conclusions have been made by studies as there are studies available.

Social systems concept and the family

The social systems concept is one that is applicable to an understanding of the Mexican-American family. *Webster's Third New International Dictionary* defines *system* as "an aggregation or assemblage of objects joined in regular interaction or interdependence." [4] The Mexican-American family, as any other family, should be an open system, sustaining relationships with other systems in the total transactional field. [5]

This concept recognizes the psychological unit of the family with its functional interaction in a variety of combinations and meanings. It also gives due importance to the variety and meanings of the family's functions in relating to the multiplicity of systems and subsystems outside itself, and it acknowledges the effects that the outside structures can have on the family unit's ability to function.

Socialization process

It is generally agreed that one of the family's primary functions is the socialization of the children, which is usually regarded as a process of transmitting and conserving sociocultural traditions from generation to generation. It is also agreed that the values, beliefs, roles, and functions of individuals and the manner in which they promote socialization of their children depend in large measure on variations in social conditions.

In this highly technological society with its history of extreme contrasts—a society firmly embedded in a competitive economic system and characterized by constant and sharp changes—the socialization process has become one in which the child acquires skills, not always effective, to deal with abrupt and contradictory change rather than one in which the child is encouraged to promote tradition. As a result, emphasis has been placed on the development of individualistic, personalistic, and polarized values rather than on the traditional kinship and group values.

This historical perspective of the American identity provides the base for Erik H. Erikson's formulation of an American national character within a psychosocial framework. This formulation begins to explain this country's inability to tolerate "differentness," which is often expressed in institutionalized racism. He says that "the patient, as a baby, was not made to feel at home in this world except under the condition that he behave himself in certain definite ways, which were inconsistent with the timetable of an infant's needs and potentialities and contradictory in themselves." [6] Erikson also says that the mother "stands for the superior values of tradition, yet she herself does not want to become 'old.' " [7]

This socialization process, once a purview of the extended family, has been delegated to outside structures—or institutions—of society. This societal machinery is necessary to maintain the social system as a system, in order to prevent society from being torn by the forces of individual self-interest; institutions, therefore, are essential in maintaining the internal harmony of society and in harnessing the individual to community action. Within this context, human society can be viewed as a system of organization in which the individual and his range of needs, at all phases and levels, are both satisfied and held in check. These needs can be met only by man in a social interaction system, which is conducted through institutions that are established to meet, repress, or oppress the needs of those individuals that compose them or through those that permit the fulfillment of the potentiality of its members.[8]

Participation within society

The second function of the family is to participate within society. Through its participation in community life and through the support it receives from the community, a family is motivated to adhere to the norms of the community, including norms regarding its own stability.[9] It is the norms of the community that ascribe status to specific families. That status, with all its implications, becomes the focus of reference for the family and determines the types of relationships it will have with the community as a whole and with its parts. It is this ascribed status that determines not only the economic, political, and educational aspirations of the family but also its relationship with society's institutions.

The institutions designed to meet the needs of society and to allow, with their systems of checks and balances, for the maximum development of individual potentiality have failed the Mexican-American family. Existing institutions are color blind; they endorse policies that exclude those who are different, that bar admission to educational systems, and that adhere to merit systems ("merit" defined from a narrow point of view without consideration of the total perspective of the Mexican American). These institutions support the "melting pot" concept with its racist core; they value individualistic, competitive achievement that systematically and consistently excludes the Mexican American from participation.

A colonized people

If the Mexican-American family is to be understood, it has to be within the historical perspective of a colonized people in its native country and in this country. In this perspective the Mexican Americans have many of the characteristics of other colonized people, with the majority society relating to them as outsiders. The inferior status of the colonized people results in damage to self-esteem, destruction of native cultural traits and adoption of foreign cultural traits, disintegration of the family unit with particular disparagement of the male, and, finally, loss of social cohesion among so-called inferior groups because of their inability to retain their own culture.[10]

All of these symptoms have been identified to some degree in a considerable number of Mexican-American families. There is sufficient evidence of the damage that institutional policies and procedures have inflicted upon Mexican Americans. In an article in the *Los Angeles Times,* Ruben Salazar summarized the plight of Mexican Americans.

> The Mexican American has an average of 8 years of schooling, [and] a significant number of farm workers who are excluded from the National Labor Relations Act, unlike any other group of workers. Mexican Americans often have to compete for low wages with their Mexican brothers below the border, with limited skills in a highly technological, competitive society. Mexican Americans have to live with the stinging fact that the word "Mexican" is the synonym for inferior in

> many parts of the southwest. Mexican Americans through
> their large population are so politically impotent that in Los
> Angeles where the country's largest single concentration lives
> we have not one representative in the City Council.[11]

Ordinarily the family participates in community activities in exchange for the support of the community. One functional interchange
consists of mutual give and take on a daily interaction basis. The
extent and quality of the interaction determines the solidarity of
bonds between society and the family unit. This daily interaction with
the external system has been blocked for many Mexican-American
families, and, as a result, they have withdrawn from participation in community affairs. The merits of withdrawal from or involvement with a hostile environment are open for discussion.

The external community has given the Mexican-American family
an inferior status and has defined that status as one with inferior
standards of behaviors and rewards. In a functional society the
community gives the family a significant status and identity by
means of support and acceptance. The present societal structure
denies the Mexican-American family a positive status and identity,
excludes it from community activities, and gives it the feeling of
alienation, marginality, and anomie.

Interchanges with social systems

The type and quality of the interchanges between the family and
the external social system determine to a considerable extent the
internal family activities and its integration. The Mexican-American
head of the household often has been unemployed or underem-
ployed in menial tasks that constantly remind him of his inferior
status. He has practically no access to the decision-making process
that could change his situation, and he has no effective means of
making those vital institutions respond to his needs. This damaging,
limiting process invariably affects the internal functioning and the
role arrangement within his family. It has an adverse effect on
family leadership, on the maintenance of expected patterns of behavior, and on the integration and solidarity of specific families and
their individual members.

Task performance and expected patterns of behavior clearly reflect the family's relationship with external systems. These task
performances are regulated in part by the requirements of the

interchanges between those systems and the family and the tangible goods obtained from these interchanges. Performance of the expected, assigned tasks in turn affects the quality and integration of the relationships within the family.[12]

The adequate performance of expected tasks is intrinsically related to other goals of the family. When these goals are limited by decisions of a system over which the individual family has no control, the equilibrium of relationships within the Mexican-American family suffers, including the degree of closeness of family bonds and the expected familial leadership. These factors affect the Mexican-American father's role as provider, disciplinarian, and protector. His authority, to be effective, has to be couched in strong effective bonds that successfully resolve the problems of the individual's identity.

The patterns of decision making are thwarted and distorted for many Mexican-American families when decisions that involve meeting the basic, essential needs of family members are beyond the control of the expected patterns. These conditions have a circular effect in disrupting the family's equilibrium and in preventing the family from reorganizing and mobilizing its internal resources to deal with a rejecting, destructive external system. The pattern thus is perpetuated.

Other forms of dealing with external systems are attempted with no actual opportunity of testing them to discover effects or alternatives. The interchanges afforded other families and the processes learned in the successful completion of those interchanges are not available for many Mexican Americans because society does not offer them that "testing ground." Is it possible that the high proportion of inmates of correctional institutions, the number of narcotic addicts, and the high percentage of school dropouts among Mexican Americans can be explained not merely on the basis of individual deviancy but more as a result of attempts to achieve some type of interaction with a destructive external system? In many instances, the only knowledge the Mexican American has of those institutions outside of his barrio is that they repress and oppress him, and the skills he develops to deal with those institutions have to be limited to responding to repression and oppression.

The strong movement for *chicanismo* within prison walls, the recruitment of Mexican-American school dropouts by young Mexican-

American students, and the involvement of Mexican-American ex-addicts in the counseling of other Mexican-American addicts—all self-help groups—present the themes typical of an interactional process that mutually affects family and society. The following themes appear repeatedly in the Chicano movement: open and better employment opportunities, change of policies that have excluded Mexican Americans from the normal activities of society, greater status for Spanish as a spoken language, respect for the Mexican American as an individual of value, cohesion and solidarity of a group united by a cause, pride in the culture and heritage of one's ancestors, and reevaluation of roles and functions of men and women.

Within this perspective, what is the function of the social worker in working with Mexican-American families? This perspective does not totally reject the psychoanalytic model; in fact, there are many Mexican-American families and individuals—particularly those who have achieved considerable mobility within the majority community —who benefit from this traditional counseling approach. The exclusive use of this approach, however, is a narrow one in view of the other factors that dramatically affect the opportunities for Mexican-American families to function adequately.

An attempt has been made to show how a significant number of weaknesses that had been attributed to the internal dynamics of the Mexican-American family can now, through the systems approach, be ascribed to the limitations placed upon the Mexican Americans by external systems. An attempt has also been made to point out how these limitations affect the internal integration of the family unit.

Identifying supportive elements

Social workers must be able to identify those elements within the Mexican-American family that have given and promoted group cohesion and individual integration. Having identified these elements, our social workers can then function effectively in encouraging desirable family relationships. The same process applies in working with external systems. Only several elements that have given support to the Mexican-American family will be discussed in this article; others have to be identified; all require further elaboration.

Extended family pattern

One element that appears consistently in the Mexican-American family is the extended family pattern. It is a supportive and flexible structure assuming functions in dealing with the environment and with the emotional and psychological aspects of the family unit and individuals. This system is compatible with the present emphasis of the Mexican American on the importance of the group; for example, *Movimiento Estudiantil Chicano de Aztlan* (MECHA), Mexican Youth Organization (MAYO), and Crusade for Justice —all group oriented and having many characteristics of a "tribe."

In the extended family pattern, the members often rescue the head of a household by sharing their goods to meet the daily needs of his family. The head of the household does not lose face, but the extended family pattern couches his feeling of failure. The feeling of isolation of the nuclear family in similar situations is diluted by the support and help of the variety of members of the extended family. Various members of the family assume the physical and affective care of the child when stress from the external system causes self-preoccupation of an individual parent. This process is also present at times of internal crisis, such as the birth of a new child, when the extended family gives care to the mother during her convalescence and to the older youngsters. In addition, the extended family provides the daily care that the father expects and continues the routines of family functions within a familiar setting.

The *compadrazgo* relationship has many similar characteristics and functions; relationships assume familial overtones in which the emotional and physical responsibilities for children are also shared. Although it is true that many Mexican Americans who migrated to this country (and others who were in the Southwest before United States expansion into these territories) brought with them the extended family pattern and the phenomenon of *compadrazgo,* with its emphasis on kinship and deep, lasting relationships, the changes experienced in this society have greatly diluted, if not modified, such structures and their accompanying relationships.

Respect for the aged

The aged are greatly respected among Mexican Americans; positions of authority are assigned to them regardless of their sex. Through the continued participation of the elderly in the decision-making process, the issue of authority is diluted among extended family relationships. This practice is in contradiction to the patriarchal model, in which it is assumed that the father is the only source of authority. Mexican Americans have strong convictions that commit them to taking care of aged parents and grandparents.

Family role patterns

The mother is given a significant position within the family. Respect for the mother is expressed symbolically by her children's using her family name in conjunction with that of the father. This custom is prevalent in Latin America but is totally overlooked in the United States with the usage of only the father's last name.

The function of the oldest son and oldest daughter to participate actively in the parental function in relation to the younger siblings continues to exist. This pattern is often interpreted by social workers as overdependency, and great efforts are made to "emancipate" such family members from their "unfair" burdens of family responsibilities.

With the exclusive use of the patriarchal model we have overlooked additional role patterns, quality and levels of relationships, sharing of parental functions, and meanings of sibling relationships. A multiplicity of variations exists in these relationships and arrangements, just as they exist in any other ethnic group.

The barrio

The barrio, like the ghetto, has become a negative concept, often destroyed by urban renewal projects that methodically appear to disperse the barrio residents by the intricate construction of freeways. For a group of pepole who have been consistently rejected by the environment and who value the group and tend to cluster in familial and neighborhood arrangements, the barrio has offered a feeling of belonging and cohesion.

The negative aspect of the barrio is not the clustering of Mexican Americans but the almost total lack of resources coming into the confined community to meet the needs of its residents. With opportunities to reach out of the barrio also limited, there are relatively few alternatives for the expression and development of the potentiality of the Mexican American.

Use of Spanish

The persistent use of Spanish, a descriptive language suitable to promoting intensive relationships in a ranking order (that is, use of *tu* and *usted*), has served to maintain and emphasize satisfying, close human relationships that have helped to provide emotional stability for many Mexican Americans.

Certainly there are many reasons for the persistence to continue to speak Spanish in the home and in the barrio. The type of interchanges between the individual and a hostile, rejecting external system raises the question of whether the language is also utilized as protection from outside threatening forces. If a person does not understand English, he does not understand the negative messages coming in, although verbal communication is certainly not the only type of communication available in the interaction with external systems. Institutions, including social service delivery systems, have misunderstood, minimized, and often participated in the destruction of many positive factors presented by the Mexican-American sociocultural framework.

Social work function

Social work traditionally has accepted its function of involvement in the process of change; its function to preserve is often overlooked or overemphasized. Effective social work intervention requires careful assessment of areas that require change and areas that should be preserved, encouraged, or supported. The sociocultural strengths of the Mexican-American family, therefore, need to be closely identified, evaluated, and supported. More often than not, the positive factors of the (Mexican-American) family have provided the only strengths available in the life experiences of the Mexican-American people. We do not have to minimize the internal functioning of the family as a system; however, in understanding the degree of negative effect of the external system upon the integration of the family unit, the profession's first priority is to intervene and change those destructive external forces.

In open forum discussions of the consequences of racism, there has been a tendency to assume that if only the laws of this country could be changed or enforced, all its problems would be resolved.

This position assumes that many institutions as they exist today are valid and viable. If social work is to be effective in giving service to the disadvantaged Mexican-American families, intervention has to take place at many levels and in many areas requiring institutional change.

New models of decision making have to be supported—specifically, the decentralization of the functions of government and the delivery of services. Accompanying rearrangements of power will bring about "community control," which will not only strengthen the barrios but will bring the decision making to the individuals who are directly affected by the policies of such structures and who hopefully are more responsive to the needs of the Mexican American. This decentralization will affect primarily the educational and service delivery systems.

These local community organizations should have direct access to the central authority. Mexican Americans, therefore, should be supported in their politization process to make this access possible and to begin to influence the political system—an opportunity that until now has been denied them.

The self-help process characteristic of the Chicano movement should be recognized and encouraged. It is only through the careful assessment of internal and external forces and their effects upon each other that internal resources can be mobilized, tested, and refined in the transactional field of families, individuals, and society.

Notes

1 Murray A. Straus, *Family Analysis: Readings and Replication of Selected Studies* (Chicago: Rand McNally & Co., 1969), p. 38.
2 Miguel Montiel, "The Social Science Myth of the Mexican American Family," *El Grito*, 3:56 (Summer 1970).
3 Ibid.
4 See *Webster's Third New International Dictionary*, s.v. "system."
5 John P. Spiegel, "A Model for Relationships Among Systems," in *Toward a Unified Theory of Human Behavior*, ed. Roy R. Grinker (New York: Basic Books, 1956), pp. 22–27.
6 Erik H. Erikson, *Childhood and Society* (New York: W. W. Norton & Co., 1950), p. 247.
7 Ibid., p. 249.
8 See Walter Goldschmidt, *Comparative Functionalism, An Essay in Anthropological Theory* (Berkeley-Los Angeles: University of California Press, 1966), pp. 58–59.

[9] See Norman W. Bell and Ezra F. Vogel, "Toward a Framework for Functional Analysis of Family Behavior," in *A Modern Introduction to the Family,* ed. Bell and Vogel (New York: Free Press, 1968), pp. 1–34.

[10] See A. Kardiner and L. Ovesey, *The Mark of Oppression: Explorations in the Personality of the American Negro* (New York: Meridian Books, 1962), p. 47.

[11] *Los Angeles Times,* February 6, 1970.

[12] See Bell and Vogel, "Functional Analysis of Family Behavior," pp. 1–34.

The Mexican Community of Detroit

Gumecindo Salas and Isabel Salas

Little or nothing has been written about the Mexican people of Detroit. Basically, Detroit is considered a black-white city in which other ethnic groups are categorized as either one or the other. Where does the Mexican-American group fit in? The answer varies. The light-skinned Mexican is usually. considered white; the medium-brown Mexican may be considered Italian, Syrian, Lebanese, Maltese, or Greek, a foreigner but nevertheless white; and the dark-skinned Mexican is identified as black. Most Detroit Anglos outside the barrio do not know what a Mexican is and until recently never bothered to find out. The shock to the Anglo community upon discovering that there are 50,000 or more Chicanos in the Detroit metropolitan area has just begun to penetrate. It has initiated a flurry of activities aimed at learning more about the entire Latin-American community comprised mostly of Mexican, Puerto Rican, and Cuban people.

The number of Mexicans in Detroit has never been reported accurately because there has never been an effort to ascertain a true figure. The 1970 census is inaccurate. It is based on surname only in identifying Latin-American people. In Michigan, the census forms provided identification for Caucasian, black, Korean, Filipino,

Chinese, and Japanese people but did not offer identification for Mexican Americans or Puerto Ricans. According to the 1960 census the largest of the Asiatic groups in Detroit, the Chinese, number about 2,000; the second largest, the Japanese, about 1,800. The question is, Why were the Mexican Americans and Puerto Ricans, whose numbers far exceed the Asians in the city, left out?

Census forms specifying both Mexican-American and Puerto Rican categories were available and used in the Southwest and New York. Why were they not used in Detroit and other midwestern cities? As a result many Latin Americans were counted as part of the Caucasian group. In some cases Mexican Americans and Puerto Ricans simply checked Caucasian and did not notice the space provided to write in their own ethnic group; some checked Caucasian because they want to be and consider themselves white. The census bureau adds to the confusion when it is unable to recognize Spanish surnames. Names such as Ballestero, Lujan, Carillo, and Vidaurri often are mistaken for Italian and therefore counted as part of the white population. Another major fault of the census bureau is that it cannot identify Latinos who have Anglo names. The writers know Chicanos with names such as VanHorn, Brewster, McKnight, Sievers, and Witherow. These Chicanos are also counted as white.

Based on these facts, the Chicano community charges that the 1970 census cannot be accurate. It rejects the bureau's projected figure of 20,000, which is strikingly similar to the 1960 census of 19,542, and places the actual number between 50,000 to 90,000.

The new interest of Anglo professionals puzzles the old residents of the barrio. Mexican people have lived in Detroit for more than fifty years. They have determinedly retained their language, heritage, culture, values, and religion. Their answer to the question "What are you?" invariably has been "I'm Mexican." There was seldom any mention of the term *Mexican American* until the last three years when it was imported by the news media from the Southwest. The term *Chicano,* however, was not unfamiliar here in Detroit; many remember hearing it and using it long before arriving in Detroit.

In 1918, Mexican migrant workers from Texas came to Michigan to work in the sugar beet fields. Carey McWilliams, in *North From Mexico,* writes that several hundred Mexicans arrived in Detroit about that time to work in the automobile factories.[1] Willard A. Heaps, in *Wandering Workers,* describes migratory labor during the

World War I years of 1914 to 1918 as a "significant source of seasonal labor." [2] Because little written information on the early migration of Mexican people to Michigan is available, the writers decided to ask the local Mexican people themselves. Surely the people who made the long trip, who worked in the fields and factories, and who settled in Detroit can relate what happened as well or better than can the historian, the sociologist, or the anthropologist who acquires information secondhand.

By questioning many friends and neighbors, the writers verified the fact that Mexicans did arrive in Michigan as long ago as 1918. Most were migrant workers who returned to their homes after the season, but a small number came to Detroit, found work, and remained. From 1918 to the present time, an unknown number of Mexican Americans, working for the railroads, in steel mills, and in automobile factories, has remained behind each year to make Detroit their new home. The story of one Mexican family can describe the conditions and reasons that brought these people to Michigan, and ultimately to Detroit. It is a story that can be duplicated thousands of times in many communities other than Detroit.

One family's story

As early as 1918, the Pablo Martinez family heard of *mejicanos* (Mexicans) traveling to Illinois, Michigan, and Ohio to work in the fields. Living conditions for *mejicanos* in Texas were intolerable. Entire families moved about as best as they could looking for work in the cotton and strawberry fields or wherever work was available. Pablo feared traveling so far north with his family, but by 1929 four of Pablo's twelve children had died; there were days when there was no food at all. As a sharecropper in Lockhart, Texas, he and his family planted cotton, tended the fields, and picked the cotton. In return he received a share of the profits. However, one year was a very good year for cotton, and rather than share the profits, the farmer decided to get rid of the family. Using anger as a pretext, he ordered the family to leave. He was a German and carried a gun and a whip to keep his farm hands in line. He is still remembered as being *muy desgraciado* (cold and cruel). There was no choice, not in Texas, and so the family began to wander from town to town looking for a way to subsist.

In 1929 the Martinez family was working in the strawberry fields near Houston when they heard of a special train to Michigan and of a contractor signing up *mejicanos* for the sugar beet fields. Pablo signed. The family boarded the train in June 1929, along with many other Mexican families. Pablo, his wife Antonia, and their children —twenty-seven-year-old Carlota with her seven-year-old daughter Maria, eighteen-year-old Lola, twelve-year-old Margarita, seven-year-old Raul, five-year-old Rodolfo, and two-year-old Beatriz—found themselves speeding to a new place, a new destiny, and hopefully a new and better future.

The family members slept as well as they could in their seats. The food provided was bologna and bread. On the fourth day the train arrived in Caro, Michigan. It was the last time the Martinez family would see another Mexican face during their entire stay in the new state.

Quickly the families were rounded up and dispersed to the nearby farms. The local residents gaped in amazement at the brown faces marching through their town, but there was little to fear; arrangements had been made so that the migrants would seldom be seen in the town itself.

The Martinez family was housed in a small shack, away from the other families on the train. From June to August all worked in the fields—all except Antonia, Carlota who was ill, and the baby Beatriz. From sunrise to sunset, day after day, Saturdays and Sundays, they blocked, thinned, and hoed the rows of sugar beets. No money was paid until that part of the season was over. It was another miserable experience for the family: the work was much too heavy for the children; Carlota's health was failing rapidly; they were completely isolated; and they did not speak English. It was a very lonely existence.

Pablo decided to use his wages to buy an old model T Ford car and return to Texas. He hoped to be able to work his way back, but bad luck in Ohio delayed the return trip and the family was stranded in Freemont, Ohio, until April 1931 when they finally arrived in Houston. Carlota had died in Ohio; a month after they returned to Texas Lola died. Margarita explained her death simply: *Murio porque estaba muy cansada, cansada de trabajar tan duro toda su vida.* ("She died because she was very tired, tired of working so hard all her life.")

Back in Texas, the family worked once again in the cotton and strawberry fields. These were the depression years, and life was worse than ever before. In desperation Pablo decided in 1937 to return to Michigan.

This time they arrived in Imlay City, Michigan, where they found work picking onions, carrots, tomatoes, and sugar beets. Pablo heard rumors of much work and better wages in Detroit. He packed up his family for the last time and went to the city. By 1939 most of his relatives had migrated from Texas to Detroit, where they still live today.

World War II migration

In the early 1940s the labor shortage in Detroit became critical because of World War II. *Mejicanos* were streaming in from the farm areas, from Texas, and from Mexico to work in the steel mills, the automobile factories, and the railroads. Willis F. Dunbar, in *Michigan: A History of the Wolverine State,* points out that during the war years there was a tremendous influx of people to Detroit from rural areas and other states, although he does not specifically mention the Mexican migrants.[3] It is interesting that from 1918 to the present time, many small Mexican communities have sprouted up throughout the state. Leaving the migrant stream, *mejicanos* have settled in Imlay City, Capac, Holland, Bad Axe, Caseville, Muskegon, Erie, Pontiac, Monroe, Adrian, and Port Huron. Michigan history seldom mentions these settlements of a people who have been here for years and now total about 200,000 in the state.

A new phenomenon began to take place in the 1940s. In addition to the farmworkers moving to the city, industrial migrants from the Southwest and Mexico bypassed the usual migrant route and came directly to Detroit to work in the factories. The Mexican barrio began to grow. Another barrio sprang up in Ecorse, a small suburban town ten miles from downtown Detroit, located near the Great Lakes Steel Plant that hired a large number of Mexicans.

Social and fraternal clubs

Although far from "home," be it Mexico or Texas, the Mexican community in Detroit formed religious, social, and fraternal clubs which have always been an integral part of Mexican community and society. These groups are needed both for the role they fulfill and for their membership that includes the oldest and the most respected families. The main objective of these groups was to focus on the ancestral cultural heritage. *Los bailes* (dances), *las fiestas* (holidays), *la reina para el 16th de Septiembre y el cinco de Mayo* (the Queen for September 16 and May 5), *el dia de la Virgen de Guadalupe* (the holy day for the Virgin of Guadalupe), *las bodas* (weddings), and *los bautismos* (baptismal parties) were all celebrated Mexican style.

Some of the earliest social clubs were *el Comite Patriotico* (the Patriotic Committee), *el Comite Democratico* (the Democratic Club), American G.I. Forum, *el Circulo Mutualista* (the Mutual Circle Club), and Post 505 of the Veterans of Foreign Wars. Their involvement over the years has been primarily centered on cultural activities. *El Comite Patriotico* sponsors the annual Independence Day festivities for May 5 and September 16. *El Circulo Mutualista* sponsors the annual Debutantes Ball and many social parties throughout the year. The American G.I. Forum, Post 505, and *el Comite Democratico* sponsor fund-raising dances and parties. All cooperate with *el Comite Patriotico* during the Independence Day activities which are held at the riverfront in downtown Detroit during the ethnic festival. These groups have kept the Mexican cultural traditions alive.

The earliest religious groups, still in existence, were *los Caballeros Catolicos* (Knights of Columbus), *las Guadalupanas,* and *los Cursillistas.* Most parishes now have their own chapters of these groups. In the 1940s these religious groups were responsible for specific religious functions. The majority of the Mexican migrants were Catholic. The Church maintained lines of communication with the Mexican community through these groups.

The *Caballeros Catolicos* was the first religious group to exert pressure against the Detroit Archdiocese. The late Cardinal Mooney, Archbishop of Detroit from 1937 to 1958, adhered to the policy that all people be Americanized and dictated that no special recognition or consideration be given to the Mexican community.[4] Nevertheless, the power of the Archbishop failed. It did not destroy the language and the culture of a people determined to remain *mejicanos.*

One parish, which had originally been French and later Irish, was not ready to accept the Mexicans who were moving in from another parish. New immigrants put added pressure on the parish priests. The Church had the responsibility to provide adequate services to the parishioners, and the Mexican parishioners wanted a Spanish-speaking priest. The *Caballeros Catolicos* requested that a Mass be conducted in Spanish and that the Mexican patron saint, the Virgin of Guadalupe, be brought into the church as had been done in their former church in another section of Detroit. The pastor was caught in the middle; he eventually complied with the request, but designated the chapel located in the back of the church as the place for Mexican services. It was some years before Mass in Spanish was celebrated in the main chapel.

While this struggle was going on between the Archbishop and the people, the composition of the area continued to change. The Mexicans were migrating into southwest Detroit. They were one of the last ethnic groups to occupy the area, and their immigration was not well received by the Irish, the Polish, and the German people. By the 1960s the church that the *Caballeros Catolicos* and others had fought to change had become predominantly Mexican. It has now become the only Catholic church in the area to be 80 percent Mexican.

In addition to fighting for religious freedom, the *Caballeros Catolicos* in conjunction with the *Guadalupanas* carried on the religious traditions revered by the Mexican people. The most important event was, and still is, the celebration of the feast of the Virgin of Guadalupe. The mass was followed by a procession from the church to the school's auditorium to see a play produced by the parishioners concerning the appearance of the Virgin to the Indian, Juan Diego. After the play, the ladies usually served a Mexican dinner.

Very few social services were available for Mexicans in the early years. These societies also attempted to fill in the gap by providing the people of the barrio with medical assistance, legal aid, financial help, housing information, and employment counseling. Thus, they were involved in the civil rights movement even then.

Several Spanish newspapers were published, and Spanish radio shows were broadcast at that time. The Spanish papers did not succeed, perhaps for lack of money. Recently, however, a new Spanish newspaper, NOSOTROS, has been published and seems to be thriving. The Spanish radio shows have been very popular in Detroit. Today there are six: *Serenata De Mi Barrio* (A Serenade to My Neighborhood) is a daily morning show featuring music; *Mañanitas Mejicanas* (Mexican Mornings) is a Sunday morning show with music and news; *Los Latinos* (The Latin Americans) is broadcast three days a week and features a popular young announcer; *Mejico Musical* (Musical Mexico), *La Hora de Olivia Galan* (The Olivia Galan Hour), and *Música, Alegria y Canciónes* (Music, Joy, and Songs) are broadcast once a week and play mostly *música nortena* (Mexican polka music). A new radio program about to be introduced to the community will be produced by a college group called *Latino En Marcha* (Latins on the March). Their program will be aired over Wayne State University's radio station and called *El Grito de Mi Raza* (The Cry of My People). It will include music, news, and interviews with Chicanos from the barrio.

Labor unions

While the community organizations were keeping cultural traditions alive, a leadership training process was taking place in the labor unions. The Mexican population grew steadily during the war production years of the 1940s through the boom years of the middle 1950s. Most Mexican men were laborers in factories; factories were quickly being unionized. By the middle of the 1950s, Detroit was a union city. The emergence of powerful, organized labor unions in the 1950s was to be a significant factor for the Mexican community in the 1960s.

The American Federation of Labor–Congress of Industrial Organizations (AFL-CIO), the United Auto Workers (UAW), and the United Steelworkers of America (USA) proved to be powerful forces with sophisticated political action committees who promised and delivered votes in important elections.[5] Recognizing the importance of political action, the unions had set about training their members in organizational skills. Mexican factory workers learned the meaning of organizing and began to organize their own people in order to move into elected union positions. An example is the Great Lakes Steel Corporation located in Ecorse. Mexican labor leaders at Great Lakes Steel organized a bargaining bloc within the union in order to successfully elect Mexican men as committeemen, grievance men, and shop stewards.

Union involvement could not have happened at a better time. The civil rights movement was beginning to make great strides. The 1967 Detroit riots blasted the Anglo community out of its "It won't happen here" attitude. National attention was focused on black demands for equal opportunities in employment, education, social services, housing, and so on. In Detroit, where blacks number about 45 percent of the population, immediate attention was given to their increasing demands, and New Detroit, Inc., was formed. This civic group brought together the industrial giants of the city: Henry Ford II, president of the Ford Motor Company; Lynn Townsend, president of Chrysler Corporation; James Roche, president of General Motors; Joseph L. Hudson, president of Hudson's Department Stores; Max Fisher, industrialist; Walter Cisler, president of Edison; Stanley Winkleman, president of Winkleman Stores; and many others who sought to save the city from any further devastation from rioting.

Assumption of leadership by Chicanos

Although most of the burning and looting occurred in the black neighborhoods, there was riot activity in the barrio, where Mexican and Appalachian whites took advantage of the opportunity to vent their anger and frustration. The Mexican union men stepped in and assumed leadership for their community. They began to analyze the community's social, political, and economic problems and to develop plans that would include Latinos in all new city programs. They began to explore the possibilities of creating an agency within the community, staffed by *mejicanos,* that would deal with these specific problems. The need for social services, educational programs, economic development, and political representation was long overdue. Two options became apparent: either established institutions would have to hire Mexican personnel to begin to deal with problems directly related to *mejicanos* or a similar institution within the community would have to be created to serve as a liaison between the community and outside service institutions.

The *patrones* (self-appointed leaders) of the community had made many overtures to Anglo agencies, with little or no success. The lesson the Latino community had to learn was that Anglo institutions recognize and relate to similar institutions rather than to individuals. By the end of 1968 it was apparent that no resources would flow into the Chicano community unless a well-organized effort was undertaken.

In 1968 the Archdiocese of Detroit allocated $1 million for program monies for the black community; none of it was earmarked for the Latin-American community. The *mejicanos* of one Roman

Catholic parish arranged a meeting with their priests to discuss how to channel some of that money into the barrio. They invited the chairman of the Latin Americans United for Political Action (LA-UPA) who was an employee of the Great Lakes Steel Corporation and an active unionist in the USA. Although the parish priests called the first meeting and hoped it would become a parish group, the people had other ideas. They took control of the meetings, set up a steering committee, and invited representatives from all the Chicano clubs in every parish. Representatives from twenty clubs joined in the struggle to bring church funds to the barrio.

Formation of LA SED

Three members of the steering committee were appointed to write a proposal as soon as possible; one was a priest, the other two were members of the USA. The proposal was written, approved, signed by the steering committee, and presented to the Archdiocese. It called for $48,000 to create an organization that would serve as a multiple-service center dealing specifically with Chicano problems. The Church could hardly say no to such a modest request after its $1 million commitment to the black community. The proposal was approved, and Latin Americans for Social and Economic Development (LA SED) became a reality.

The next step was to appoint a board of directors. The original board consisted of six members—president, vice-president, secretary, treasurer, and two trustees; all were chosen from the original steering committee. All were active union men.

The first director of LA SED hired by the board of directors was one of the original proposal writers, a strong union man who was at that time a member of the executive board of his local, the editor of the union paper, the chairman of the union education and incentive committee, and the chairman of LAUPA. His staff at LA SED included a full-time secretary and two field representatives.

LA SED became operational in April 1969 in a one-room storefront. The field representatives handled problems related to public assistance, police brutality, immigration, housing, employment, driver's licenses, and so forth. The director's task was to legitimize LA SED in the eyes of city and state agencies and to persuade these agencies to bring their services into the barrio. Within six months the director obtained $10,000 from New Detroit, Inc. to buy an old, vacant bank building. It was renovated and remodeled at cost by local unions.

LA SED is a nonprofit corporation. It has 501-03 tax exempt status and is completely controlled and run by the Chicano community. It is the first Chicano institution in Detroit to successfully compete for program monies. LA SED has given the Latin-American community a recognized and respectable institutional voice. The building today not only houses LA SED's staff of five members but also provides space for the Michigan Employment Security Commission, Neighborhood Legal Services, Consumer Protection Service, Michigan Civil Rights Commission, the Neighborhood Youth Corps, and the Social Security Aid Office. This is a total of thirteen full-time service people; most of them are of Latin extraction, but several are Caucasian and black bilingual personnel. The funding of LA SED has been assumed by the United Community Service, a United Fund agency, and its permanency seems to be assured.

Development of the Latin American Secretariat

Detroit has a dedicated group of priests and nuns in the barrio who are completely bilingual and have chosen to side with the people at the risk of being censured by the Church. Soon after LA SED was established, this group of church people met once again with community leaders to discuss the creation of an office within the Archdiocese that would truly represent and relate to all Latinos in the state. The church people were spurred on by the growing frustration that they and the Church were still not doing enough. The Church, with its tremendous resources and prestige, should not be allowed to become complacent because it had contributed a modest $48,000 to LA SED.

A core group of six people from the community asked for a meeting with the Bishop. They were instructed to write a constitution, document the needs of Chicanos in various counties, and submit a proposal for such a community office. Such a proposal was promptly written and submitted to the Human Relations Council for the Archdiocese. It was not approved. The reason given was that no funds were available for such an office. The members of the group decided to do some rejecting of their own. They rejected the decision of the Human Relations Council and once again petitioned the Bishop for a hearing. More determined than ever, they called every area in the Archdiocese with a Chicano community and requested two representatives from each. Twenty representatives from eight counties responded. The Bishop and the Human Relations Council met with the twenty laymen, two priests, and two nuns. In June 1969 the Church acquiesced to their demands. The important issue was the decision to establish an autonomous Latin American Office within the Archdiocese to be responsible only to the Bishop.

On July 1, 1969 the Latin American Secretariat was officially opened in downtown Detroit. The small staff consisted of the executive director who was a union man from the United Steelworkers, an assistant, and a secretary. The Executive Board was appointed by the Cardinal and comprised the twenty laymen, two priests, and two nuns. After their first-year appointment, the officers of the board will be elected by the Latin-American community for two-year terms. The officers include a chairman, vice-chairman, secretary, and treasurer. The board of directors informs the Secretariat of the needs of the local community, and together they pick the target area and plan what action to take in any given situation.

The mandate of the Secretariat is twofold. It represents the local Chicanos in formal negotiations with the Church, the city, and the state, and it is a voice for the Latino community. The Secretariat's second major task is the referral of personal and community problems to proper agencies. It acts as a lobbyist for the local inhabitants, using the prestige of the Church to support its position. It has established satellite centers in various communities to deal at the grass-roots level with problems affecting the migrant farmworkers and Chicanos who have left the migrant stream to settle in Michigan.

The Detroit office concentrates on securing monies for educational and leadership programs for the various areas. In the summer of 1971, it sponsored a three-day leadership training conference. Ninety Chicano families from throughout the state participated in workshops and discussions, reacted to speakers from around the state, and watched movies and filmstrips dealing with Chicano affairs around the country. It was a new experience for many of the participants.

The Secretariat, along with LA SED, has been influential in broadening the policies of New Detroit, Inc., which, as noted earlier, came into existence because of the riots of 1967. The New Detroit board was composed of forty-nine members; more than twelve were from the black community but there was not one Chicano representative. This gross disregard brought swift action from the Chicanos. Letters, petitions, statements to the press, and pressure from LA SED and the Secretariat prompted New Detroit, Inc. to take a second look at its composition and to rectify its mistake by including the Chicano community in its plans. It appointed Mexican representatives to every subcommittee. Without the existence of LA SED and the Secretariat to inspire and generate concerted action, this step forward would not have been possible. The Secretariat has thus far aided in placing Chicanos in twenty city agencies.

Committee of Concerned Spanish-Speaking Americans

In 1968 the Mexican teachers and the grass-roots activists formed a committee to investigate educational problems. The news media followed the activities of the group closely and called it the Committee of Concerned Spanish Americans; this name did not appeal to most members, but it stuck because of the publicity and because the group included Cubans and Puerto Ricans. The name has since been changed to the Committee of Concerned Spanish-Speaking Americans. Today, CCSSA is recognized as the spokesman in educational matters. Working closely with LA SED and the Secretariat, it has successfully lobbied for an intensive teacher training program for the Spanish speaking that raised the number of Mexican teachers in the barrio from two to twenty-nine within one year. CCSSA also organized a slate consisting of representatives of the major ethnic groups in the area (Mexican, Polish, Negro) for the regional school board election and almost succeeded in getting the first *mejicano* elected to such a position. The fact that Chicanos were involved in this political race has increased respect for and awareness of Chicano demands. CCSSA negotiated and won from the board of education in March 1971 the right to send a Chicano representative to recruit in New Mexico and Texas for bilingual teachers for the Detroit region. It then requested that such recruiting be included on the permanent list of procedures for the board. Unfortunately the recruitment effort in the Southwest was not successful, and the board of education is reluctant to try again.

At the insistence of CCSSA, two new classes have been introduced at a high school that has 17 percent Chicano students. The

Spanish heritage class is designed to teach the reading and writing
of Spanish along with the study of Mexican culture. The Latin-
American history class deals with all the Spanish-speaking countries.
The idea for these two classes met with a great deal of enthusiasm
from students and parents. However, the high school did not have
personnel qualified to teach such classes, and students have expressed much disappointment in how the classes are conducted and
by whom. Chicano educators have written a new proposal to establish a real Chicano Studies program at the school, taught by Chicano
teachers. Although it was approved, implementation depends on
whether the school budget passes in 1972; chances for the proposed
mill rate are very slim. CCSSA is bracing itself for a new fight.

Sensitivity workshops for area teachers was another CCSSA recommendation. Mexican parents were brought in as consultants. At last
Mexican mothers had an opportunity to educate teachers about *nuestra cultura* (our culture) and to voice their opinions about local
school curriculum. The old way of keeping quiet and allowing the
school to decide what is best for children is disappearing. Mexican
mothers visit the schools, sit in on classes, help in the program planning, and seem to enjoy every minute of it. In several schools, the
summer fiesta is becoming a regular event. The ladies prepare *tacos,
enchiladas,* and *tamales.* The breaking of the *piñata* is a favorite
game with all the children. Anglos in the barrio, both teachers and
neighbors, are learning about Chicano culture from the people themselves rather than from books. The CCSSA has been instrumental in
changing the educative process but it does not neglect other civic
affairs. For example, it participates in the neighborhood Fourth of
July parade. Each year it enters a float depicting a historical or cultural aspect of Mexico. In 1971, it won first prize with a float decorated
to resemble the floating gardens of Xochimilco.

Political life

The Michigan chapter of *La Raza Unida* was organized in 1968.
The Detroit chapter is even newer, but it is working diligently to
unite the different groups to speak as one voice on important issues.
Members of CCSSA, *el Circulo Mutualista,* G.I. Forum, American
Post 505, *Caballeros Catolicos, el Comite Patriotico, las Cursillistas,*
and the Brown Berets meet on the first Friday of the month at the

Latin American House to report on their activities, discuss current issues, and formulate new policies affecting the community. *La Raza* hopes to plant deep roots in the community and move the Chicano cause *adelante* (forward).

A new type of politics is emerging in the barrio. The patron system by which the community had to rely on the self-appointed leader, never very popular to begin with but nevertheless imposed on a people trying to adjust to a new environment, new roles, and a new life, has been cast aside. The *patrones* (patrons) have not given up easily. They too now call themselves Chicanos. A few have successfully formed their own organizations and have recruited many members. The point is that the old patron recognizes the mood of the community. The "I" in Chicano politics has changed to "We."

A look at the early political picture may explain why the Mexican people of Detroit have had no political power. Political involvement began through the efforts of LAUPA and were mostly fund-raising activities and candidate promotion for Democrats in major city, state, and national campaigns. Mayoral candidates, gubernatorial candidates, aspiring councilmen, judges, and so on were paraded through the barrio and introduced to the people, usually at a dance or fiesta. LAUPA was not consulted or included in candidate selection, but was merely used for promotional purposes.

By the early 1960s the Chicanos from the United Steelworkers union began to move into the political sphere. At the same time the "patron politicians" appeared, calling themselves the voice of the community. Articulate, better educated than the majority of the barrio people, it was easier for them to be heard and accepted by the Anglo society. They did not consult with the people even though they professed to speak for them. They did not attempt to register Chicanos or politically educate them, and, as a result, they were never very successful in delivering votes or gaining political power, except for a few minor appointments for themselves and a certain amount of personal prestige. It was, however, politically wise to have minority people visible during campaigns, so the "patron politicians" were used by the party to give the illusion that the party was addressing itself to all minorities. As the Chicano community began to grow politically sophisticated, dissatisfaction with the *patrones* grew.

The union men, who had been building up their strength, decided to act in 1968. To test their strength they ran two Chicanos for councilmen in two suburbs. The candidate for the city of Ecorse lost his first bid for election but came back to win the second time and is still in office. The other candidate in Riverview, Michigan, won and became a candidate for mayor.

At the State Democratic Convention held in Grand Rapids in 1970, the union men ran a Chicano for the board of governors of Wayne State University. Chicanos from all over the state were contacted and persuaded to add their support. This new political element alarmed and surprised the other candidates. There was little chance to win, but the union men wanted to demonstrate they had enough votes to affect the election. The strategy of the Chicano Caucus at that convention lead to the development of a Chicano Studies program at Wayne State University. The Caucus threw its support behind the two candidates who were most sympathetic to its educational goals. LA SED had written a proposal for a leadership training program which it hoped New Detroit, Inc. would fund. It had already appealed to Wayne University for assistance in developing the training components; now it could count on support from the board of governors.

Latino En Marcha

LA SED named the new program *Latino En Marcha* (Latins on the March), succeeded in obtaining funds from New Detroit, Inc., and enlisted the services of a local Chicano professor at Monteith College to take over the actual implementation. A selection committee consisting of Chicano teachers, students, and grass-roots people screened and selected forty applicants for the program. The forty prospective students included recent graduates, veterans, housewives, and adults in their early twenties who had been out of school three or four years. They were selected on the basis of their past involvement in community activities, their interest in Chicano history and culture, and their willingness to continue serving the community. High school records were reviewed but not considered the primary criteria for selection; in fact, many of those selected had barely a D average at graduation.

The students were to attend classes in Chicano history and culture and social and political problems of the barrio and to assist in research projects which would uncover the most serious problems of the community. The director concluded that this was truly more than a leadership training program. The academic work required was considerable. Why not give the students college credit and Wayne University the opportunity to be truly responsive to the Chicano community? The idea appealed to all the students.

It was not easy to persuade the University to accept the idea. There were many problems concerning admission of what Wayne termed "substandard students." Other problems involved securing financial aid, hiring Chicano personnel, and meeting operating expenses, but the support of two of the board governors made *Latino En Marcha* a reality. After completing the first year, the students of *Latino En Marcha* had: (1) established an educational information center at the LA SED building to assist any Latino, young or old, who wants to continue his education; (2) established a scholarship fund which is quickly growing through the efforts of both students and community people; (3) acquired radio time at Wayne University's WDET and begun airing a weekly show called *El Grito De Mi Raza;* (4) begun plans to write an in-depth history of the barrio and its people; (5) pushed through a Latino Studies program at Monteith College with permanent funding by Wayne University which will admit a minimum of thirty Latino students beginning September 1973; and (6) pressured the University into hiring a Chicano recruiter.

These achievements may seem minor to Chicanos in the Southwest, but in the Midwest they are significant accomplishments by a minority group that is small, scattered, and almost invisible to the Anglo world. Small wonder that there is great pride in the community in the *Latino En Marcha* program.

The efforts of LA SED and the Latin American Secretariat of the Archdiocese of Detroit have also been responsible for placing key people in the Justice Department, the Civil Rights Commission, and the Department of Migrant Education. There is still much to be done, and no Detroit Chicano is foolish enough to believe that the road ahead will be easy. Serious problems still exist within the community and within the leadership. There is still too much division, petty jealousies, and quarreling among the different factions. But one thing is clear; Detroit Chicanos are on the move, striving in the same spirit of *Aztlan* and *La Raza* of the Southwest for freedom and justice for all our people.

Notes

1 Carey McWilliams, *North From Mexico: The Spanish-Speaking People of the United States* (New York: Greenwood Press, 1948), p. 184.
2 Willard A. Heaps, *Wandering Workers* (New York: Crown Publishing Co., 1968), p. 155.
3 Willis F. Dunbar, *Michigan: A History of the Wolverine State* (Grand Rapids: W. B. Erdmans Publishing Co., 1965), p. 575.
4 McWilliams, *North From Mexico,* p. 222.
5 Dunbar, *Michigan,* p. 605.

Socioeconomic and Cultural Conditions of Migrant Workers

Faustina Solis

The plaintive and indignant cry of the migrant farm worker is at last being heard in our rapidly advancing technological society. A poem by Ricardo Sanchez expresses the migrant's mood.

as visualized
by ever being
mexi-colored moods
vis-à-vis
america the
hurt-in-full

and brother,
i can tell you
picking cotton
in texas
is as rotten
as picking it
in alabam . . .

and
i can tell,
my brothers,
how it is
you also hurt

when
it
is
the same
for me . . .

i am
the
sum
and
total
of
social brutalization . . .[1]

For many years the humanistic goals of the United States have seemed incompatible with the indifference manifested toward the deplorable living and working conditions of the migrant population. The insignificant power of this group, as well as the fact that field workers are usually recruited from among those ranking lowest in socioeconomic status, have enabled the nation to dismiss collectively the hardships imposed by the migrant way of life.

It is not the purpose of this article to dwell in detail on the plight and problems of the seasonal and agricultural migratory populations; their hardships have been grippingly and dramatically reported since the early 1900s. The purpose is to delineate major socioeconomic and cultural factors that are basic for an understanding of the farm workers' efforts to utilize services and mobilize their own quests for a viable community. Focus will be on the worker of Mexican descent or the citizens of Mexico living or working in the Southwest.

Unfortunately, statistics concerning the agricultural migratory population are generally unreliable. Data collection methods are questionable because most sources of information document a partial sample of the population. Ethnic, age, and sex distribution is usually not available, and the counts on migrants are not consistently kept for peak and low harvest months. A discussion of the ethnic backgrounds of migratory workers before the Senate Subcommittee on Migratory Labor in April 1970 suggested that only 40 percent of the labor force is made up of members of minority groups (Mexican and black).[2] This estimate undoubtedly ignores the increases in commuter, "green carder" (resident alien), and illegal entry migrants from Mexico.

Historical overview

The increasing need for a constant labor supply for the developing agricultural areas in the country, particularly in the southwestern states, initiated the importation of foreign laborers primarily from China, Japan, and the Philippines from the late 1870s through the 1920s. The Mexican immigrants hired as laborers at the turn of the century were primarily employed as members of "extra gangs" and as section hands on the railroads. Approximately 90 percent of the Mexicans immigrating to the United States between 1920 and 1928 were unskilled laborers. A "cheap" farm labor supply therefore became readily available.

During the mid-1930s, residents of the Great Plains states and other areas, who either fled from the drought or sought employment during the depression era, constituted another significant supply of migrant farm laborers to the West. Thousands of people from Oklahoma, Arkansas, Texas, Arizona, Missouri, and Kansas moved westward to augment an already burgeoning labor supply.

In 1942 foreign labor importation legislation was passed as an emergency measure to assure the harvesting of crops during the war years. The *bracero* (farm laborer) imported from Mexico produced a dependable labor supply in California and other southwestern states for over twenty years. Following the repeal of this legislation in 1964, attention had to be directed toward hiring the existing domestic labor supply. The foreign labor importation legislation had given rise to expressed dissatisfaction by domestic farm workers. Contractual benefits guaranteed to the *bracero* but not available to the domestic worker were a minimum wage, housing, medical care, and transportation to and from the border. There were instances, however, when contractual agreements were violated and exploitative maneuverings resulted against *braceros*.

Unionization of farm workers

The National Labor Relations Act, enacted in 1935, excluded agricultural workers from its basic coverage, which guaranteed the right to organize or not, to bargain collectively through representation of choice, and to engage in those activities that promoted mutual assistance and protection. The reasons for excluding the agricultural labor force from the enforcement of this act have never been quite clear, although it is generally assumed that the exclusion stemmed from political rather than from administrative factors. The farm lobby was powerful and strongly opposed this legislation.

Despite the lack of substantive support from the National Labor Relations Board, which is responsible for the enforcement of the act, sporadic attempts were made in the last four decades to organize farm labor. These efforts resulted in repeated failures, which perhaps were due to the fact that trade union methods were used to organize workers. Because most farm workers were unfamiliar with these techniques, it was necessary to import professional organizers who invariably left the area defeated by such overwhelming obstacles as politically powerful farmers, forming ruthless opposition that at times threatened their lives, and a farm labor force, grossly lacking in organizational skills and caught desperately in a struggle for survival.

These professional organizers failed not because they lacked organizational prowess or commitment but because they were unwilling to modify their approach for agricultural workers. They failed to observe how the workers' strong social and cultural values were inconsistent with the patterns of trade unionism, and, most important, they did not develop able leadership within the ranks of farm laborers themselves.

In the early 1960s, two important developments took place in farm worker organization. Both took place in California, the setting for numerous past unionization efforts and particularly suitable for union organizing because of several factors: (1) the state employs more farm workers and pays higher wages than other states; (2) agriculture is one of the state's top industries because of its gross receipts; and (3) there is year-round and seasonal harvesting, as well as a large variety of crops grown.

The first important development occurred in 1960, when the Agricultural Workers Organizing Committee (AWOC), in an attempt to seek more effective methods of stimulating unionization, directed its efforts to include labor contractors. At about the same time César Chávez organized the National Farm Workers Association (NFWA). Chávez believed that the initial job of the association was to organize farm workers in a community of interests and endeavors that would instill in them a greater sense of self-worth and confidence and would enrich the quality of their family and community lives. Integrated into the plan was the development of leadership on various levels of activities. The organization was formed intentionally as an association because many workers had witnessed or experienced punitive measures following abortive attempts at union organization and were thus fearful of unions. Chávez's efforts were more effective because of his identification with the ethnic and cultural patterns of the farm labor force. He was keenly aware of the long process of community evolvement that would have to precede the constructive participation of the farm worker. Formal programs of community training in management and organizational skills were launched. When the first labor dispute arose in Delano in 1965, the NFWA had the backing of a small but strong contingent of farm workers well aware of the price their commitment would cost them and their families.

In 1966 a merger of AWOC and NFWA resulted in the United Farm Workers Organizing Committee (UFWOC). Members are primarily California resident farm workers—seasonal and migrant. It would not have been organizationally feasible to concentrate on interstate migrants as a resource for early membership, although these workers are joining the committee in increasing numbers.

Simultaneous with the activities to seek nationwide support for *La Causa* was the necessary task of recruiting professional and non-professional staff and volunteers to organize in those areas still unfamiliar to the workers—effective picketing, organization of boycotts, use of mass media communications, and fund raising. Grassroots impact was demonstrated in the setting of priorities in union negotiations, in the implementation of the Robert Kennedy Health Plan, and in the continuing development of Forty Acres, a community complex of employment, social, legal, and health services operated and maintained by union membership.

The present UFWOC membership, which is not so numerous as the general public might surmise, may constitute less than 15 percent of the total agricultural force in California. There are significant numbers of farm workers who are not UFWOC sympathizers and others who remain distrustful of unionization. It is significant, however, that the reawakening of the public conscience to long-standing injustices took place only when farm workers could express themselves through an organization.

Current conditions

The more than one million migrant agricultural workers and their dependents in this country—including the blacks and Puerto Ricans who are currently available as farm workers on the eastern seaboard and in the middle western states—have estimated annual family incomes ranging from $1,400 to $3,600. During harvest periods the families may not be eligible for public assistance or medical care. They continue to live in substandard, dilapidated housing with inadequate sanitation facilities and are exposed to environmental hazards that breed disease. Local educational programs and attitudes of school personnel discourage rather than encourage the participation of the migratory children and youth in the schools. The rate of infant mortality and the incidence of morbidity of certain disease categories are higher than in any other occupational group. Occupational injuries in agriculture are second only to those in the construction industry.

Migrant workers are usually surrounded by a society that is insensitive to them, to their problems, and to their aspirations, values, and needs. They have no political power because their mobility and economic struggles do not allow them to establish the community cohesiveness that is essential both to organization and to the mobilization of political effort. Migrant farm workers are discriminated against by the dominant group and often by their own ethnic group. Historically they have been considered desirable as laborers but not as citizens. It is, therefore, difficult for this population to believe that perseverance and hard work will insure financial success.

Employment patterns

Four general types of migrant farm laborers can be identified according to employment patterns: (1) United States resident families that have depended on migrancy in agricultural work for two or three successive generations and consider themselves locked into the system for the future; (2) seasonal agricultural workers who do not wish to pursue their lives as farm workers but whose circumstances, such as their limited skills and their responsibility for support of their families, allow little time and funds to pursue other educational, training, or employment endeavors; (3) workers who want to stop doing farm work but must reenter the migrant labor force periodically because of fluctuations in the general labor market; and (4) workers whose homes are in Mexico or "green carders" whose earnings in the United States are considerably higher than the wages they could possibly earn in Mexico. Attitudes toward farm labor will vary within the group, depending on mobility patterns, distances traveled, and opportunities for upgrading of employment in home base areas. Not all farm workers consider their plight irreversible. The spectrum of attitudes is wide, ranging from quiet resignation to demonstrated impatience for raising the status and opportunities for farm workers through organizational methods. Workers as a whole do not consider farm labor a degrading occupation, but they do consider the conditions under which they work degrading.

Competition and some animosity exist between local seasonal agricultural workers and workers from Mexico. The worker whose home base is Mexico tends to express less dissatisfaction with his working and living conditions. He isolates himself more from the domestic migrant community and the community at large. His lack of proficiency in English, as well as the strangeness of institutional structures, creates for him a world of uncertainties. He relies heavily on his countrymen and relatives for advice.

Migrants whose homes are in Texas and Arizona usually establish a pattern of mobility built through their own experiences or through envoys who make explorative visits to evaluate promising harvest areas and to make housing arrangements. The ability to negotiate employment is one general indicator of the worker and his family's increasing ability to identify opportunities and services within the communities. Families or individuals who negotiate their work through labor contractors and crew leaders narrow their interaction with the community and know less about their benefits because they depend on employers to assist them.

Workers on the move are seldom known to take risks. They have developed a communications system for passing along information regarding matters that enhance or threaten their economic survival. Unlike most of the single men who travel alone, families traveling separately tend to follow the itineraries of other families from their home states. Migrant workers do not always take unfamiliar co-workers into their confidence, and, therefore, important helpful information may not reach all workers in one specific location. Workers also may not divulge even innocuous information about neighbors and relatives; they do not wish to give information that may be used against one or all of them at some future date.

Although the origin of residence may differ considerably in the groupings described, the economic plight is severe for all. Even for those workers who regularly return to the same fields of harvest with the same employers, economic uncertainty looms annually. The winter months cause an accumulation of debts—particularly for food, transportation, and emergency medical care. There is always talk about whether winter frosts, too much rain, or an early spring will ruin crops or will precipitate their ripening. Reaching a harvest area to find that a crop may be two or three weeks late for picking can be catastrophic for a family whose financial resources at hand may not be sufficient to cover one week's living costs.

In recent years alternative considerations have been given to planning for family mobility. As a result, there has been an array of groupings—single, unattached men or women, partial familes that may include one older person to care for the very young, and total families, especially when contracts are made for "family crops." Family crops include selected tree crops, such as cherries, and row crops, such as berries and cucumbers; farmers with these crops can usually employ all family members who are able to work.

The family that travels together may not always stay together. The Mexican family resists camping in orchards, river beds, or ditches, but when there is a need for two or more units in a crowded farm labor center, some members of the family may have to be distributed among relatives and friends not residing in the center. The family computes its earnings as a group. In fact, it is not uncommon for the father to compute all earnings under his social security number, not understanding the individual benefits that may accrue to all other members if each were to use his own number. Accepting wage deductions today for benefits in the far future is a difficult concept, particularly when the future, as well as the benefits, is undependable and uncertain.

Social and cultural considerations

Common to most farm worker groupings is the dominance of Mexican tradition, with its more conservative behavior patterns. Because mobility does not encourage close and intimate friendships, there tends to be great reliance on family dependency and independence from the surrounding community. The reluctance of some parents to send children to school may be based on economic need. Nevertheless, the economic need may be a guise to keep children and youth from losing respect for their families and their cultural inheritance, which many parents believe to be the primary mission of some schools. As Chicanos, these parents have experienced discrimination on many levels, and their perception of continued harassment colors the degree to which they will allow any intervention with their families. Generally, however, they hope for improved opportunities for their children and, therefore, support educational endeavors. Departure from and return to the home base are planned with schooling in mind, and it is not infrequent for adolescents to be sent home with younger children so that they can start school while their parents remain to pick the autumn harvest.

If one were to generalize about this population, one could say that migrants are individualistic and self-sufficient. Their physical pain or emotional agony must be unbearable before they seek assistance; for their children, however, they will often seek help earlier. Their endurance tolerance is such that children, rarely hearing their parents complain of their hurts, will also endure pain and discomfort.

Individuals and families that follow the crops learn to adapt to new surroundings but maintain their own system of values. The farm worker acknowledges his fear and despair, at times expressing powerlessness to effect change in his life. His demands and his expectations are minimal. His approach to services, when they do exist, is one of skepticism. He is unable to adjust to the values of those providing services, which, in essence, he is expected to do, although reciprocal understanding is not always evident. He is often described by agency workers as unobtrusive, undemanding, and easy to work with. His demeanor may well be a method for limiting unwelcome intrusions into his life.

Patterns of services

Although services have been provided sporadically for migrant populations for several decades, they have been limited in scope and usually have been under the auspices of voluntary agencies. Unless special funds are appropriated, public services appear to be incidental, accidental, or provided to meet only certain crisis situations. Agencies, as well as communities, do not consider specialized services for migrants important. They too believe that migrants should be educated to avail themselves of all mainstream services as do other citizens. In reality, of course, migrants cannot be compared to other citizens.

In the last decade, legislation enacted on behalf of the poor has earmarked funds for seasonal and agricultural workers and their families. Particularly important have been the Migrant Health Act of 1963, the Economic Opportunity Act of 1964, and federal grants for compensatory education which provide special educational programs to migrant children. The latter include remedial education as well as preschool and day care services; day care facilities have offered social services as a fringe program component in some areas.

Needless to say, funding for crucially needed programs has been discouragingly limited and uncertain. Health funds available cannot possibly provide comprehensive health care for even 15 percent of the population in need. Because these funds, representing a decided improvement, are so limited, sponsors of services tend to concentrate their efforts in farm labor centers and definable migrant streams. In those states in which seasonal and migratory populations do not follow a stream but are dispersed over large geographic areas, hundreds of families remain unreached during peak harvest months.

Rural areas traditionally structure programs using the philosophy of service and staffing models of the urban areas and ignoring the following special features of the rural areas: lack of public transportation, distances, political barriers, and dearth of professional manpower. Little consideration is given to programming for people on the move, although all society has become increasing mobile. Social services are often designed for long-term activity. Families are not trusted to diagnose their own problems, and the service process is therefore unnecessarily prolonged and ineffectual. Services are expensive for the client even when he does not pay a fee. Free care is costly when the family must pay expenses for private transportation, interpreting, child care, and meals.

Broken appointments and failure to follow through with referrals are especially frustrating to professionals, but many professional workers are unaware that referrals undergo a series of procedural steps when they involve migrants or residents new to an area. Before a final disposition is made, the referral is usually discussed both with family members and friends or relatives whom the individual trusts.

A public health nurse could not understand a note that was left for her by a bilingual community health worker, which read: "Mrs. G has not had time to talk with Mrs. C about your referral to the clinic; therefore, at her request, I cancelled her appointment for today's clinic." The explanation is quite simple when it is understood. Mrs. G would like to consider following through with the referral, enough to seek the counsel of her friend, Mrs. C. If her friend has not attended the clinic, she would locate, if possible, more than one person who had attended and would report on the services.

Mrs. G could then make her decision on the basis of additional knowledge.

Contributing to the lack of communication between social workers and migrant clients are the differing definitions they give to the word *crisis,* which reflect, of course, basic differences in their value systems. A family may experience severe anxiety and panic because it will not be in Texas when a relative is scheduled to arrive. The social worker may be more concerned about the fact that the family is not seeking needed medical care for a particular condition.

The description that migrants and other poor people give of agencies is noteworthy. While working as project director at the Farm Workers Health Service, Berkeley, California, the writer was assigned a Spanish-speaking international social worker for placement. As an orientation to a California rural community, the worker was asked to assess the need for a day care center in a specific migrant neighborhood. Purposefully no explanation was given to her of voluntary and public agencies and how they function in the state. She was to learn about services from the people in the community. After two weeks she called the writer, troubled that the people did not know what a social worker was and that many of them did not know that public services, such as public health services, existed. She was also troubled by the fact that most people identified an agency through the services received from the efforts of a particular worker rather than through an understanding, even theoretical, of the scope of services provided by the agency. From what families reported, she had identified youth corrections as residential centers for emotionally disturbed youth and the welfare department as a correctional system. Most astounding to her was the number of serious problems that had gone unattended because they were either not identified or because the family resisted acknowledging them to professionals in the neighborhood, fearing that it would lose all power to make decisions.

Attitudes toward recipients of service are also reflected in facilities and their arrangements. Poor people and those who work with them are the endurance testers for facilities that are inadequately equipped, crowded, unattractive, and depressing but that are expected to provide quality services. Complaints lodged against facilities center primarily on the reception areas, in which clients are stripped of all their dignity. The lack of privacy—a luxury that many families cannot afford in their own housing arrangements—is more acutely experienced when they seek assistance.

The social work task

The task facing social work today is immense and its position is precarious.

> When a class of our citizens—farm workers—are not able to drive its roots into a community; when they can be driven out of farm labor camps, as they were after World War II; when they can be told there are literally 200 crop areas in California where they can expect no lodging if they are traveling with their families, [this] obviously creates the atmosphere in which services—social services—are needed, including social assistance and public health. . . . The migrant farm workers are a sand dune, and the winds that blow them from place to place are deliberately created by social and economic forces in our society.[3]

Although there has been inordinate and sometimes unjust criticism made of social work and its role in these changing times—particularly in economically deprived areas—there is also restiveness within the ranks of the profession itself. This restiveness threatens the profession even more than accusations made by the communities. It certainly demands a response. The dissatisfaction is not related to a specific agency or to a group of social workers whatever their specialty might be; it relates to the profession as a whole.

Is social work demonstrating a concerned, active, and assertive role in relation to broad social issues? It is folly to respond defensively to irresponsible accusations, but it is apparent that there is a societal and professional demand for reorganizing and redirecting skills. The duality of responsibility to the individual and to the community becomes even more intense because it is no longer possible to ignore the physical, social, and political reality of people's lives while trying to concentrate on symptoms and conditions that are created in great part by society. Social work can and must, through its advocacy programs, bring into partnership the providers and consumers of service. It must help to reorganize and reorder national and regional priorities for planning, programming, and implementing service mechanisms.

Migrant workers and the general farm labor community are striving for an opportunity to experience freedom in establishing a community that will allow the enjoyment of collective economic advantages, humane support, emotional and cultural contacts, and mutual understanding. The field of social work has keys to open the storehouse of limitless possibilities of assistance, advocacy, and action on behalf of people. The power that turns the keys, however, is not merely an understanding of individual and social behavior and social work methods but a disciplined commitment to people throughout cycles of social change.

Notes

1 Ricardo Sanchez, Mi Unica Manera de Virir, *El Grito,* 3:32 (Winter 1970). Reprinted by permission of the publisher.
2 U.S., Congress, Senate, Committee on Labor and Public Welfare, *Migrant and Seasonal Farm Worker Powerlessness, Hearings,* before a subcommittee of the Committee on Labor and Public Welfare, Senate, 91st Cong., 1st and 2d sess., 1970, Manpower and Economic Problems, Part 7-A, April 14, 1970, pp. 4094–98.
3 Ernesto Galarza, The Farm Laborer: His Economic and Social Outlook (Address to the Western Region Migrant Health Conference, University of California at Los Angeles, Los Angeles, Calif., June 26–28, 1967).

Communication: the Key to Social Change

Gloria López McKnight

Chicanos' identification with *La Causa* (The Cause) requires that we first ascertain who we are and from where we came. We must seek to communicate our history to one another and from our elders learn about our heritage and our culture. From them we can hear also the tales of the Alamo, the Mexican Revolution, Benito Juarez, Pancho Villa, and Emiliano Zapata. We must keep open the lines of communication between the generations and enable our *abuelitos* (grandparents) to relate to us *los cuentos de su juventud* (the tales of their youth).

Suppression of Mexican-American history

So many of us feel cut off from the past, confused with the present, and uneasy about the future. The Mexican American came into existence by default in 1848. Before that he belonged to the Republic of Mexico and earlier to Spain. Mexican-American history, in its 124 years, has been suppressed and distorted. Any history textbook will disclose the extent to which Mexican Americans have been completely ignored or, at best, treated negatively.

Distortion of our history has resulted from nativistic Anglo-Saxon

Protestants who are markedly different from us culturally and racially. The United States, soon after independence, was molded by many peoples; but the Anglo-Saxon attitude tended to minimize and suppress other cultural groups. The Anglo-Saxon minority sought to form an authentic American culture, and any other group was not admitted into the Anglo culture until it became Americanized. Mexican Americans tried to win acceptance by changing their names, shedding their accents, dyeing their hair, surrendering their language, discarding their past, denying their culture, and moving into the alien world of the Anglo. In the United States they were even permitted to classify themselves as "Caucasian."

We tend to regard ourselves as a conquered people rather than as immigrants who freely chose to come to the United States. Many of us are descended from families that lived in the Southwest for generations before the territory became part of the United States after the Mexican-American War. Others have forebears who fled Mexico in the wake of the Mexican Revolution or emigrated to escape the dire effects of poverty. We are therefore considered a new immigrant group. We are different, however, from other immigrant American groups because we are the only ethnic group with which the United States has been at war. The psychological aspects of being a conquered people can be found especially in Texas because the Texan Chicano can never forget the Alamo.

Mexico lies just across the border; therefore, the cultural ties of Mexican Americans with the homeland are stronger than they are for most descendants of European immigrants. We have retained qualities that impede our progress: the tendency to substitute *machismo* (manliness) rhetoric for action and the suspicion, nurtured by memories of Latin American politics, that every leader is a potential betrayer. Perhaps the incorporation of Chicano Studies at schools and universities will clarify our history and assist us to understand ourselves better.

We are one of the most mixed and complex groups of people in the United States. To some degree we are Indian, Spanish, German, French, and black. We come from many Indian groups, each of which is complex. In Spain there is a great variety of subgroups; perhaps that is why we have such difficulty in organizing and standing united. Intermarriage between Aztecs and the Spaniards, to cite one example, brought another combination into existence. Many Mexicans are black; this fact has been documented and proved.

Similarity in the music, clothes, and dances of Mexico reflects the Mexican-black thought. We are a cosmic race as we have everything in us.[1]

Our history is important, as is evidenced by the continued existence of the *Adelitas* of the Mexican Revolution.[2] The beautiful Chicanas are the mothers of the new generation and the sweethearts *del gran movimiento* (of the grand movement). The composer and musician Miguel Francisco Barragan has said, "Many are the valiant American women of Mexican descent in the urban and rural battlefronts of America. They, too, sacrifice for justice and seek equal opportunity for the oppressed." [3] His song, "Mujer Valiente," pays tribute to our revolutionary spirit and Aztec beauty.

Parental denial of cultural identity

So many of our parents in an honest effort to make a living have urged us to assimilate and have therefore deprived us of our history and *cuentos* (folktales) of the past. The phrases are familiar: "Don't learn Spanish; don't let them know you're a Mexican; just tell them you have a good tan; get lost in the crowd." Many Chicanos have achieved economic stability, especially if they shed their identities. Many have become accustomed to it and simply have become "lost." Nevertheless, somewhere, great Chicano architects, painters, and writers do exist.

Our lost brothers and sisters have been leading double lives trying to pretend to be what they are not. Denying one's true identity can have deleterious psychological effects. The parents must be told that the people want programs, that the people are tired of poverty, and that the people are no longer going to let themselves be ridiculed about their eating, speaking, or living habits.

Questions may be raised about the feelings of parents who have raised children who are ashamed of their own background and of their own parents. Denial of our culture, our language, and our heritage is denial of our own parents. Through this kind of questioning, *el movimiento* is going to gain even more momentum and induce some of our people to return home. They will be proud of being Chicanos. *Que viva La Raza!* (Long live the people!)

Consideration must be given to the older generation who still call themselves Mexican Americans. Many soldiers, during World War

II, fought hard to be recognized by that name. Many lost their jobs just to win that fight. The Chicano generation has become *el movimiento*. There need be no quarrel about terms. The important thing is that the generations relate to each other and communicate with each other. What matters is not the name but what each has to do in order to achieve unity of purpose through *La Causa Chicana*. *La raza nueva en marcha esta* (A new generation is now on the move).

Return to the barrio

In part, the solution to this problem is found in the fact that, in the search for our past, many of our prodigal sons are returning home. They were educated in the Anglo world, learned the strategy of social, economic, and political mobility and were therefore able to become an integral part of the established system. They are needed in the barrio to assist the mobility of *la gente humilde* (the humble people) and join in the upward journey of the people.

The three dominant motives inducing prodigal sons to return to *la communidad Chicana* (The Chicano community) are reawakening of pride in our people, economic development in *el barrio,* and embarrassment when they are confronted with such questions as "What is *La Causa?*," "What is a Chicano?," and "Are you really Spanish or Mexican?" Chicanos who deny their culture are now beginning to be sensitized by the movement. As the mass media start expounding it, the lost souls will increasingly be questioned concerning their identities. It is no longer in vogue to seek to conceal one's identity and culture.

Pride of identity

La Causa has provided a sense of identity. No longer need Mexican Americans hide behind assumed Anglo names or disavow their parents' heritage. *El movimiento* has produced an identity of which to be proud.

The rate of this return depends on the rapidity of *La Causa's* momentum across the nation. Not until recent years have Mexican Americans begun to identify with the word *Chicano* that the youth conferred upon this great awakening. Not all are, as yet, committed to *La Causa,* for some have been "lost" in the process of assimilation required for acceptance into the Anglo establishment. Not until all Mexican Americans return to the fold will there be a true *movimiento*.

Economic development

Entrepreneurs who located their businesses outside the barrio are returning with the knowledge that rehabilitation of the Chicano community will be providing a service as well as a business investment, circulating money back to *la gente* (the people) by improving the economic spectrum of the community. It is better for the Chicano businessman to make his services available to the community than for the people to pay an Anglo for these services. We must help our own. We also must develop our own electricians, builders, architects, and plumbers because the rehabilitation of housing will be one of the economic booms in the coming years.

Curiosity of Anglo

The Anglo is going to help *La Causa* indirectly because he is curious. He will want to know who and what we are. The Anglo does not know anything about us. So far, the Anglo majority has failed to respond. We Chicanos are the country's least known, albeit the second largest, ethnic minority in the United States.

For example, when *Advertising Age* magazine published an article about "El Frito Bandito," an advertising man from St. Louis wrote that he could not understand why the Chicano was so upset by the image projected by the "Frito Bandito" on the television screen. He thought Chicanos were too sensitive. He did not feel offended when Davy Crockett or Daniel Boone was made into a television series. However, another advertising man responded, "Yes, he did not have to feel offended by Davy Crockett or Daniel Boone because they were depicted as heroes on the television screen, NOT AS A BANDIT." [4]

Chicano family

The Chicano family has been stereotyped by the concepts of the *machismo* of the man and the submissiveness of the woman. It is an old myth that the female was to grow up to get married, bear children, and take care of the home. Not much effort was made to educate her because it was the duty of the male to maintain the home and be the "king" of the family. The Catholic Church's paternalistic attitude extensively influenced Chicano family life. Birth control was unheard of and the woman was to bear as many children as possible because they also enhanced the virility of the man. No thought was given to the ways in which the family was to be adequately clothed, fed, or educated. Often it was a means of survival for the family to have several children because most Chicanos had a rural background. To this day, this practice persists *con el campesino* (with the farm worker).

As the Chicano became more urbanized, the need for survival emphasized other criteria. The extensively large family is no longer a necessity because 80 percent of the Chicano families reside in an urban setting. Technological advancement has changed the employment pattern, and education has become more important to the Chicano for social and economic upward mobility. The average Chicano is poor. There is no substantial middle or upper class because, to an overwhelming degree, most Chicanos are unskilled workers—a crippling handicap in an increasingly professional and business-minded society. Chicanos are woefully undereducated. Despite the fact that Chicanos constitute the second largest minority group in this country, the need for bicultural and bilingual education was not recognized by the educational systems. Insistence on assimilation for acceptance in these United States unnecessarily caused surrender of a heritage, a culture, and a language. Accordingly, there is a lack of educated Chicanos to assist in the task of social, economic, and political development.

Ashamed to speak with an accent, many Mexican Americans denied their children the privilege of being bilingual. Those fortunate enough to have Spanish as their first language in the home were humiliated and degraded in the classroom by teachers and classmates who failed to understand and recognize the advantages of having two cultures and two languages, one complementing the other. The child became caught in a web, not knowing who was right or who was wrong. Many families even changed their names, from Martinez to Martin, for example, in an attempt to rid themselves of the stigma attached to being Chicano in an Anglo society.

Although the movement is gaining momentum, many Chicanos do not know what it means. As it receives recognition, more and more Chicanos experience a feeling of pride in saying, "I am Chicano *y que Viva La Causa*" (and long live the Cause). For too many years,

Chicanos have been a forgotten people, but that time is past. We now have something with which to identify ourselves—*el despertar de mi raza* (the reawakening of my people). We find ourselves occupying a place near the bottom of the national social, economic, and political ladder with no immediate prospects of moving up. We have occupied this place for years, comforted by close family ties and sustained by a Spanish-Catholic and Indian culture that taught us to accept our fate.

Urban renewal has threatened to destroy our way of life and to destroy Chicano institutions. However, other elements in our culture, such as the close kinship ties and the habit of cooperation, offer hope.

The struggle for recognition continues. Throughout the country, communities are organizing to gain the expertise necessary for economic and social advancement. Organizations put better education ahead of all other aims, with bilingual teaching in the primary grades as a priority goal. Yesterday's occasional college graduate tended to move gratefully into an Anglo society; today he frequently elects Chicano Studies and scours the barrio for college recruits. What the movement seeks is to improve our social and economic lot while preserving our traditional values. It is a difficult task for our communities have few resources.

Those who advanced themselves in the past tended to forsake their identity. Some moved to the midwestern industrial centers of St. Paul, Chicago, and Detroit, where relatively small clusters of Chicanos suffered little of the special discrimination produced by their denser concentration in the Southwest. Still other Chicanos moved out of the group socially, rather than spatially, a movement made possible by the existence of an old established upper class, dating back to the days of Spanish conquest, which identifies itself as Spanish American and which has traditionally remained aloof from both the Chicano peasantry and the Anglo upper class. A Chicano whose racial characteristics are Castillian enough and whose educational level is high enough can identify with this respected group, regardless of whether he actually joins it socially.[5]

Of importance to the Chicano community is the fact that both these forms of movement away from the group represent serious losses in potential leadership and in models for successful adaptation. An emerging middle class, which may have improved its lot while remaining within the Chicano group, has not reached significant numbers or status to assume effective leadership. Because leadership is difficult to assume in a group which is traditionally resistant to, and suspicious of, any attempts at organization, a lack of leaders has consistently been the greatest obstacle to the goal of the movement.

It is necessary to review the past to understand why this characteristic of our culture still exists. The form of leadership the Mexican peon best understood was lost with the breakdown of the patron-peon relationship, which was familiar throughout rural Mexico and in those northern reaches of the colonial empire that later became the American Southwest. The land-owning patron had been expected to take responsibility for the entire well-being of the peons and their families, providing employment, social and economic security, and leadership for those who did the manual work. The peons, in return, had been expected to give complete loyalty and cooperation, often to get necessary communal tasks done. Stripped of this secure and dependent position, the Chicano still often reflects the values and attitudes appropriate to the lost relationship. He prefers to leave major decisions to those with the prominence of wealth or political power equivalent to a patron's, feeling that such a person is best equipped to take the responsibility involved. He still prefers friendly person-to-person relationships in a stable hierarchical social system in which mutual obligations and statuses are clearly spelled out. He resists those social and cultural changes that require personal initiative in a competitive world.[6]

Importance of leadership

Chicano leadership is vital, but potential leaders must be educated and supported. Groups develop leaders, and leaders usually respond to the demands of the group. The kind of leadership needed must be defined. Are all the present leaders accountable to the community or are some of them *Tio Tacos* (those who ride the fence) selected because of their incompetence? It is known that many Chicanos have been selected for positions because a brown face is needed in the front. David Riesman says:

> A political position may become so conventional as a class or mass phenomenon that it is accepted by people of widely different character . . . people can be mistaken or misled for the "right" emotional reasons, and conversely they can hold unexceptionable positions despite a basic inappropriateness.[7]

The community has the responsibility of developing competent and intelligent leaders who can function and use their expertise to find the key to open the door for *La Causa* to achieve its goal.

Leaders may be seen as group functionaries, who develop certain social characteristics as a result of the influence of the group they lead and of their position in the group. Groups are likely to select as leaders those who have the educational background, the vocational skills, and the prestige to make them effective leaders. Participation itself tends to be a "trait." [8] Group leaders characteristically:

1. Participate more than the general population in organizations other than those in which they are leaders.

2. Are more likely to be members of a union, professional, or business group.

3. Are often participants in a range of voluntary associations other than those in which they are leaders.

4. Have more close friends than do persons in the general population and are more socially integrated.

5. Are much less alienated than the general population in regard to knowledge of how the social system works.

6. Are constantly acquiring social knowledge, and using it to lead or control or manipulate a segment of society, no matter how small or specialized.

7. Are more inclined to support civil liberties than is the general population and more inclined to support civil rights and are less prejudiced.

8. Have a clearer and more definite idea about their personal aspirations.

9. Are different only in degree and proportion, not in kind or absolutely, from the general population, and what differences there are are due to the leaders' more active social participation.[9]

The matter of leading is better viewed as a relationship between individuals than as a quality that some individuals "have" although "talents differ." [10] A few members of a group may adequately represent the attitudes and aspirations of the rank and file. Drives for prestige can be expressed by achieving influential positions in the group. Michels has noted that the holding of an office tends to become a customary right, and an individual will "remain in office unless removed by extraordinary circumstances or in obedience to rules observed with exceptional strictness." [11] Those "extraordinary circumstances," moreover, may be long postponed if the official appears to advance the group's interests sufficiently to make his continuance in office a gesture of decent gratitude on the part of his constituents or at least sufficiently to forestall intense dissatisfaction. "Authority," as John Gaus has observed, ". . . follows the successful exercise of function." [12] The authority, it should be added, may be much more extensive than the function so exercised.[13]

The Anglo society has demanded proof of Chicanos' ability to succeed on its terms, without having provided us with the economic and social supports with which to achieve success—supports on which the rest of the nation has come to depend. The Chicanos within this nation sense that such injustices must be dealt with because we see ourselves as citizens in need of equal opportunity and representation.

Gunnar Myrdal observes:

> Despite the democratic organization of American society with its emphasis upon liberty, equality of opportunity (with a strong leaning in favor of the underdog), and individualism, the idea of leadership pervades American thought and collective action. The demand for "intelligent leadership" is raised in all political camps, social and professional groups, and indeed, in every collective activity centered around any interest or purpose. . . . The other side of this picture is, of course, the relative inertia and inarticulateness of the masses in America.[14]

Responsibility of Chicano social workers

There exists a professional group, the Chicano social workers, whose responsibility is to communicate the needs of the community and to make community organization more effective, to be more vocal in their demands to meet human needs, and to assist the Chicano community in becoming politically more aware. This commitment to effective communication is needed not only in the major urban areas, but also in the small towns and rural parts of this country where Chicanos still are suppressed and demoralized. Who, better than Chicano social workers, can understand and make others understand the problems of our people—their poverty, their cultural variances, and their lack of adequate education.

The Chicano social workers have the responsibility of making this long overdue social change a reality. They must not be afraid to advise the established agencies when they do not relate to our people; they must educate our people to understand the need for legislation in the interest of the bicultural and bilingual peoples of this nation; they must teach the people of the barrio how the political machine operates and how local, state, and national governments function.

Howard N. Lee, Mayor of Chapel Hill, North Carolina, made the following statement in his address at The National Conference on Social Welfare in Dallas, Texas:

> We must begin to make our presence felt through the political arena. We must redefine for our own age the meanings and functions of a governmental system and a society that is supposed to be structured to meet the needs of the people. We must begin to realize that in order for this to happen and for us to be able to fairly and squarely deal with the social problems of today that it will take action and pressure, which requires the involvement of individuals, institutions, associations, and organizations on practically every level of society. Social workers should lead. There is no profession in a better position to develop a broad overview of the social needs, develop strategies for meeting them and agitating for attention than the Social Workers. As social workers, we must be concerned for those individuals and families who bear the brunt of deteriorating urban life and unrest and violence it breeds. We must point up the deficiencies and inadequacies in our system of justice. We must demand a reordering of national and governmental priorities on all levels. We must assume specific responsibility for assuring access to needed community services of good quality. We should recognize that not only the lack of opportunities but also the inadequacies of essential community services have contributed to the perpetuation of poverty, frustration, and rebellion in many urban neighborhoods. The social work profession has a role to play and should be involved with planning bodies and citizens groups on a continuing basis in efforts to reduce tension, identify human problems and needs, and facilitate communication across personal, ethnical and organizational lines. . . . It is imperative now that social workers become more educated in the art of penetrating the system in order to have some impact on the decision-making process on all levels; especially in the area of politics. . . . It's required that we influence others; fellow professionals, the city council, the county commissioners, the state legislature and all other such bodies.[15]

Leadership is time consuming, and only a few can afford to spend the necessary time without remuneration. Nonprofessional leaders acquire such skills as a consequence of spending more time upon, and gaining greater familiarity with, the group's activities than can the rank and file. Professionals can give most of their time to the group because they are paid for it. The nonprofessional leader gives the time that he can spare from the activities by which he secures his livelihood. A man must have some margin of wealth and leisure to leave his position and attend conventions, to say nothing of serving on active operating committees, with trips to the state capital or to out-of-state places. Politics and the public office that goes with it take time; less, it is true, in associational politics than in the politics of the state, but too much for a man who is regularly employed to go off on a junket. Membership on key committees tends to fall disproportionately on those who can afford the leisure necessary for frequent participation in group actions.[16]

We, *los Trabajadores de la Raza* (the social workers of the people) have learned to hope, for the first time in our lives, that a society can be constructed free of poverty, abundant in educational opportunity, tolerant of racial and ethnic diversity, and liberation for the human spirit. *El movimiento* has given us this faith to move *adelante por nuestra raza* (forward for our people).

Cruel and exaggerated rhetoric of unkept promises by politicians during campaigns has threatened the very creditability of the government itself and has almost destroyed a society's stability. Since 1961, federal administrations have been charged, pressured, begged, and called upon repeatedly to provide a decent portion of the country's wealth for all the people. Yet, no administration has really committed itself to this basic human cause, which will do more to eliminate alienation and division in our communities.

Poverty, by definition, means social and economic deprivation. Over the years, however, we have somehow developed the mistaken idea that if we merely give enough advice and services to the poor they will stop being poor. No one has thought of working with the poor; knowing the problems of the individual, as well as the community in which he lives; building the self-image of the people in the barrio; assisting them *por dentro de nuestro corazon* (from the bottom of our heart) whatever the time or place. Until the goal of *La Causa* is realized—social, economic, and political advancement for every Chicano and Latino in this nation—the work will require more than the usual forty hours a week; the work will demand every minute, every hour, every day.

Political action

Communication, the key to social change, lies in the realm of voicing our needs in the political arena. The name of the game is politics; the stakes are high, the game is dirty, many throw their hats in the ring, and only a few come out winners. In all societies one fact dominates political life: there is a scarcity of most of the valued things. Some of the claims for these relatively scarce things never find their way into the political system but are satisfied through the private negotiations of, or settlements by, the persons involved. Demands for prestige may find satisfaction through the status relations of the society; claims for wealth are met in part through the economic system; aspirations for power find expression in educational, fraternal, labor, and similar private organizations. Only when specific needs require some special organized effort on the part of society to settle them authoritatively may we say that they have become inputs of the political system.[17]

For this reason, Chicanos must become politically aware, because they are not yet sufficiently sophisticated to have their own private organizations and foundations that are self-sustaining to support their educational requirements, political demands, and monetary needs for economic development. Chicanos are aware that they are lowest on the statistical totem pole except for the birth rate, which also is a factor in remaining at the poverty level.

Few bureaucratic structures in this country recognize us. Few cities in the United States in which large numbers of our population reside recognize our needs, understand our language, and try to communicate with us in the language we understand. The agencies that have implemented affirmative action programs did not do so because they felt such a need existed. Action was not taken until our own *raza* demanded that services be given to the Chicano community in a manner not degrading or dehumanizing. Throughout the United States, there still exist hundreds of agencies that fail to recognize our needs. The few Chicanos who have managed to gain employment in these agencies as staff personnel have a great responsibility to see to it that the needs of *nuestra raza* are met. We must not be afraid to speak up when one of our peers makes derogatory remarks about our own people, our language, and our culture.

The incidents that occur that are detrimental to us must not be overlooked, but must be used as test cases to open additional doors. We must assist in the organizing of communities, and teach the structure of the political game from local politics to the national power play. All of us must now realize that only through a political bloc can we be recognized. When the politician does not hear us, it is because he is not threatened by us. Yet, we have a responsibility to register, to vote, to know the person for whom we are voting, and to follow up on the political promises made during the campaigns. We have to build not only our political power but also our political representation. How many Chicanos do we have at the local, county, state, and federal levels to represent us? It is at the state and federal levels where the majority of the laws are made, where programs are implemented, and where funds are redistributed back to the people. We must be sure that we get our proper share. Today our communities lack this expertise and these resources—the line of communication to the mayor, to the governor, to the legislature, and to the Congress of the United States that is supposed to be representing Chicanos.

Politically, we are probably the most underrepresented citizens in the United States. Los Angeles lacks a single Chicano city councilman, although it has more than one million Chicano residents and has the third largest Mexican population, after Mexico City and Guadalajara. Only New Mexico with a 27 percent Chicano population has a significant number of Chicano representatives, headed by United States Senator Joseph Montoya.

On May 6, 1971, Montoya stated in Congress:

Yet, it is our Federal Government itself which has been setting the worst possible example in one instance after another. Its non-record in opening up doors to Spanish-speaking Americans is shameful. Thirty-four agencies did not have a single Hispano in any capacity under the GS pay system. The least it could do is provide the same proportion of opportunities for them to advance at home in government as it does for them to die abroad in military service. We are first in janitors, first in infantry units, last in equal opportunity. Although we are at least 5 percent of the population, we possess less than 3 percent of the Federal jobs. . . . At the National Institutes of Health, there are 59 Spanish-surnamed employees out of a total work force of 11,167. This comes to a staggering total of 0.5 percent of all workers there. . . . There are no Spanish-surnamed employees in grades 16 through 18 in the Department of State, AID [Agency for International Development], and Peace Corps. Our dealings in each of these vital areas with Spanish-speaking nations are numerous and on the up-swing. Yet, when such countries deal with us, they have few encounters at upper levels with people they can relate to directly. This is short-sighted and injurious to America as well as direct evidence of discrimination. . . . There are no Spanish-surnamed employees in GS grades 16 through 18 in the Departments of Agriculture and Commerce. The last two are particularly strange situations, in light of the fact so many Spanish-speaking Americans live close to the land, and that Commerce deals so extensively with Spanish-Americans who would be instant assets to our Government in dealing with essential areas of responsibility. . . . At the rate of progress these agencies have been making, an award of some kind should go to the Departments of Justice, Interior, and Labor. Let us call it the order of tokenism, first class, because each of these vast organizations has one Spanish-surnamed employee operating in this high area of employee responsibility. . . . Outrageous discrimination existing in higher levels of Government employment must be removed instantly. The Civil Service Commission and administration have the power to act and should immediately do so. . . . Appointments of capable Spanish Americans to an entire series of high-visibility, high-responsibility positions should come high on our agenda of reform. Such signs of recognition and accomplishment regardless of politics, are vital as a sign of the Nation's Hispano community.[18]

Some members of the Cabinet Committee on Opportunity for the Spanish Speaking People recently indicated that they cannot adequately represent Chicanos unless we communicate to them the issues that confront the barrios.[19] Yet relatively few Chicanos have supported this Cabinet Committee to the fullest extent and made recommendations to them and their superiors. A recommendation might be made to this body that a representative be appointed to each of the regional areas of the United States so that problems can begin to be resolved more efficiently at the regional level. However, the regional representatives cannot work alone; they require the support of all Chicanos in this effort. The need for better communication throughout the United States is the greatest need of *el movimiento.* Unfortunately there are insufficient volunteers to assist in this much-needed work because most community workers are employed full time. Regional representatives who are responsible to the Cabinet Committee as well as to the barrios in their regional areas would tighten up the communication lines throughout the country as they serve as liaison between the local communities and the representatives in Washington, D.C.

There is also a great need for closer communication between Chicanos and their elected representatives on state and national levels. However, unless we communicate with these elected officials and make our demands known, we cannot expect them to know our problems. Too few Chicanos organize as an effective force on local or national issues. Although some of us have consistently written to government representatives and met with them in their offices, too few of us regularly employ this means of working for social change.

Too few Chicanos really represent us in local, state, and national government. Too often these representatives are only token acknowledgment to rebut the charge of overt discrimination. Too many *Tio Tacos* never communicate with *la gente del barrio*. *La Causa Chicana* alone has supplied reason to feel pride in being a Chicano because the movement will no longer tolerate inefficiency and lack of communication.

Conclusion

Communication is the greatest ally of inter-group relations and community organization as it now exists *en el barrio*. For the first time, *la gente del barrio y la inteligencia* (the people of the barrio and the better educated) are communicating with one another in trying to find the ways and means for long overdue social, economic, and political change. The tide is beginning to change, and the community is at last letting its voice be heard. There still exist some missing links in the lines of communication, but improvement is being made constantly, *poco a poco* (little by little). *El movimiento del barrio y de la raza* has begun, and nothing can stop it. *La Causa Chicana* has restored to us the pride of our culture, the beauty of our language, and the desire to know our true heritage.

Some schools of social work may have been induced to stress community organization because of the insistent demands of the Chicano students. Community organization is justified, however, only as it aids in penetrating the system. Fundamentally all Chicanos must be educated in both cultures and both languages. Then they must communicate and relate to *el barrio* and assist *nuestra raza* in implementing programs, in meeting needs, and in teaching the means of fighting effectively for constitutional rights on a sophisticated plane. They must make a greater impact not only at governmental levels but also with community representatives.

John Gardner, founder of Common Cause, reaffirms this conviction:

> In the case of political and governmental institutions, the shake up, the process of renewal, has to start with the citizens. It cannot come from anywhere else. If we'd waited for a civil rights movement, or a peace movement, or a conservation movement to emerge from the innards of the bureaucracy, we'd still be waiting. So . . . the most important thing we can do . . . is to go back to the idea that citizen-statesmen created this country . . . and citizens have to renew it.[20]

Self-interest is vital, but personal advantage must be subordinated when the goals of the movement are at stake. It is necessary to select priorities. If the goal is equality, dignity, and self-pride, it is essential that we first make certain who we are.

The United States must recognize Chicanos as bilingual, bicultural, functional personalities capable of extracting the best of two cultures to make a significant contribution to this society. It will not be easy to achieve equality and happiness. Self-interest affects politics and encounters many obstacles. Tax laws and government representation favor certain groups and operate against others. *El movimiento* must find the way to achieve its goal.

To communicate the goals of *La Causa* to the Chicano community, to the system, and to the nation, leaders must be developed who have the expertise to draw ideas from the community and to make effective demands in the political arena. The community as a united and organized group must apply pressure on the social systems that are not now responding to our bicultural and bilingual social and economic needs. The Chicano youth, as well as the few politicians among us, require undivided support.

It will be necessary to develop channels of the mass media to communicate the meaning of the movement to *nuestra raza,* as well as to the people of the United States. National television networks will have to be sensitized concerning needed programs. Chicano professionals of stage and screen must devise means to eliminate the stereotyped Mexican from motion picture and television screens. The

Chicano must come to be viewed as a dignified human being rather than as a comic, lazy, or stupid person. New advertising methods must be utilized to eliminate the false stereotypes and myths concerning the Mexican American.

A new mass communication network must be developed to permit all Chicanos to express their demands and state the issues as a united voice. It is futile to ban "El Frito Bandito" in Los Angeles and then show it in Detroit. Effective action in relation to representation in the mass media requires that Chicanos let each other know what progress is being made in all parts of the country in breaking down the barriers to understanding.

The need for exchange of ideas and successful programs must be facilitated. Assistance must be given to many Chicano communities that are concerned and want to participate actively in the movement but lack the technical ability. Radio stations do not generally allow free time in the area of public interest for the presentation of pertinent community information concerning Mexican Americans and are thus failing to communicate effectively to the people of the barrio.

Furthermore, too few Mexican Americans have begun to publish and document their ideas and plans. Communication, however, is the key to social change. *El movimiento* might well convene a national conference so that all Chicanos and Latinos of the United States might exchange ideas and establish national priorities. The social worker is able to assist the other professional, the educator, in developing community organization and in relaying the message to the people, to sustain faith, to help to improve the self-image, and to support the sense of identity. As leaders appear, they must, with the support of the community, be articulate in informing the politicians of the Chicanos' needs. Chicanos in turn have the responsibility of questioning the credibility of persons elected to public office. They must see that officials function properly and respond adequately to the inequalities that continue to plague *nuestra raza*.

It is up to us, *la gente del movimiento* (the people of the movement). *Union es la fuerza y victoria es el ideal del pobre que pide justicia social y economica* (Unity is the power and victory is the goal of the poor who ask for social and economic justice). *La raza nueva en marcha esta. Que Viva La Causa!*

Notes

1 Presentation by Professor Julian Nava, Ph.D., at La Raza Unida de Michigan Conference, Lansing, Michigan, August 7, 1971.
2 *Adelitas* is the name given to the women who accompanied their men during the Mexican Revolution of 1910.
3 Miguel F. Barragan, *Adelante!* (Onward!), The Bronze Artists Label, Phoenix, Arizona, Copyright, 1970.
4 "The Voice of the Advertiser," *Civil Rights Digest,* 4:48 (Winter 1971).
5 Marjorie Fallows, "The Mexican-American Laborers: A Different Drummer?", in *The Aliens, A History of Ethnic Minorities in America,* ed. Leonard Dinnerstein and Frederic Cople Jaher (New York: Meredith Corporation, 1970), p. 317.
6 Ibid.
7 David Riesman, *Faces in the Crowd,* 2d ed. rev. (New Haven and London: Yale University Press, 1965), p. 69.
8 Arnold M. Rose, *The Power Structure: Political Process in American Society* (New York: Oxford University Press, 1967), pp. 167–69.
9 Ibid., pp. 167–80. The characteristics of group leadership were summarized from chapter 5, "Alienation and Participation: A Comparison of Group Leaders and the 'Mass'."
10 David B. Truman, "Tendencies Toward Minority Control in Political Interest Groups," in *American Politics: Research and Readings,* ed. Stephen V. Monsma and Jack R. Van Der Slik (New York: Holt, Rinehart & Winston, 1970), p. 647.
11 Ibid., pp. 647–48.
12 Ibid., p. 39.
13 Ibid.
14 Ibid., pp. 649–50.
15 Address by Mayor Howard N. Lee at the National Conference on Social Welfare, Dallas, Texas, May 27, 1971.
16 Truman, "Tendencies Toward Minority Control," p. 646.
17 David Easton, "An Approach to the Analysis of Political Systems," in *American Politics,* ed. Monsma and Van Der Slik, p. 9.
18 U.S., Congress, Senate, Senator Montoya speaking before Senate, 92d Cong., 1st sess., May 6, 1971, *Congressional Record,* vol. 117, no. 66.
19 The Cabinet Committee on Opportunities for the Spanish Speaking People (formerly Inter-Agency Committee on Mexican-American Affairs), 1800 G Street N.W., Washington, D.C. 20506. Henry M. Ramirez, Chairman. In 1967, the Inter-Agency Committee on Mexican-American Affairs was created by Presidential memorandum. Its purposes were to assure that federal programs reached the Mexican Americans, to provide the assistance needed to seek new programs to handle their exceptional problems, to serve as an ombudsman within the government for the Mexican-Americans, and to be the central liaison point between the communities and the federal officials. Because the Inter-Agency Committee needed a sense of continuity in order to perform its advisory and advocative roles effectively, legislation was introduced to make it a statutory agency. Included in the bill was a new agency name: "The Cabinet Committee on Opportunities for Spanish Speaking People." The new agency title reflected the expanded scope of the committee. The committee's legislative mandate directed it to encompass the affairs of all Spanish-speaking Americans, including Mexican Americans, Puerto Ricans, and Cubans. On December 18, 1969, Congress passed the bill establishing the new committee and on December 30, President Nixon signed the bill into law.
20 John W. Gardner, "The Unfinished Business of America," *Look,* July 13, 1971.

Index

212

Chrysler Corporation, 169
Circulo Mutualista, el, 166,
174–176
Cisler, Walter, 169
City of Night (Rechy), 57
Civil War, 50, 51
Claretians (religious order), 88,
92
Coalition process, 81–86; with
new allies, 84–85
Cobos, Francisco, 71
Cohen, Rosalie, 142, 143–144,
145
Colegio Altamiro, El, 53
Collective preconscious, racism
and, 17–28
Comite Democratico, el, 166
Comite Patriotico, el, 166,
174–175
Committee of Concerned Spanish-
Speaking Americans
(CCSSA), 173–174
Compadrazgo relationship, 156
Common Cause (organization),
208
Communications Act of 1934, 10
Communications media, 6–15, 24;
FCC Fairness Doctrine,
10–15; stereotypic
representations, 8–10
Compean, Mario, 31
Con Safos (publication), 57, 58
Consumer Protection Service, 171
Cortina, Juan, 50
Council on Social Work Education
(CSWE), 119–120
Crusade for Justice, 5, 156
Cultural identity, parental denial
of, 194–195
Curanderos (faith healers), 73,
111
Cursillistas, las, 174–175

Dana, Richard Henry, 49
Davis, W. W. H., 49
Dawn of Day, The (Nietzsche),
20
Del Buono, Antonio, 115–125
Delgado, Abelardo, 60
Detroit, Archdiocese of, 166–167,
169–170; Latin American
Secretariat, 171–173

Detroit area, 161–177; casework
services, 126–136; CCSSA,
173–174; *Chicano* leadership,
169–170; family agency
services, 129–134; formation
of LA SED, 170–171; labor
unions, 168–169; *Latino En
Marcha* program, 176–177;
migration to, 162–163, 165;
political life, 174–176;
population, 161, 165; Roman
Catholic Church, 166–167,
169–170, 171–173; social
and fraternal clubs, 165–168
de Vega, Lope, 47
Díaz, Porfirio, 54, 58, 59
Dobie, J. Frank, 57
Dunbar, Willis F., 165
Durkheim, Emile, 20, 23, 27

Economic Opportunity Act of
1964, 187–188
Education, 6, 53, 96, 187–188;
barrio expertise, social work
and, 115–125; school
dropout rate, 6; *See also*
Social work education
*El Grito: A Journal of Contempo-
rary Mexican American
Thought,* 56, 57–58
Employment, 6; migrant farm
laborers, 184–186
English language, Spanish words
in, 53
Erikson, Erik H., 151
*Escala de Inteligencia Wechsler
Para Niños,* 138–139
Espalier, Carlos, 46
Esparza, Gegorio, 46
*Espejo-The Mirror, El: Selected
Mexican American Literature*
(Alurista), 62

Fairness Doctrine (Federal Communications Commission),
10–15; foundation of, 11;
personal attack regulations,
14
Family, the, barrio and, 157;
historical perspective of,
152–153; interchanges with
social systems, 153–155;